AF352626

ESSENTIALISM

ESSENTIALISM

A Wittgensteinian Critique

Garth L. Hallett

State University of New York Press

Published by
State University of New York Press, Albany

For information, address State University of New York
Press, State University Plaza, Albany, N.Y. 12246

Production by Leslie Frank-Hass
Marketing by Fran Keneston

Library of Congress Cataloging-in-Publication Data

Hallett, Garth L.
    Essentialism : a Wittgensteinian critique / Garth L. Hallett.
        p.   cm. — (SUNY series in logic and language)
    Includes bibliographical references and index.
    ISBN 0–7914-0773–X (alk. paper) . — ISBN 0–7914-0774–8 (pbk.)
    1. Language and logic. 2. Essence (Philosophy) 3. Semantics
(Philosophy) 4. Wittgenstein, Ludwig. 1889–1951—Contributions in
criticism of essentialism.   I. Title. II. Series.
BC57.H34   1991
111' .1—dc20
                                                            90–46848
                                                            CIP

10 9 8 7 6 5 4 3 2 1

CONTENTS

ACKNOWLEDGMENTS

This book has profited greatly from the comments and suggestions of Michael Barber, Richard Blackwell, William Charron, Vincent Cooke, Max Hocutt, T. Michael McNulty, and readers for the State University of New York Press, and from the stylistic polishing of Jeannette Batz. Warm thanks to them all.

INTRODUCTION

When philosophers use a word—"knowledge," "being," "object," "I," "proposition," "name"—and try to grasp the *essence* of the thing, one must always ask oneself: is the word ever actually used in this way in the language-game which is its original home?[1]

Struggling free from his early, pseudo-scientific mode of philosophizing, Wittgenstein realized the error not only of his former theses but also of his former ways: philosophy could not be done in the manner of the *Tractatus Logico-Philosophicus*. Few, however, have shared Wittgenstein's paradigm experience; and those acquainted with it often appear not to have grasped its full significance. After a momentary decline, Tractarian thinking has rebounded. With a deferential nod to the nebulous, if genial, deliverances of the *Philosophical Investigations*, contemporary philosophers frequently revert to a style of thought Wittgenstein saw good reason to abjure.

It is regrettable, though understandable, that Wittgenstein did not spell out more fully and clearly the motives for his radical shift of method from the *Tractatus* to the *Investigations*. If he had, he doubtless would have dwelt on the methodological implications of the linguistic instruments philosophers are obliged to employ, whether in stating their positions or in fashioning new verbal instruments. As Wittgenstein remarked, "When I talk about language (words, sentences, etc.) I must speak the language of every day. Is this language somehow too coarse and material for what we want to say? *Then how is another one to be constructed?*"[2] Can it be done nonlinguistically, in the privacy of the mind, without relying on any existing idiom?

The Wittgensteinian view of existing languages as composed of shifting, indefinite, heterogeneous concepts has far-reaching implications—more far-reaching, I believe, than is generally recognized. While I would prefer to indicate these implications positively rather than negatively, I have found that road blocked. Given the diversity of human thought and its expression, the only way I see to achieve a unified yet fairly comprehensive treatment is to center on a single object of concern—what I term "essentialism"—and let the implications appear from a critique of that broad and varied yet relatively focused target. This critique occupies chapters 1 to 5. Chapters 6 and 7 then complement critique with diagnosis and prognosis, explaining the criticized phenomenon and considering its prospects. Here, I shall first indicate more clearly what phenomenon it is that I intend to explore.

"Essentialism" can mean many things, as can its root term *essence*. In one sense, "an essence is the 'quiddity' of a thing . . . An essence is any character of a thing whereby that thing is what it is."[3] It is the fuzziness of a peach, the splendor of a sunset, the keenness of a person's wit. With such essences, there can be little quarrel. Similarly innocuous are the frequent formulations which assume that all members of a class have *something* in common—however various, irregular, or ill-defined—that makes them all members of that class (a shared "family resemblance," for example). More problematic is the essentialism that interests modal logicians, namely, "the view that some attributes belong to an object by necessity whereas others belong to it contingently."[4] Although they are sometimes termed "essential," such necessary attributes do not qualify as "essences" unless, singly or collectively, they constitute sufficient as well as necessary conditions of membership in a class. Essences in the traditional sense are core properties or clusters of properties present, necessarily, in all and only those things which bear the common name. Knowledge is one thing; language is one thing; beauty, meaning, humanity, life, law, justice—each is a single, invariant reality, present in the most varied instances, or in a separate realm of forms.

Even the later Wittgenstein has been accused of such reductive simplification, for instance with regard to the nature of philosophy. "Philosophy," he declared, "is a battle against the bewitchment of our intelligence by means of language."[5] Hence it "leaves everything as it is";[6] it "simply puts everything before us, and neither explains nor deduces anything."[7] Surely philosophy is and has been more varied than these assertions allow. However, "allow" is the right word: Wittgenstein's pronouncements prescribe; they do not describe. He would not maintain that all philosophies have proceeded in the manner indicated; nor would he deny the name "philosophy" to those which have not. Accordingly, few samples of this prescriptive sort will be found in this book. For I shall focus not only on the fourth, one-thing-only, core-reality kind of essentialism, but more specifically on its descriptive form. Prescriptive analogs call for different treatment.

Despite these successive restrictions, the type of essentialism I have targeted reveals great diversity. It invites comparison, not with chicken pox or appendicitis, but with the varied forms of cancer (carcinoma, sarcoma, leukemia, or lymphoma, in skin, lungs, brain, prostate, cervix, colon, breast, blood, bone, . . .). Hence I shall not attempt a precise definition, lest, in doing so, I unrealistically restrict the field of inquiry. A critique of essentialism ought not to be essentialistic.

Essentialism, thus broadly understood, has been a prominent feature of Western thought and, I think, for the most part a regrettable one. As my comparisons suggest, I incline to call it pathological. In any case, its history has been so long and its influence so great, that its current status merits scrutiny. The present study will not linger on popular versions of the past (Platonic, Aristotelian, Thomistic, Lockean, etc.) but will attend principally to recent forms, both explicit and especially implicit.

Previous reporting and assessment have centered on explicit theory rather than on implicit practice; the larger life of essentialism has gone largely unobserved and uncritiqued. Here, the emphasis is reversed: two chapters survey essentialistic theories (general then particular), whereas three chapters then scrutinize the essentialism implicit in varied forms of reasoning. Since critique, too, has predominated over explanation, the final two chapters, drawing on those that precede, undertake a fuller inquiry into the etiology of essentialism than has previously been attempted.

Chapter One

THE DECLINE OF EXPLICIT ESSENTIALISM

Upon examining "Moore's and Russell's principal argument for the reality of universals, in order to determine whether any spark of life remains in it"—"Is it truly dead, or only neglected?"—A. Donagan concludes that it is still very much alive. And surely this is what the history of philosophy would lead one to expect: philosophical positions—except for scientific theories classified as philosophical, e.g. Aristotle's theory of the ethereal spheres—rarely, if ever, perish. Being criticism-resistant, as it were, they remain to be taken up by anyone attracted to them; which is one of the great enigmas of philosophy.[1]

From just explicit formulations, it might appear that essentialism, after a bright Platonic dawn, medieval high noon, and modern decline, has finally entered its twilight time and is fading from view. At best, this picture is partial. A better metaphor, in view of recent developments, might be an ocean whose successive waves surged ever higher as the tide of essentialism rose and now lap ever lower as the tide runs out, but which leave the sand damp with their passing. The waves are successive essentialistic theories; the dampness is the essentialistic practice that endures after the waves have subsided. In the present chapter I shall speak of theoretical developments within the present century which illustrate this metaphor of successive, retreating waves. In subsequent chapters I shall turn to varied forms of philosophical practice which attest the lingering power of essentialistic thinking.

A Theoretical Sampling

In the first part of the century, broad essentialistic claims were still common. Listen, for example, to Sir David Ross:

The essence of the theory of Ideas lay in the conscious recognition of the fact that there is a class of entities, for which the best name is probably "universals," that are entirely different from sensible things. Any use of language involves the recognition, either conscious or unconscious, of the fact that there are such entities; for every word used, except proper names—every abstract noun, every general noun, every adjective, every verb, even every pronoun and every preposition—is a name for something of which there are or may be instances. The first step towards the conscious recognition of this class of entities was, if we may believe Aristotle, taken by Socrates when he concentrated on the search for definitions; to ask for the meaning of a general word was a step from the mere use of such a word towards the recognition of universals as a distinct class of entities.[2]

Ross here goes beyond Socrates or Plato. Even Aquinas might have hesitated to speak with such assurance of "any use of language" and "every word used," attentive as he was to analogous concepts.

In its breadth, Ross's view echoes Russell's in *The Problems of Philosophy*. "We succeed in avoiding all notice of universals as such," Russell wrote, "until the study of philosophy forces them upon our attention."[3] Plato pioneered their exploration; the theory Russell advocated was, he acknowledged, "largely Plato's, with merely such modifications as time has shown to be necessary."[4] Developments since Spinoza have shown the need to generalize Plato's essentialism. "When we examine common words, we find that, broadly speaking, proper names stand for particulars, while other substantives, adjectives, prepositions, and verbs stand for universals."[5] The latter categories merit special emphasis. "Even among philosophers, we may say, broadly, that only those universals which are named by adjectives or substantives have been much or often recognized, while those named by verbs and prepositions have been usually overlooked. This omission has had a very great effect upon philosophy."[6]

Talk of "universals," like talk of "essences," can have a stronger or weaker sense; it may or may not express the kind of unifying, simplifying, one-thing-only conception that concerns us in this study. The same is true of "general ideas," the term Moore used to express a similarly comprehensive viewpoint. There can be little doubt, however, about the genuineness of Moore's essentialism. His treatment of color concepts is particularly revealing:

This character wh. we express by "is a shade of blue," is, of course, something which is common to all shades of blue—something which they have "in common." Some people seem loth to admit that they have anything "in

common." And of course this character is not "in common" to both of 2 blue shades, in the sense that it is a
part or constituent of both . . . Obviously this character
also is not identical with any shade which possesses it,
nor yet with any other shade of colour that we *see*. It is
not similar in shade to any shade that we *see*. So that, if
it is "seen" at all, it is only in a completely different
sense.[7]

"*All* the shades we *see* occupy some position in the colour octahedron; but 'blue,' in the sense in which many of the shades in the
octahedron are 'blue,' occupies *no* position in it: therefore it is not
seen."[8]

Moore was not thinking of a hidden cause. "Consider yellow," he
wrote. "We may try to define it, by describing its physical equivalent; we may state what kind of light-vibrations must stimulate the
normal eye, in order that we may perceive it. But a moment's reflection is sufficient to shew that those light-vibrations are not themselves what we mean by yellow. *They* are not what we perceive."[9]

The like holds for *good*. "It may be true that all things which are
good are *also* something else, just as it is true that all things which
are yellow produce a certain kind of vibration in the light . . . But far
too many philosophers have thought that when they named those
other properties they were actually defining good; that these properties, in fact, were simply not 'other,' but absolutely and entirely
the same with goodness."[10] "My point is that 'good' is a simple
notion, just as 'yellow' is a simple notion; that, just as you cannot, by
any manner of means, explain to any one who does not already
know it, what yellow is, so you cannot explain what good is."[11]

Were it suggested that neither yellow nor good is simple—that
there are different shades of yellow and different species of good—
doubtless Moore would respond in the way just seen: as yellow or
blue is invisible and distinct from visible hues, so good is a nonnat-
ural entity, distinct from any natural, descriptive properties. Specific goods may vary, but not *the good*. Not the essence they all
share.

Various indications[12] suggest that Russell understood "universals" as essentialistically as Moore did "general ideas." Scheler's
remarks bespeak still more clearly the unitary, non-disjunctive
nature of the essences he espoused. For Scheler, "that a man or a
deed is 'noble' or 'base,' 'courageous' or 'cowardly,' 'innocent' or
'guilty,' 'good' or 'evil,' is not made certain for us by constant characteristics which can be discerned in such things and events; nor

do such values *consist* in such characteristics. In certain circumstances a *single* deed or a *single* person is all that we need to grasp the *essence* of the value in question."[13] And what holds for value concepts holds for all.

> An essence, or whatness, is in this sense *as such* neither universal nor particular. The essence red, for example, is given in the universal concept as well as in each perceivable nuance of this color. The differences between universal and particular meanings come about only in relation to the objects in which an essence comes to the fore. Thus, an essence becomes *universal* if it comes to the fore in a plurality of otherwise different objects as an identical essence: in all and everything that "has" or "bears" this essence. The essence can, on the other hand, also constitute the nature of an *individual thing* without ceasing to be such an *essence.*[14]

In *Ideas,* Husserl used other illustrations to express a similar viewpoint:

> An individual object is not simply and quite generally an individual, a "this-there" something unique; but being constituted thus and thus *"in itself"* it has *its own proper mode of being,* its own supply of *essential* predicables which must qualify it (*qua* "Being as it is in itself"), if other secondary relative determinations are to qualify it also. Thus, for example, every tone in and for itself has an essential nature, and at the limit the universal meaning-essence "tone in general," or rather the acoustic in general—understood in the pure sense of a phase or aspect intuitively derivable from the individual tone (either in its singleness, or through comparison with others as a "common element").[15]

"An instance of the essence 'colour' and an instance of the essence 'sound' are intuitively 'present,' and indeed *as* instancing their own essences."[16]

Husserl went further and noted that we can recognize such essences even if the instantiating samples are not real ones.

> If in the play of fancy we bring spatial shapes of one sort or another to birth, melodies, social happenings, and so forth, or live through fictitious acts of everyday life, of satisfaction or dissatisfaction, of volition and the like,

we can through "ideation" secure from this source primordial and even on occasion adequate insight into pure essences in manifold variety: essences, it may be, of spatial shape *in general,* of melody *as such,* of social happening *as such,* and so forth, or of the shape, melody, etc., of the relevant special *type.* It is a matter of indifference in this connexion whether such things have ever been given in actual experience or not.[17]

Wittgenstein's Critique

A characteristic feature of twentieth-century views like those just sampled and of similar views in earlier centuries was their slight attention to language and to the customary use of the terms the authors employed. When, for example, Russell, Moore, or Scheler alluded to the various shades of some color—red, white, yellow, blue—and alleged an essence present in all members of the class, he did not state explicitly that the class in question was the one picked out by the standard employment of that particular English term (*red, white, yellow, blue*) or by its German equivalent (*rot, weiss, gelb, blau*). So long as one does not look beyond one's native tongue and its near neighbors and envisage a different color cartography (joining red and pink, say, or red and orange, under a single predicate), this silence about usage may appear relatively unproblematic. More evidently questionable is Scheler's assertion that "in certain circumstances a *single* deed or a *single* person is all that we need to grasp the *essence* of the value in question."

If an essence, to qualify as an essence of X, must be present in all X's, then there is no telling from any single member of the class that the essence present in it is the essence of X. Perhaps Scheler meant merely that a person can become acquainted with an essence through acquaintance with any instance in which the essence is present. (One could, for instance, become acquainted with the essence of nobility, if it has one, by observing a single noble deed.) However, the further difficulty would remain that the use of terms like *noble, courageous, innocent,* and *good* reveals much diversity from speaker to speaker, in both intension and extension.

So the question arises: What relation is the purported essence supposed to have to the current or past use of the term applied to it? What relationship holds between the essence of X and the use of the word *X*? Must the essence be found in all the things so named, or just in some of them? If just in some, in which ones, and why? Or does usage matter? If not, why speak of the essence of X rather than of Y or Z?

These queries take on a special urgency when Husserl asserts that the "play of fancy," not restricted to real cases, may reveal the essence of melody *as such* or of social happening *as such*. Does it make no difference whether, in order to characterize the nonlinguistic phenomenon Husserl alludes to, one speaks of "*melody* as such" or "*tune* as such" or "*melodic line* as such"—or for that matter of "*music* as such" or "*sound* as such"? Does it make no difference whether the expression *melody* or *social happening* has ever been employed or has been applied to such a phenomenon (as his closing remark would seem to suggest)? If it does make a difference, should not actual samples and actual usage be consulted to ascertain whether this or that aspect of the contemplated fiction instantiates a given essence? What does the expression "as such" signify if it has no connection with familiar applications of the terms Husserl employs (*melody, social happening*)? And if there is a connection, what is its character? How does the essence of X relate to the word *X*?[18]

Essentialists before Wittgenstein seldom addressed considerations like these, and when they did, their explanations did little or nothing to clarify the status of the "essences" they alleged.[19] Moore, for example, said he was concerned with "that which is meant by 'good'"[20]—with "that object or idea, which I hold, rightly or wrongly, that the word is generally used to stand for"[21]—yet declared, "At the same time I am not anxious to discuss whether I am right in thinking that it is so used."[22] The good, we can imagine Moore explaining, would still be the good even if called by some other name, just as fish would still be fish if called figs, or bison would still be bison if called candelabra. This sounds reasonable enough, except that Moore has taken away with one hand what he gave with the other. To verify what he says about the good, we must examine what, if anything, the word *good* customarily designates, and see whether he accurately describes it; yet we are also advised that we need not concern ourselves with whether the word does in fact stand for the entity Moore says it does. Perhaps no finer illustration can be found of what Wittgenstein had in mind when he wrote: "The essential thing about metaphysics: it obliterates the distinction between factual and conceptual investigations."[23] Not merely ignores: obliterates, systematically obfuscates.[24]

Other remarks of Moore sound more sensible. "I should, indeed, be foolish," he wrote, "if I tried to use [the word *good*] for something which it did not usually denote; if, for instance, I were to announce that, whenever I used the word 'good,' I must be understood to be thinking of that object which is usually denoted by the word 'table.'"[25] It would be similarly misleading to speak of "all X's" and mean only some of the things so designated; or to speak of "the essence of X's" and mean a trait found in some X's but not all, or in all X's but also in some Y's and Z's; or to speak of what the word *X* denotes or stands for when the word does not typically denote or stand for anything but has a different function.

For reasons like these, Wittgenstein advised that when philosophers employ some term and "try to grasp the *essence* of the thing, one must always ask oneself: is the word ever actually used in this way in the language-game which is its original home? What *we* do is to bring words back from their metaphysical to their everyday use."[26] Not that everyday use is sacrosanct;[27] but if another use seems more opportune—practically or theoretically, contextually or generally—let it be introduced as a new word-use, not paraded as an essence.

To recognize the actual, everyday use of words, Wittgenstein advised that we *look,* not *think.*[28] His meaning can be gathered from preceding samples. An invisible blue distinct from all shades of blue, for example, is not seen with the eyes but with the mind. It arises from the thought that varied blues—cobalt, turquoise, aquamarine—are, after all, all instances of blueness. They share this trait, have it in common. So it must be somehow perceptible in each instance.

Wittgenstein recognized that there is such a thing as spotting what is common and abstracting it from varied instances. "Suppose I shew someone various multi-coloured pictures, and say: 'The colour you see in all these is called "yellow ochre"'... Then he can look *at,* can point *to,* the common thing." But "compare this case: I shew him samples of different shades of blue and say: 'The colour that is common to all these is what I call "blue".'"[29] Now what can be looked at or pointed to save the varied hues of blue? And don't say, "There *must* be something common, or they would not be called 'blue,'" "but *look and see* whether there is anything common to all."[30]

With regard to "games" Wittgenstein reached the well-known verdict that nothing common to all games makes us name them so, "but similarities, relationships, and a whole series of them at that."[31] To this "complicated network of similarities, overlapping and criss-crossing," he applied the label "family-resemblances," explaining that "the various resemblances between members of a family: build, features, colour of eyes, gait, temperament, etc., overlap and criss-cross in the same way."[32] Blues, however, do not relate in this way. Neither do the members of many other classes.[33] Wittgenstein recognized a variety of conceptual structures besides the family-resemblance configuration. But a single-essence, all-and-only structure, permitting the statement of sufficient and necessary conditions of application, did not figure among them. Still, he did not demonstrate the impossibility of such a structure—did not even attempt to. And for all a few samples like *blue* and *game* demonstrate, essences might be common. So it is not immediately evident why Wittgenstein's critique had the impact it did or merited so much attention.

One reason emerges from the quotations with which we began our sampling of essentialistic thinking. When Russell and Ross alleged the omnipresence of essences and universals, for nouns, verbs, adjectives, adverbs, and even prepositions, their claim did not result from empirical inquiry. They had not perused samples of each class of expression, in representative languages, and found that time after time these samples revealed such essentialistic uniformity. No, they supposed—a priori—that it had to be so. The significance of Wittgenstein's jejune examples derives from the challenge they pose to this underlying assumption.[34] If color predicates, proposed as paradigmatic by essentialists like Russell, Moore, and Scheler, reveal no essence when scrutinized a posteriori, and neither does a "univocal" concept as typical as *game*,[35] perhaps essences are rare or nonexistent. Indeed, the all-or-nothing essentialistic mode of thought would tend to reinforce this negative conclusion. According to Moore, if there are any essences, there are tremendous numbers of them;[36] a *modus tollens* argument would therefore suggest that if there are not tremendous numbers, there are not any.

Wittgenstein's impact also stemmed from his stress on the neglected linguistic parameters of essentialism. If an essence does not correlate with the word an essentialist uses to label it, then he should label it differently. If it does and must correlate with the label, then its existence is not just a fact of nature but also a fact of language. The *concept X* reveals the existence or nonexistence of an essence of X.[37] But the concept belongs to a language; and that language is the common property and common creation of a vast and varied population, whose employment of expressions, on various occasions and for varied purposes, cannot be expected to manifest the austere uniformity required to establish or perpetuate essences. When children, housewives, mechanics, poets, journalists, and mystics are the speakers, a similarity from shade to shade of some color, or a family resemblance between various games, may suffice for the common appellation "blue" or "game." Indeed, in metaphysically licentious moments such folk may speak of "feeling blue," "singing the blues," "war games," "a war of nerves," or "the game of politics." Hence, when viewed as a matter of linguistic usage, and not of metaphysics, the essentialistic structure of language, thought, and world appears extremely dubious.[38]

Carnapian "Explication"

Vagaries of usage have not deterred scientifically-minded theorists. "There is still the opportunity," writes Ian McGreal, "which Wittgenstein tended to ignore or overlook, of constructing a definition of 'games' by the use of which one could give a definitive (but creative) answer to a question as to the essence of games. One might take advantage of the ambiguity of such a term as 'amusing,' or one might, by stipulation, rule out many of those cases now conventionally called 'games.'"[39] In science, notes Joseph Margolis, "'family resemblances' between different kinds of energy, for example, [have] had to give way gradually to an empirically adequate definition of the necessary and sufficient properties of energy."[40] Philosophers, it would seem, may follow suit. However, when they have attempted to do so, they have generally been as unclear as traditional metaphysicians concerning the nature of their enterprise. The intended relation of their theories or definitions to the concepts or terms they employed has remained obscure.[41] Often, when they have offered something by way of explanation for their partial or total disregard of usage, they have characterized their undertaking as Carnapian "explication."

"If there is one concept that might be said to provide a key to Carnap's philosophy," observes Peter Achinstein, "it is *explication*, a concept that has had considerable influence on many philosophers."[42] "By an explication," writes Carnap, "I understand the replacement of a pre-scientific inexact concept (which I call 'explicandum') by an exact concept ('explicatum'), which frequently belongs to the scientific language . . . Although explications are often given also by scientists, it seems to me particularly characteristic of philosophical work that a great part of it is devoted to proposing and discussing explications of certain basic, general concepts."[43] At least the proposals look more plausible viewed this way. For in explication "the only essential requirement is that the explicatum be more precise than the explicandum."[44] Hence, "the interpretation which we shall adopt . . . deviates deliberately from the meaning of descriptions in the ordinary language. Generally speaking, it is not required that an explicatum have, as nearly as possible, the same meaning as the explicandum."[45] Rather, it suffices that the explicandum satisfy the following four requirements, "to a sufficient degree":

> 1. The explicatum is to be *similar to the explicandum* in such a way that, in most cases in which the explicandum has so far been used, the explicatum can be used; however, close similarity is not required, and considerable differences are permitted.
>
> 2. The characterization of the explicatum, that is, the rules of its use (for instance, in the form of a definition), is to be given in an *exact* form, so as to introduce the explicatum into a well-connected system of scientific concepts.
>
> 3. The explicatum is to be a *fruitful* concept, that is, useful for the formulation of many universal statements (empirical laws in the case of a nonlogical concept, logical theorems in the case of a logical concept).
>
> 4. The explicatum should be as *simple* as possible; this means as simple as the more important requirements (1), (2), and (3) permit.[46]

"Philosophers, scientists, and mathematicians," Carnap adds, "make explications very frequently. But they do not often discuss explicitly the general rules which they follow implicitly."[47] In philosophy, one frequently has the impression that the tag *explication* serves as a warrant to do business as usual in the essentialistic manner. With the constraints of standard usage loosened, the theorist can continue to equate his explicandum with some single explicatum, and do so with an appearance of scientific rigor. But with the rules of the game left ill-defined,[48] or the rules once stated thereafter ignored,[49] the reality of the enterprise contradicts the appearances. In fairness to Carnap it should be said that most of the explications that have failed have not been genuinely Carnapian; they have not adhered to the guidelines just cited. However, the fog surrounding the explicative enterprise,[50] the obscurity of individual specimens, and the tendency to conceive explication essentialistically are traceable in part to Carnap's own characterizations.

First, the very name *explication* suggests something more than merely stipulating a handy sense for a term. Yet basically that is all explication, as stated, amounts to. Consider a simple case. The interpretation of "if . . . then" in the sense of material implication satisfies all four of Carnap's conditions and has been cited by Carnap and others as an instance of explication.[51] Yet clearly such a sharpening does not explain the existing concept, as the term *explication* suggests. The process is the familiar one of stipulating or specifying the sense an expression will have within a given context, work, or discipline. One sense among several gets singled out for its utility.[52]

Second, as an exception to the general failure to clarify the rules of explication, Carnap cites the "good explicit formulation ... given by Karl Menger in connection with his explication of the concept of dimension":

> He states the following requirements. The explicatum "must include all entities which are always denoted and must exclude all entities which are never denoted" by the explicandum. The explication "should extend the use of the word by dealing with objects not known or not dealt with in ordinary language. With regard to such entities, a definition [explication] cannot help being arbitrary." The explication "must yield many consequences," theorems possessing "generality and simplicity" and connecting the explicatum with concepts of other theories.[53]

As reported by Carnap, these stipulations of Menger look inconsistent; in any case, they clearly do not agree with Carnap's own four requirements. Carnap's first prescription says nothing about extending the range of the explicandum nor, more essentialistically, about including all entities which are always denoted and excluding all which are never denoted. He stipulates more flexibly. For in his own conception no explicatory formula—no inclusion or exclusion—is to be arbitrary; each is to be fruitful, and fruitfulness may require narrowing in one instance, stretching in another.

Third, given the looseness of Carnap's conditions and their pragmatic motivation, it is not clear why any specific set, stated any specific way, should qualify as *the* requirements for worthwile explication. He cites increased precision as "the only essential requirement"; yet often that can be achieved without any attention to fruitfulness. On the other hand, greater fruitfulness can sometimes be had without increased precision; a sense may simply be narrowed or extended. More realistic than Carnap's requirements would be a list of desiderata to consider when stipulating senses; and such a list would have to be much longer than his. It would need to speak, for example, of the "explication's" context, of its recipients, and of how it is conveyed to them.[54] A once-and-for-all listing like Carnap's, suggesting that all stipulations of sense should satisfy all these criteria,[55] ignores context and to that extent is imperfectly pragmatic. It betrays a lingering essentialism.

Fourth, the listing of all four conditions to be met, simultaneously, suggests that there can be only one successful explicatum for any explicandum. But this is not the case, as Carnap is aware. "In a problem of explication," he writes,

> the datum, viz., the explicandum, is not given in exact terms; if it were, no explication would be necessary. Since the datum is inexact, the problem itself is not stated in exact terms; and yet we are asked to give an exact solution. This is one of the puzzling peculiarities of explication. It follows that, if a solution for a problem of explication is proposed, we cannot decide in an exact way whether it is right or wrong. Strictly speaking, the question whether the solution is right or wrong makes no good sense because there is no clear-cut answer.[56]

The imprecision lies more in Carnap's prescriptions than in the data to which they are applied. All four of his conditions may, on occasion, conflict with one another, and he assigns no respective weights to them, save to prescribe that the first three conditions take precedence, individually, over the fourth condition of simplicity. His stipulations give no indication whether an explication that is more precise but less fruitful should be preferred to one that is more fruitful but less precise; whether one that departs notably from standard usage but is fruitful should be preferred to one that is closer to usage but somewhat less fruitful; and so forth.

Within this collective imprecision further indefiniteness appears with regard to the individual conditions. The fourth requirement, of simplicity, may be variously interpreted, and the different interpretations will yield different verdicts.[57] For example, does an explicatum employing fewer but more complex concepts count as more or less simple than one employing more numerous but less complex concepts?[58] In the first requirement, uncertainty arises from the fact that proximity to existing usage varies with the degree of precision with which the explicandum is identified (for example, as the concept *meaning*, or the concept *meaning* as applied to expressions, or the concept *meaning* as applied to complete utterances, or the concept *meaning* as applied to complete empirical utterances).[59]

These and other reasons account for my conjecture that the

imprecision Carnap recognized lies more in his account of explication than in the explicanda. But whatever the nature or source of the indefiniteness, the upshot is the same: If explication is understood as Carnap defined it, no explicatum can be proposed as the uniquely correct one.

Hence it comes as no surprise that the Carnapian wave was followed by a more clearly essentialistic wavelet. Treating Carnap's account as an explication of explication, Joseph Hanna faulted both Carnap's choice of explicandum and his formulation of the explicatum, and proposed instead a more restricted, uniform account. With regard to the explicandum, he suggested: "Although Carnap frequently speaks of explicating concepts, it seems more perspicacious to follow Quine and view the method as applying fundamentally to linguistic terms (i.e. predicates, operators, names, etc.) and as applying only derivatively to concepts. Concepts are mysterious entities and it is best to avoid them when the same point can be made by referring to predicates."[60] Carnap's explicatum, which does not require close similarity, likewise needs tightening. "Carnap appears to be assimilating all cases in which presystematic terms are adapted for scientific use to cases of explication."[61] But such assimilation looks doubly objectionable. "In the first place, this use of 'explication' does not seem to be consistent with the method of analysis actually employed by other 'ideal-language' philosophers (the school of which Carnap is spiritual father)."[62] Hanna acknowledged that "it would be difficult to substantiate this claim because of the conflicting and not very detailed remarks that various 'ideal-language' philosophers have addressed to this issue," then proceeded to "a second, though related, objection to Carnap's assimilation of all cases of 'scientific reconstruction' to explication," namely the objection "that the resulting notion is vague, and it is not apparent how this vagueness is to be remedied."[63]

Hanna's own presentation supposedly avoids both these difficulties when, for instance, it prescribes that the explicatum should "agree with" the explicandum "in those cases where our intuitions concerning the meaning of the latter term are not defective. In the remaining cases, the explicatum serves to educate our intuitions or re-educate our intuitions, as the case may be. In short, the explicatum systematically fills in the gaps and corrects the inconsistencies of the explicandum."[64]

Hanna's account looks still more defective than Carnap's. For one thing, substituting the word *meaning* for the word *concept* (as in the preceding quotation) hardly removes all vagueness from the discussion. And if the test of adequacy is agreement with the term to be explicated, why are Carnap's stipulations criticized for their disagreement with the "method of analysis" employed by kindred thinkers rather than for their disagreement with these thinkers' or others' use of the term *explication*? It seems odder still that Hanna's own explication of the term *explication* is not based in any empirical sampling of usage, and that, instead, the explicandum is identified as "the brand of philosophic analysis variously called explication, rational reconstruction, formal analysis, etc."[65]

With regard to the word *explication,* Hanna briefly noted that in its presystematic usage it has a variety of senses, then explained that only one of these senses was the primary concern of his paper.[66] It was the sense *characterized* by his explicatum and also, it appears, the sense *identified* by that characterization. Hence his explication looks indefeasible, and if indefeasible, uninteresting (save, perhaps, for other, nondescriptive purposes). Where agreement with the explicandum is the aim of explication or the criterion of success, the explicatum cannot also serve to pinpoint the explicandum it "agrees with." Where, on the contrary, fruitfulness figures as at least a co-determinant, the test of agreement must be loosened, as in Carnap's treatment.

Had Hanna been genuinely concerned about close descriptive equivalence (closer than Carnap prescribed), he would have attended more carefully to the use of the term to be described. Had he attended more carefully to the vagaries of that term's employment, I think he would have recognized that such messy linguistic data really did not interest him. His proposal amounts to a stipulation, for the sake of greater precision; and though the stipulation may be less precise than Hanna imagined, so far as agreement with familiar usage is concerned it does look preferable to Carnap's. To apply the label *explication* to a mere conceptual revision such as that of the concept *fish* does indeed sound odd. But a stipulated sense of *explication* neither reveals nor generates an essence of explication. And with regard to the type of analysis he commended, Hanna's own sample—the explication of *explication*—does not look promising. It offers no reason to surmise that other samples may succeed any better in satisfying essentialistic aspirations.

Whatever Hanna's motivation may have been, his account responds to two basic essentialistic urges. First, an essence must be uniform and sharp, whereas Carnap's characterization admitted considerable variety, with no clear limit; the explicatum would just need to resemble the explicandum to some unstated extent. Second, essential definition must capture an existing essence, not merely stipulate a useful meaning for a term, whereas Carnap's prescriptions pointed in the latter direction. Had they done so still more clearly, they would have been less apt to perpetuate essentialistic expectations.

Essences and "Rigid Designators"

The doctrine of "rigid designation" advanced in the 70's by Saul Kripke and Hilary Putnam gave rise to another surge of essentialistic thinking. Putnam explained the doctrine by means of the term *water*. "Kripke calls a designator 'rigid' (in a given sentence) if (in that sentence) it refers to the same individual in every possible world in which the designator designates. If we extend the notion of rigidity [from proper names] to substance names, then we may express Kripke's theory and mine by saying that the term 'water' is *rigid*."[67] For, "once we have discovered that water (in the actual world) is H_2O, *nothing counts as a possible world in which water isn't H_2O*."[68] Thus water is necessarily H_2O; H_2O constitutes its essence. The word *water* rigidly designates H_2O regardless of what superficial properties the H_2O may or may not have. In Putnam's opinion, similar, essentialistic rigidity characterizes not only other natural-kind terms like *gold, lemon, tiger,* and *acid,*[69] but also "the great majority of all nouns," for instance "the names of artifacts—words like 'pencil,' 'chair,' 'bottle,' etc.," and "other parts of speech as well."[70] In each instance, the extension of the term is fixed by the "important physical properties"[71] or "hidden structure"[72] revealed, or still to be revealed, by science.[73]

This alleged fact of language Putnam sought to demonstrate through various thought experiments, of which his Twin-Earth fantasy is the best known. Let us imagine, he suggested, that somewhere a planet exists which exactly duplicates ours, except that the liquid there called "water," which in all superficial respects resembles what we call "water," does not consist of H_2O but rather of XYZ (an abbreviated formula for something very long and complicated). Having further spelled out this hypothesis, Putnam considered it evident that the word *water* does not have the same meaning in both places;[74] that in our sense of the word their stuff is not water;[75] and that we would not and should not call it water once the discrepancy was noted.[76] The Twin-Earth scenario thus highlights the essential meaning of the word *water* and, more generally, the functioning of similar expressions.[77]

What Putnam took as evident has not seemed so to others. We

do in fact extend words to specimens with different structures. And the plausibility of Putnam's surmise appears to derive from some unwitting sleight of hand.[78] As he himself noted elsewhere, hidden structure looks important because of its connection with surface features (specific gravity, fluidity, freezing point, taste, characteristic feel, etc.).[79] But his Twin-Earth fiction cuts this connection; the difference in microstructure makes no perceptible difference between the two liquids. Anyone who noted this further difference, and not just the one Putnam focused on, might not attach the customary importance to hidden structure. For some strange reason, the structural dissimilarity between H_2O and XYZ would have even fewer consequences than that between H_2O (ordinary water) and D_2O (heavy water). The term *water* might therefore be extended to Putnam's Twin-Earth liquid as it actually was, for instance, to heavy water. Indeed, suppose we alter Putnam's fictional hypothesis and imagine that Twin-Earth "water" was all D_2O. Would Putnam still refuse to call it "water"? Would other people?

It may be suggested that with this counter-example, the war is lost but the battle, at least, may be won. Putnam may be wrong in his essentialism but right about Twin-Earth water. For the similarity between D_2O and H_2O is internal, not external, whereas that in his example is external. However, once this much flexibility is recognized and similarity replaces sameness, there is no reason to suppose that similarity will function more rigidly here than on other occasions.

In a previous work I proposed a "principle of relative similarity" (PRS for short), according to which "for a statement of fact, or informative utterance, to be true it suffices that its use of terms resemble more closely the established uses of those terms than it does those of rival, incompatible terms."[81] Calling the Twin-Earth liquid "water" would satisfy this condition; *water* would conform with current usage more closely than any other existing name. Not only would the appellation satisfy the principle, but it would agree with the facts of usage on which the principle rests—with our familiar use of terms in making assertions and with our familiar use of *true* in assessing the assertions. It would resemble countless other instances in which a term has been extended from familiar paradigms to new ones on the basis of relative similarity.[82]

Often, even this basis is lacking: we speak, for instance, of "deep sorrow," "thin excuses," "sharp regrets," and "tender mercies." Some may wish to characterize such extensions as "figurative" or "metaphorical"; nonetheless, we do make them, readily and repeatedly. Hence to predict that we would not extend a term like *water* even where extensive similarity obtains—more extensive than for any other term available—would reveal more about the persons who make the prediction than about speakers of the language at large. The doctrine of rigid designation not only arises from a selective sampling of cases but also demands a selective sampling of speakers. Doubtless it would contain more truth, and Kripke's and Putnam's intuitions would agree better with those of the populace as a whole, were everyone as scientifically, essentialistically minded as are these philosophers of science.[83]

The importance of a carefully restricted population within selectively scientific settings, for Putnam's doctrine to have a semblance of realism, appears, for instance, when he writes: "It is logically possible (although empirically unlikely, perhaps) that a species of fruit biologically unrelated to lemons might be indistinguishable from lemons in taste and appearance. In such a case, there would be two possibilities: (1) to call them *lemons*, and thus let 'lemon' be a word for any one of a number of natural kinds; or (2) to say that they are not lemons (which is what, I suspect, biologists would decide to do)." This closing reference to biologists elicits three queries: (1) Does the doctrine of rigid designation apply just to scientific speakers, in scientific contexts, or to speakers generally? (2) If the former, does it surmise what scientific speakers would "decide to do" merely in the sense of what meaning-stipulations they might introduce, or in the sense of what they would assert ("They are not lemons") without stipulating new meanings? (3) If the latter, would their assertions be correct, or would they reveal the kind of conceptual intolerance Carnap,[84] Achinstein,[85] and others have criticized?

The doctrine of rigid designators seems to suggest the wrong answers to all three of these queries. And even with regard to scientific speakers in scientific contexts its claims appear unrealistic. Listing "three strategies that might be attempted for identifying privileged sameness relations between the members of a species"—strategies "based, respectively, on intrinsic properties of the individuals, on reproductive isolation of a group of individuals, and on evolutionary descent of a group of individuals"—John Dupré observes: "There are many sameness relations that serve to distinguish classes of organisms in ways that are relevant to various concerns . . . none of these relations is privileged."[87] Similar flexibility has been noted in other sciences.[88] For example,

> In the context of investigating electronic energy levels in
> the atom, one might define "electron" as a term referring

to charged particles orbiting about the atomic nucleus. In other situations definitions of this sort would be different, e.g., "particles emitted from a cathode," "fundamental units of electricity," "particles shared by atoms to form chemical bonds." Any or all of these might be considered "definitional" characteristics in a given context, though in others they might constitute hypotheses to be subjected to experimental verification.[89]

Suppose, by way of comparison, that we envisage an empiricist rather than a scientific theory of rigid designation, and apply it to the term *chess*. Chess, a theorist might say, requires a board and pieces. Such is the essence of chess; such are its components in any possible world. Granted, speakers might loosely extend the term *chess* to cover chess by mail or chess in one's head or chess played with a computer; in fact, they have thus twisted "fibre on fibre," despite the absence of board and pieces. However, these variants are not chess in the same sense of the word; they are not genuine instances of *chess*. (Here the word is uttered with emphasis, so as to carry conviction or convey an impression of rigor.) Such a theory would tell us more about the fixed mind-set of the theorist than about the fixity of the language or its terms.[90] And the theory's vogue, if it found a following, would reveal the current prevalence of similarly essentialistic thinking.[91]

Variations

The Kripke-Putnam theory has had a mixed reception. Most commentators have reacted negatively;[92] but some have limited their criticism to Putnam's extension of the theory beyond natural-kind words,[93] while others have argued for a more rigorous or plausible version of the theory. Robert Hollinger has written that rather than assert conceptual rigidity, he "would allow for the possibility—which Putnam does not seriously consider or rule out—that the laws which define a term like 'gold' are such that all and only gold (or at least all gold) conform to them. Such laws would specify empirically necessary and sufficient laws and properties, which would be scientifically defended, and would characterize natural kinds. This possibility is needed to defend essentialism."[94] Hollinger does not allege that scientists have discovered such laws. "My only claim is that it is a possibility that they might, and that if they did, essentialism would be true. If there are to be 'real essences,' such laws must in principle be discoverable, and the view of science based on the view that they can be must be a regulative ideal if essentialism is to be defensible."[95]

If Hollinger's essentialism looks more plausible than the version it replaces, that is because it makes such generous concessions that it barely merits the label "essentialism." Abandoning conceptual necessity and substituting contingent, empirical necessity marks one retreat from traditional essentialism; waiving the requirement that only members of the class—things of the named kind—can possess the essence constitutes another. Even so, if there are to be essences of the type envisaged, nature will no doubt need some help from definitions. The resulting essences may reflect the essentialistic preferences of those who speak of them as much as they reflect the uniformity of nature.

Consider isotopes. In opposition to a view he labels "Wittgensteinian," Hollinger rightly argues that no new meaning-stipulation was required—no "more or less arbitrary linguistic decision"—when scientists announced "that most, if not all, elements are really mixtures of isotopes, and always have been."[96] Wittgenstein would raise no objection here, nor would PRS. For, as Hollinger notes, "isotopes resemble their twins in all chemical respects."[97] Similar flexibility, natural and reasonable, might countenance many another diversification of inner structure without change of name, as for instance in the case of heavy water. But at this point the would-be essentialist faces a dilemma. Either the resulting "essences" will be disjunctive, in which case they will resemble still less the uniform realities traditionally labeled essences, or some linguistic adjustment will need to be made: the name will have to be accorded to just one kind of water, hydrogen, or the like, or be restricted to some aspect of the inner structure that is common to all varieties of the substance. From this dilemma one can sense why Hollinger proposes no actual samples as Kripke and Putnam did, but merely a schema for possible instantiation: "I will . . . construe schema[ta] such as 'Gold is an element with properties $P_1 \ldots P_n$ (which conforms to laws $l_1 \ldots l_n$)' as empirical/theoretical identification, analogous to 'Water is an aggregation of H_2O molecules.'"[98]

Hollinger would apparently grasp the second, more restrictive horn of the dilemma, and assert, more specifically, that real essences, if found, would make our linguistic decisions for us. They would determine what was gold, what was water, and so forth. For the only correct linguistic route is the scientific one, and the only correct, or optimal, way of doing science is the essentialistic way.[99]

Thus the adoption of essentialistic classifications would be neither arbitrary nor conventional.

> One way of bringing out this point is by noting the process-product ambiguity in the term "classification." Classification may be the activity of collecting things into groups, or the product of such activities. (I shall call these, respectively, "classification-1" and "classification-2.") Now, as an activity, classification-1 can be either natural or unnatural. Classification-1 is natural only if it serves as a means—ideally the best or only means—of achieving certain ends . . . I claim that there are some ends, e.g., the scientific goals of explanation, prediction, systematization, which can be best achieved—perhaps only achieved—by classifying-1 things into natural kinds, since doing so allows us to gain the most knowledge. If this is so, the fact that our interests put constraints on admissible classifications in no way shows that classifications-1, much less classifications-2, are conventional or arbitrary, or invented rather than discovered.[100]

Hollinger's thinking is thus doubly essentialistic: natural kinds have essences, because science has a single, ideal essence. "On this view, in which the conventional element is assumed to be at a minimum, the discovery of real essences amounts, in principle, to the discovery of the ultimate science which is, for Peirce, the ideal limit of scientific inquiry. Thus, if the Peircean ideal is legitimate, so is essentialism."[101]

To define science, which presently explains so much, in terms of an ideal which has no present instances, sounds suspiciously Platonic. Still, it opens interesting avenues of reflection. Does this contrast between actual science and the alleged ideal attest to present immaturity and incompleteness, or does it bespeak other possibilities than Hollinger envisions? May science continue to enunciate general explanatory laws in terms of bodies, movements, charges, and the like, or must it eventually pass to more specific laws, with regard to tigers, gold, quarks, and other natural kinds, and cluster them in rigid, essentialistic definitions?

It might appear that were specific laws added to the present general laws the result would be "the most knowledge." In support of this conclusion, Hollinger proposes that "the concepts 'essential property,' 'natural kind,' and 'natural necessity' play an explanatory role in theory,"[102] and offers the following illustrative schema:

> Gold dissolves in aqua regia because it has chemical structure S.
> It is reasonable for us to believe that anything which is gold would dissolve in aqua regia.
> The hypothesis that S constitutes gold's real essence is the only or best available hypothesis which (relative to what we now know) satisfactorily explains why this belief is true.

> It is reasonable to accept the hypothesis that S constitutes gold's real essence (ideally, we would know that it does), for this hypothesis provides the best available (ideally, the best possible) explanation of gold's behavior in aqua regia.[103]

I would suggest that at best this way of doing science would introduce a handier terminology; substantively it would add nothing to science's explanatory power. Consider the still simpler example Hollinger cites as analogous to this one. Were we to define water as "an aggregation of H_2O molecules," thus excluding heavy water and various other varieties, we might then explain the freezing point, boiling point, and other behavior of water by citing this "real essence." All water would behave the same way because it shared the same chemical structure. However, the identical facts could be explained by referring, not to "all water," but simply to "all H_2O." A more complex defining structure than H_2O might be more conveniently expressed by means of a single substantive (*cryolite, gamete,* or the like); but no explanatory power would be sacrificed by foregoing the shorthand expression—and certainly not by eschewing all reference to "real essences."

Hollinger does not stand alone. T. E. Wilkerson expresses a similar viewpoint.[104] So does Irving Copi, who agrees with Aristotle that "definition is a scientific process" and that "the definition of a thing should state its essence."[105] The first of these assertions, ignoring the varied forms and purposes of definition, suggests an essentialistic view of definition; the second, simplifying the needs and possibilities of science, betrays an essentialistic view of science. In response it may be noted, first, that not all defining is scientific; second, that even scientific discourse should allow for varied settings, aims, and interests; third, that only some natural kinds look like promising candidates for essentialistic definition; fourth, that even these may be bypassed by the genuine needs of science. It may be neither accident nor proof of immaturity that

science has managed until now without constant, uniform definitions of natural kinds. In the absence of any proof to the contrary,
then, classifications such as Hollinger and Copi defend should be
viewed as mere proposals. They are not the only correct classifications, dictated by nature, but more or less reasonable stipulations,
akin to Carnapian explications.

More recently, John Weckert has proposed a less narrowly scientific revision of Putnam's theory:

> Two objects have the same essence, let us say, if and only
> if they resemble each other in some important respect.
> Putnam cashes this in terms of the hidden or chemical
> structure of the objects. Two objects have the same
> essence if and only if they have the same, or very similar,
> hidden structures ... What we ought to say is that two
> objects have the same essence if and only if they resem-
> ble each other in certain ways which the linguistic com-
> munity considers to be important. Here essences are
> more likely to be cashed in terms of something like
> stereotypes. For example, bits of water on W_1 would have
> the same essence as bits of the W_2 liquid, XYZ.[106]

Weckert's essentialism is more modest than Putnam's. He does
not claim that all general terms, or even all those of a given category (for instance, natural-kind terms), are consistently governed
by importance and never, say, by mere resemblance (for instance,
between one shade of "blue" and another). He does not claim that
importance always attaches to underlying structures, or to
microstructures rather than to surface features, or that it holds
constant from culture to culture. ("It is quite plausible, for
instance, that in some community, even if not in ours, the only
resemblances important for some liquid to be water concern the
property of thirst-quenchingness."[107]) Weckert does not maintain,
as Putnam does, that "if A and B are members of the same kind,
they are so regardless of what anyone, anywhere, at any time,
believes about them."[108]

He does not notice, however, that importance may extend as
well as restrict a term's coverage; for example, given the importance of human health, climates and diets and complexions may
also seem important, and the same term, *healthy*, may therefore be
extended to them. Moreover, he too readily supposes, on the
strength of certain favorable examples, that importance, when present, inevitably prevails. And he takes no note of the fact that what
seems important to one person may seem unimportant or less

important to another, not only within the same general linguistic community, but even, for instance, within the scientific community, where emphasis may vary from context to context. Even for the same person importance is not fixed once and for all, but may shift from one scientific context to another or from a scientific to a non-scientific setting. A simple illustration can be derived from his own remark about water. Weckert speaks of importance, and Hollinger of interest, as determining the essences of things; but from such variable factors no uniform, invariant essences can result, any more than they can from sheer scientific fact.

Summary Reflections

As these post-Wittgensteinian samplings attest, general essentialistic doctrines, positing large numbers of essences, have not disappeared. However, Hollinger's, Copi's, and Weckert's versions of essentialism appear less widespread than the essentialism of Kripke and Putnam; and their theory, in turn, proved less popular and influential than Carnap's doctrine of explication; and his approach enjoyed a lesser vogue by far than traditional, pre-Wittgensteinian essentialism, sampled at the start of the chapter. Furthermore, the more recent varieties of essentialism have become progressively less general and less essentialistic. Although Carnap's prescription is entirely general, its application is not; only individual terms are affected, one by one, in philosophy, anthropology, physics, or elsewhere, as the occasion suggests. Putnam's theory extends to a great many terms, Kripke's to fewer, Hollinger and Copi's to still fewer.

Reasons for this broad retreat can be discerned in Wittgenstein's critique. Philosophers could, of course, continue to ignore the linguistic problems he posed for essentialism; and many have. Some continue to insist that they are interested in the realities words stand for, not in the words themselves; others declare concern for usage a mere anachronism, now that the heyday of ordinary-language philosophy has passed. However, all the post-Wittgensteinian essentialists whose views we have sampled have been aware of the linguistic challenge, and have taken the linguistic parameters of inquiry more seriously than their predecessors did. As a consequence, only a limited range of solutions has remained open to them. They could loosen the bonds of usage somewhat, as Carnap did; or claim that usage was in fact essentialistic, deep down, as Kripke and Putnam did; or allege that nature dictates usage and nature is—somehow or to some degree—essentialistic, as Hollinger, Copi, and Weckert did. None of these responses has proved satisfactory, and none, for reasons such as those suggested, has retained a broad following. Since few if any essentialistic alternatives remain to be tried, we may surmise that essentialism will continue to decline—at least in the form of general essentialistic theories, holding for language generally or for large categories of expressions.

Prospects look slight, however, that essentialism will soon cease to figure as an intellectual force. As empiricist thinking has been far commoner than the enunciation of general empiricist theories like the verification principle, and as teleological moral thinking has been far commoner than the enunciation of general teleological principles such as Mill's, so essentialistic thinking has been far commoner than the formulation of explicit, general essentialistic doctrines such as those reviewed in this chapter. These doctrines are but surface waves; the sands beneath are drenched with essentialistic practice—with piecemeal essentialistic theorizing and implicitly essentialistic reasoning. More extensive, more diffuse, and less obvious, hence less exposed to effective criticism, this underlying essentialism may long survive the surface variety. Yet it has received scant attention. Accordingly, essentialistic practice, not essentialistic theory, will occupy the next four chapters of this study.

Chapter Two

THE PERSISTENCE OF ESSENTIALISTIC THEORIZING

> How readily people suppose some single reality for each single
> term, common to all members of the class the term designates!
> How readily they suppose that a successful definition of the
> class would demonstrate the existence of such a common core!
> How readily they continue to believe that worthwile knowl-
> edge should take the form of universal formulae![1]

Essentialism has figured massively in Western thought—still more massively than a perusal of its explicit formulations would suggest, plentiful and influential though they have been. Present in practice as well as in theory, it has proved more resistant to critique and contrary evidence than one might expect. Hence essentialistic practice may continue when and if essentialistic theory is finally discredited. That this is so, and why it is so, will start to appear from this chapter's illustrations. They will also permit a fuller, more detailed critique than that developed in the preceding chapter.

Cajetan on Analogy

An impressive illustration of essentialism's power of endurance comes from an earlier age. "Cajetan's well-known work *de Nominum Analogia*," writes Henry Koren, "contains the first and still unsurpassed systematization of the Aristotelian-Thomistic theory of analogy. As such, it is the classical treatise of analogy and forms the basis of practically all modern discussions of the arduous problem of analogy."[2] Of special interest here is the manner in which Cajetan conducted his inquiry. The term *analogia*, he first notes, as received from the Greeks, meant a proportion or a proportionality. Now, alas, it has lost its unity. Cajetan identifies three current uses of *analogia*—analogy of inequality, analogy of attribution, and analogy of proportionality—and, discussing each, moves from what is least properly analogy to what is truly analogy.[3] For Cajetan, the first two members of this trilogy are abusively termed *analogia*; only the third merits the name.[4]

Perhaps the most striking feature of this doctrine is that Cajetan does not question the legitimacy of the verbal extensions he
catalogs, yet contests and rejects any extension of the term *analogia* regardless of whether it belongs to one or the other of these
three varieties, indeed without even considering or discussing such
a possible vindication. The practice of the Greeks decides the matter for him—despite the fact that the Greeks wrote Greek and the
authors he criticized wrote Latin,[5] and the fact that the Greeks
themselves extended the Greek word much as the Latins extended
the Latin term *analogia*.[6] How are we to explain such anomalies in
Cajetan's thought? How can we account for this dissonance
between his essentialistic manner and the facts of analogy which
stared him in the face—facts which he not only knew and accepted, but took as the subject matter of his discussion?

Whatever the reasons, they are likely to prove interesting. I
cite Cajetan's strange case, not as an historical oddity, but as representative of much past and contemporary practice. His case is
representative, specifically, with regard to the treatment of analogy, since "those who have constructed 'theories' of analogy have
usually construed 'analogy' as itself a univocal term."[7] More generally, his approach resembles many others' in its terminological
narrowness. It is not just ancient, pre-analytic thinkers who,
resisting familiar extensions by analogy, have insisted on the
"proper," "true," "strict" sense of terms and have trimmed discussion accordingly.

Russell, for example, used similarly restrictive expressions to
declare that what we customarily call names are not really names.
"In the *proper strict logical* sense of the word," he maintained, a
name is the sign for some simple item (or "particular") within immediate consciousness;[8] the things we customarily call names are not
in fact such. The most revealing of the restrictive expressions I have
italicized is the third: *logical*. For the proper sense of the term *name*
Russell looks, not to the ancients, but to logicians— and to idealized
logicians at that, just as Cajetan's Greeks were idealized Greeks.
Why we should be bound by the usage of logicians, or regard their
usage as normative, Russell does not indicate.

Wittgenstein spoke of bringing words back from their metaphysical to their everyday use. Why such a restoration should be
necessary, and why "metaphysicians" like Cajetan and Russell
depart so freely from everyday usage, is something of a
mystery—especially when they are as aware as these two were of
everyday usage and cite it in their discussions. Wittgenstein's
early thought, in which much the same phenomenon appears, is

less mysterious, since the author himself provides a subsequent depth analysis—or conceptual psychoanalysis—of his personal pathology. I shall here attend to the pathology, and its kinship with Cajetan's, and shall later return to consider its etiology.

Wittgenstein on Language and Propositions

"My *whole* task," Wittgenstein declared in an early notebook, "consists in explaining the nature of the proposition."[9] From the nature of the proposition he might discern the nature of language and thought, and of the world they represent. For already when he wrote these words, thought and language appeared to him "as the unique correlate, picture, of the world. These concepts: proposition, language, thought, world, stand in line one behind the other, each equivalent to each."[10]

The key to the last three concepts was the first; for according to the *Tractatus*, language and thought consist of propositions, and "in the proposition a world is as it were put together experimentally."[11] In a specific proposition the structure of a specific world or state of affairs stands revealed. From the nature of all propositions the nature of all possible worlds or states of affairs shines forth.

What young Wittgenstein had to determine, then, was the *general form* of the proposition *as such*. The form common to some propositions might be Fx, to others xRy, to others (Ex)Fx, and so on; but the form common to them all could not contain such details. "It is clear that *only* what is essential to the most general propositional form may be included in its description—for otherwise it would not be the most general form" (4.5). But what constitutes this elusive quintessence of propositions?

Halfway through the *Tractatus*, Wittgenstein declared: "It now seems possible to give the most general propositional form: that is, to give a description of the propositions of *any* sign-language *whatsoever* in such a way that every possible sense can be expressed by a symbol satisfying the description, and every symbol satisfying the description can express a sense, provided that the meanings of the names are suitably chosen...The general form of a proposition is: This is how things stand" (4.5). That is, a proposition is a logical picture of reality, a model of a possible state of affairs which it affirms (4.01, 4.064). And the totality of such propositions is language (*Sprache*) (4.001).

Wittgenstein's later reaction to these doctrines of his youth was to emphasize differences. There are "countless different kinds of use of what we call 'symbols,' 'words,' 'sentences'. And this multiplicity is not something fixed, given once for all; but new types of language, new language-games, as we may say, come into existence, and others become obsolete and get forgotten."[12] No one essence, no general form, pervades this multiplicity.[13] Rather, the concept *language* resembles the concept *game*: "We see a complicated network of similarities overlapping and criss-crossing: sometimes overall similarities, sometimes similarities of detail."[14] No single similarity, common to all games and to them alone, accounts for the common label.

The same holds for the concept *proposition* (and still more for the German concept *Satz*). A paraphrase of *Investigations* §66, on games, might run: "Look, for example, at empirical propositions (historical, introspective, scientific, predictive, and so forth), with their multifarious relationships. Now pass to mathematical propositions; here you find many correspondences with the first group, but many common features drop out, and others appear. When we pass next to propositions concerning nonexistent entities (Hamlet, Santa Claus, Cyclops, and the like), much that is common is retained, but much is lost.—Do they all picture the world? Compare propositions of logic with descriptions of the weather. Or are there always verification and falsification, or descriptive criteria to go by? Think of avowals. In science there is observation and experiment; logical propositions have no such backing. Look at the importance of context for some propositions and the irrelevance of context for others . . . We can go through the many, many other types of proposition in the same way; can see how similarities crop up and disappear."

How, then, could the *Tractatus* have erred so egregiously? How could it ignore its own warnings? "In everyday language," its author noted, "it very frequently happens that the same word has different modes of signification, and so belongs to different symbols—or two words that have different modes of signification are employed in propositions in what is superficially the same way" (3.323). "In this way the most fundamental confusions are easily produced (the whole of philosophy is full of them)" (3.324). Yet this realization apparently had scant effect on Wittgenstein's own mode of philosophizing. He was untroubled by the thought (if it ever came to him) that the words *Satz* and *Sprache* may also have varying uses, precluding the discovery of any single essence, "general concept," or "general form" which alone legitimizes the appellation. Despite the warnings of 3.323-3.324, in Wittgenstein's early doctrine no qualifications appear in the manner of *Philosophical Investigations* §43

("For a *large* class of cases—though not for all—in which we employ the word 'meaning' it can be defined thus: the meaning of a word is its use in the language"). The *Tractatus* simply declares, apodictically, what language is and what propositions are, without any reference to usage or acknowledgement of its variations.

"The essential thing about metaphysics," we have seen Wittgenstein remark, is that "it obliterates the distinction between factual and conceptual investigations." The *Tractatus* attended little to this distinction—indeed, so little that it is not immediately evident that its deliverances disagree with those of the *Investigations*. The *Investigations* denies that there is "something common to all that we call language" and claims, instead, that "these phenomena have no one thing in common which makes us use the same word for all." The *Tractatus* contains no such references to what we *call* language or to what makes us *use the same word*. It does not pretend to be doing conceptual analysis; it does not propose to trace the borderline of the German concept *Satz* or the meanderings of the English concept *proposition*. But neither, on the other hand, does it propose to furnish a factual description of those things which fall within the borders of the concepts it employs (*Satz, Gedanke, Sprache*). That, too, would require some attention to the actual use of the terms; and Wittgenstein was not interested in mere verbal usage. So what *was* he doing?

Like Cajetan, Russell, and so many other speculative thinkers, he left his language-game undefined; even as he scrutinized the use of words, he failed to pay attention to his own use of words.[15] Does 4.5 trace the borderline of *Satz* in German usage? Obviously not. That's not the game being played. Does it describe the things that fall within that boundary? Again, surely not. In everyday use, the term *Satz* extends to sentences, propositions, and statements, to countless varieties of each; and young Wittgenstein knew it did.[16] As a description of that usage-defined class, his statement would be grossly, obviously inaccurate. But what class, then, does 4.5 describe? Whatever fits its description? Is it a mere tautology: "Propositions that picture reality all picture reality; those that say how things stand all say how things stand"? Surely not. With both conceptual and factual description precluded, there remains the possibility that 4.5 should be read as a mere stipulation of sense: "Let us apply the term *Satz* to utterances that say how things stand in the world." But this interpretation of Wittgenstein's meaning looks still less realistic.

Running through all conceivable interpretations, we realize that an utterance like 4.5 is not plausibly explained by any one of them. Wittgenstein had no coherent conception of what he was doing; he simply disregarded the verbal aspect of his theorizing and stared, unheeding, through his verbal spectacles. Such is his own verdict on his youthful classic.[17]

Once he attended not merely to concepts in general but to the concepts that he himself employed—*Satz, Sprache, Gedanke,* and the rest—he recognized their shifting diversity. Once he recognized their diversity, he saw the implication. Philosophy could not be done in the manner of the *Tractatus.* Were there uniform, sharply defined essences, and many of them, the attempt to discover and formulate essences might make sense. But if we cease thinking long enough to look, we find no such essences. Hence the essentialistic mode of theorizing exemplified by the *Tractatus* is not viable.

Williams on Knowledge

This lesson has not taken hold as widely as one might expect. Even among those familiar with Wittgenstein's paradigm experience, speculation has continued in the Tractarian mode. As one example among many, consider the exchange some years ago between Bernard Williams and A. J. Ayer on the subject of knowledge. "I shall be concerned," Williams explained, "only with what I shall call *propositional* knowledge, knowledge whose paradigmatic expression in language-users is the confident assertion of truths, and where the claim that it is knowledge that is being expressed involves as a necessary condition that what is asserted is true."[18] For the speakers in question to be knowers, they must have good reasons for what they assert. But how are these "good reasons" to be defined?

> What is necessary—and what represents the undoubted fact that knowledge differs from mere true belief—is that one or more of a class of conditions should obtain, which relate the fact that A has this belief to the fact that the belief is true: conditions which can best be summarised by the formula that, given the truth of p, it is no accident that A believes p rather than not-p. This formula is vague and over-generous, but it gets us, I think, on the right line.[19]

That the formula is "vague and over-generous" as an analysis of knowledge appears, Williams suggests, from an example like the following:

Suppose that A, being from Guinea, tells B falsely that he is from Ghana; but (let us fancifully suppose) owing to features of A's spoken English which are peculiar to Guineans, B takes him to have said "Guinea" when he said "Ghana." Then B has come truly to believe that A is from Guinea, and (in an obvious sense) it is no accident, relative to A's being from Guinea, that this has come about; but B can scarcely be said to have acquired knowledge in this way, as opposed (for instance) to a situation in which, familiar with the Guinean accent, he sees through the pretense.[20]

From this and similar counterexamples, Williams does not conclude, with the later Wittgenstein, that precise, definitional analysis should be abandoned. Instead, he expresses the hope that further investigation may provide some appropriate types of restriction, such as those needed to distinguish between the passage of a piece of information and the more general notion of a causal chain with the same proposition at each end of it. In the absence of the required restrictions, he offers the "no accident" clause "not as part of an analysis but (as I said before) as a label for a class of conditions, the general requirements on which need to be spelled out with greater precision."[21]

Ayer responds to Williams as Wittgenstein might have. "I think," he writes,

> that there are various different grounds on which claims to knowledge can be accredited, and I therefore suspect that if one is trying to define knowledge, in its personal aspect, one may have to be content with some such vague formula as my own 'having the right to be sure.' If one ventures on anything more precise, one is likely to be faced with counter-examples . . . We are usually able to decide the question in particular cases, though even here there may be differences of opinion, but I have some doubt whether these particular decisions can be fitted tidily under any general rule.[22]

This response looks realistic, but needs to be spelled out to carry full conviction. Let us ask: Is the ideal precision which Williams aims at a precision which he believes presently exists in usage—that is, in the customary use of *know, knowledge,* and the like—or is it a precision he aims to introduce, by veiled or explicit stipulation of a new, more precise sense of these terms? Does he see himself as *tracing* a sharp border or *drawing* a sharp border? His reference to "analysis" suggests the former, as does the absence of any arguments or explanations he might have used to propose a new idiom. Yet what are the chances that English usage draws such a sharp border, or that we could detect the border if it did exist, or that we could express it accurately, in a precise defining formula, if we did detect it?

First, how likely is it that the English-speaking population has, through consistent linguistic practice, drawn a boundary more precise than the ones Williams and Ayer proposed? This question can be broken into three sub-queries: How frequent are cases lying just one side or the other of this more precise border, so that application of *know* or *knowledge* on one side and nonapplication on the other would trace a conceptual borderline between them? When and if such cases occur, how frequently do people analyze them closely, then publicly confer or withhold the label *know* or *knowledge*? When and if they so discriminate, do their scattered verdicts agree? Merely formulating these queries suffices to suggest how doubtful is the existence of the sharp border Williams envisages.[23]

The queries also suggest how unlikely it is that such a border would be known to any speaker of the language, or could be discovered through linguistic inquiry. (This improbability reinforces the unlikelihood of the border's existence, since the regularity of the usage would not result, as in most instances, from acquaintance with an existing standard.) Who among us can recall a single such borderline predication (outside the imaginings of philosophers)? Who among us knows how to gather even half a dozen such specimens of actual linguistic usage? As for the method of questionnaires proposing imaginary cases and asking people's verdicts, even if no falsification resulted from the artificiality of the situation and the wording of the inquiries, the "verdicts" elicited would more likely *create* a borderline than reveal an existing one.[24] And what grounds do we have to expect that the responses would all agree? Suppose the instances used to test the "good reasons" aspect of knowledge were religious, political, or ethical ones: could unanimity be expected? Suppose such instances were avoided: would the result be representative?

Finally, if the border of the concept *know* were in fact razor-sharp and if we were able to verify its existence (both very big *if*s), there still would be no guarantee that other terms could be discovered with which to trace the concept's border precisely. By comparison, suppose that we set out to discover the final shade this side of *orange* which falls within the concept *red* and the first precise shade beyond it which falls within the concept *orange*. The unlikelihood of such a border, unknown to speakers of the language, is comparable to the unlikelihood of a precise border for *know*. But assume that somehow we did in fact spot it. With what other words might we then indicate this borderline? Would any single terms other than *red* and *orange* draw that precise boundary? Does any *combination* of terms exist which would pinpoint that dividing line?

This comparison with color concepts brings up further difficulties. To draw a precise border between red and orange is not to draw a precise border between red and pink, red and blue, red and black, and so on. Thus a single fine discrimination between red and some one bordering color would not trace the whole borderline of *red*. Something similar might hold, and probably does, for the concept *know*. In one direction, *direct evidence* grows weaker and weaker, in another *testimony*, in another *argumentation*, in relation to paradigm instances of knowledge. Presumably, then, in Williams's view, at some precise point in each of these directions the border is crossed from knowing to not knowing. However, even this would not suffice. In other directions, varied combinations of reasons—of direct evidence and testimony, of testimony and argumentation, of direct evidence and argumentation, or of all these reasons combined—also taper off imperceptibly (as in the spaces between orange and pink, purple and black, and so forth, along the border with red). Thus no single pinpoint verdict between case and case would trace the entire border of the concept *know*.

The more closely we examine Williams's apparent goal, the more it appears not only unattainable but pointless. Suppose we had both detected and accurately drawn such a border between *red* and *orange*, or between *orange* and *pink*: what purpose, practical or theoretical, would the delineation serve? Suppose we were to labor and bring forth a similar result for *know*: what significance would such a semantic discovery have? Immediately on one side of the border, the reasons—personal experiences, authorities, arguments—would be slightly stronger, on the other slightly weaker. So? What utility would that discovery possess? Even if the slight difference in degree were a useful thing to know, couldn't we make the same discrimination (this stronger, that weaker) without paying any attention to the concept *know* or its borderline?[25]

One suspects that this search—this pursuit of "the strict sense of knowledge which has exercised philosophers through the centuries"[26] (and many another like it)—reveals a lingering essentialism. A single formula is pursued because it would reveal a single essence, common to all instances of knowledge, and not a heterogeneous grouping within the concept's ample boundary. Once we had the formula, we would perceive the nature of all knowledge, not simply the borderline between some not very interesting and not very representative examples. But this underlying essentialist supposition is warranted neither with regard to the concept to be analyzed nor with regard to the concepts used to analyze it. This is the lesson of the later Wittgenstein's critique. In the absence of numerous, precise, uniform essences, the enterprise of precise, bordertracing "analysis" no longer looks either feasible or profitable.[27]

It may seem unlikely that a thinker as intelligent as Williams was engaged in a wild-goose chase. But the author of the *Tractatus* was equally intelligent. So it is not unrealistic to suggest, in view of countless inquiries similar to Williams's, that something may still be learned from Wittgenstein's experience. At first glance the *Investigations* looks regrettably woolly and imprecise in comparison with the *Tractatus*. But the contrary is in fact the case.[28]

Consider a comparison with cartography. The borders of the runways at O'Hare may be mapped with great precision, but not the borders of the Mississippi River. Sometimes the river is high; sometimes it is low; sometimes it floods and spreads for miles; every so often it shifts its bed. Now which cartographer is more accurate: one who, as in the maps in our atlases, gives a general indication of the river's course, or one who, without regard for nature's fluctuations, maps the river's contours as precisely as the runways at O'Hare? Who has a more realistic understanding: the map-maker who rests content with a rough indication or the one who aspires to pinpoint accuracy? The same contrast holds between the *Tractatus*'s pronouncements and the *Investigations'* rough sketches, and between Williams's analytic aspirations and Ayer's more modest expectations. Ayer, I would say, showed better understanding of the methodological implications of analogy—that is, of the shifting, indefinite heterogeneity of our concepts, stressed by the later Wittgenstein.

Dretske on Knowledge

Essentialism has not proved an unmitigated misfortune. Had Ponce de Léon not believed in the fountain of youth, he might never have learned about Florida; had Plato not proposed a definition of knowledge and had critics not sought to refine or improve it, many an interesting epistemological fact might have gone undetected. A believer in the Platonic account has something to learn, for example, from the kind of case Fred Dretske cites, proposed by Gilbert Harman. Suppose a man, S, has only one among thousands of tickets in a lottery, hence has little chance of winning. Even if S correctly predicts that he is going to lose, we would deny that he *knows* he is going to lose if the only basis for his belief is the fact that his chances of winning are so slight. This is puzzling. For where a belief is based solely on testimony, and the testimony, though fallible, looks sure, we may grant a claim of knowledge. Yet the probabilities in both instances may be comparable. "Why, then," asks Dretske, "are we prepared to say that we know in the one case but not in the other?"[29] Neither Plato's nor Williams's formulation explains this difference. Dretske thinks he can account for it, by noting the presence of a "conclusive reason" in the second case but not in the first. More generally and fully,

> Let us call R a conclusive reason for P if and only if R would not be the case unless P were the case . . . Of course, R may *be* a conclusive reason for believing P without anyone believing P, much less having R as their reason for believing. I shall say, therefore, that S *has conclusive reasons*, R, for believing P if and only if:
>
> (A) R is a conclusive reason for P . . .
> (B) S believes, without doubt, reservation, or question, that P is the case and he believes this on the basis of R,
> (C) (i) S knows that R is the case or
>   (ii) R is some experimental state of S (about which it may not make sense to suppose that S *knows* that R is the case; at least it no longer makes much sense to ask *how* he knows).
>
> With only minor embellishments, to be mentioned in a moment, I believe that S's having conclusive reasons for believing P is *both* a necessary and a sufficient condition for his knowing that P is the case.[30]

True to his word, Dretske merely mentions but does not provide these missing "embellishments"; and they sound less minor when he concludes:

> I think both of the above qualifications can be summarized by saying that when one has conclusive reasons, then this is sufficient for knowing that P is the case when those reasons are *properly specific*, both with regard to *what it is* that displays the particular features

on which one relies *and* on the particular features themselves. A complete statement of these restrictions is,
however, far beyond the scope of this paper. Suffice it to
say that the possession of conclusive reasons for believing is a necessary condition for knowledge and, properly
qualified along the lines suggested here, also (I think)
sufficient.[31]

These words have a familiarly inconclusive sound. Like
Williams and many others,[32] Dretske harbors high aspirations, yet
recognizes that somehow the grail of perfect precision and adequacy has eluded him. And indeed, with the sufficient and necessary
conditions of knowledge still not "properly qualified," subsequent
authors have found flaws in Dretske's account and thought up
counterexamples. Having formulated situations which satisfy his
stipulations as stated, they deny knowledge,[33] or, in situations
which fail to meet his demands, they assert knowledge.[34]

How are such disagreements to be decided? *Can* they be decided? Does a correct answer exist, either for individual contested
cases or for knowledge generally? Who or what can arbitrate conflicting "intuitions"?

According to the correspondence criterion of truth I proposed,
refined, and defended in *Language and Truth*, established word-
uses typically do serve, and regularly should serve, as neutral
arbiters of truth. This criterion is not as restrictive as it sounds.
Established uses need not be rigidly fixed. Nor need they be standard. They may originate either by customary practice or by stipulation. However, neither of these alternatives permits a verdict in
borderline disputes like those in which Williams, Dretske, and others have engaged.[35] The customary uses of words like *know* and
knowledge have fuzzy edges, hence yield no verdict for or against
borderline cases; and the theorists who debate the cases stipulate
no special, more precise senses of their own by which the truth of
their assertions might be judged. Their answers, then, presumably
are true by virtue of some other, unstated standard. But what this
other standard might be—this apparently nonlinguistic standard
by which linguistic acts might be judged—is far from clear. So long
as the criterion of linguistic correspondence is spurned or ignored
and no rational alternative replaces it, debates like the one concerning the *precise* nature of knowledge may be expected to continue interminably, unresolved and unresolvable.[36]

Insisting on linguistic standards for linguistic acts elicits
impatience in many: they feel forced, willy-nilly, into a linguistic

straitjacket. Yet, suppose somebody proposed to play a game, without naming it or specifying the rules, and suppose those invited asked, "What game? What are its rules? Will there be scoring, will there be winning? If so, how will the score be tallied, how will the winner be determined?" Such queries would not be unreasonable. They would elicit no complaints about an arbitrary "ludistic principle of immanence" from which there is no escape, comparable to the "linguistic principle of immanence" others have complained of. Similarly, if somebody proposes to engage in linguistic activity, it is not unreasonable to suppose that the activity will be subject to rules, either familiar or stipulated, and to inquire what those rules are. In familiar discourse, in familiar settings, such clarifications may not be necessary: everybody knows what game is being played. But in speculative inquiry no such supposition can be made. It is often evident that the language-game is not played by familiar rules, yet no substitute rules are specified. It then becomes unclear not only how to play the game, but why. What is the point?

Essence-seeking made sense, supposing there were such things as essences. If, as Moore opined, essences or real universals are among "the most important kinds of things in the Universe"—if "there are tremendous numbers of them, and we are all constantly thinking and talking of them"—then let us by all means pursue them, though the search should prove as arduous as that for ultimate particles. It is clear, however, that the pursuit of sufficient and necessary conditions, as conducted by a seeker like Dretske, is disconnected from the pursuit of essences as traditionally conceived. Traditional essentialists often assumed, wrongly, that a perfectly accurate definition, restricting a term to all and only members of some class, would demonstrate or reveal an essence. But it is evident from Dretske's account that his formula, if successful, would not capture a single essence, in the sense of a single, uniform reality present in all instances of knowledge. Dretske's condition C, above, is disjunctive, and so is his condition A, with regard to the "conclusive reason for P." Some conclusive reasons are logically conclusive, he notes; others are empirically conclusive.[37]

If, then, the formulation of precise necessary and sufficient conditions of knowledge neither captures a concept of the English language nor reveals an essence, what is its point? So far as I can see, the statement of such conditions would furnish no help in discovering the truth; conclusive reasons for beliefs would be just as difficult to establish, whether or not they figured in the definition of knowledge. For the same reason, the proposed conditions would offer no help in answering skeptical attacks on knowledge. Nor would they assist in sorting out justified beliefs from unjustified; the lottery example demonstrates how strong a person's reasons for belief may be without counting as conclusive or warranting a knowledge claim. In the absence, then, of any satisfactory explanation—or any attempt at an explanation—one may suspect that this continuing effort to formulate necessary and sufficient conditions is the lingering ghost of a long-popular enterprise: the formulation of real, essential definitions, applying to all and only the members of some class.

If so, Wittgenstein's misgivings may be justified: "We are opposed above all to the idea that the question 'What is knowledge?'—for instance—is a burning issue. For *such* it appears to be, and it seems as though we didn't know anything at all until we can answer *it*. In our philosophical investigation we would like, as it were, to finish off something in the greatest haste, since everything else appears to hang in the air till it is completed."[38]

Overview

It may be unfair to criticize theorists like Dretske for failing to explicate the nature and purpose of their enterprise. To illuminate such questions, we should perhaps look to general methodological inquiries, not to particular discussions concerning knowledge, meaning, reference, and the like. However, when we do turn to such inquiries, for instance those in the last chapter, no light is shed. To judge from their expectations and mode of argumentation, neither Williams nor Dretske saw himself as engaged in linguistic analysis. Neither saw himself as proposing a Carnapian explication, satisfying criteria of simplicity, precision, fruitfulness, and proximity to usage. Neither viewed knowledge as a natural kind to be treated in the manner Putnam prescribed. What, then, was the game being played?

At the start of the article Dretske cited, Gilbert Harman may have revealed the mentality of other participants in the debate about knowledge, and not just his personal perspective:

> I take an analysis to be any interesting set of necessary and sufficient conditions. Although I shall not offer an analysis of the meaning of "know" (whatever that would be), I shall appeal to your intuitions about hypothetical cases. I shall claim, for example, that a person can come

> to know something when he is told it, or when he reads
> it in the newspaper. Although I may seem to appeal to
> what one would ordinarily say about such cases and for
> this reason may seem to be doing "linguistic analysis," I
> am interested in what is true about such cases and not
> just in what we say about such cases.[39]

What is true about Harman's hypothetical cases (for instance, the lottery case) is, first of all, what he freely stipulates about them (for instance, the number of tickets, S's single ticket). What is also true is the improbability of S's having won the lottery and the reasonableness of supposing that he didn't. But beyond these evident truths, Harman wishes to know whether such a supposition qualifies as *knowledge*. And this is to be determined, apparently, not by consulting "what we say" but through an appeal to our "intuitions."

To some extent, this makes sense. While it would be odd to speak of an "intuition" that it is raining when drops are pouring down, or of an "intuition" that a student knows the answer when he has set it down, flawlessly, in his examination paper, somehow discernment of the truth becomes more delicate and difficult in the cases Harman cites. The reason, I think, is clear. No amount of water, by itself, no quantity of scribbling, alone, would establish the truth of "It's raining" or "He knows the answer." The statement's words are also relevant: the downpour is a clear instance of what we call rain; the student's answer is a clear example of the kind of evidence on which we base assertions of knowledge. Harman appeals to our "intuitions" because familiar usage will no longer provide comparable, unreflective guidance in the borderland into which his imaginings lead us. Hence any judgments of "truth" he may evoke from us will have a new status: they will not have the backing of existing word-use, nor report agreement with it, but will establish new agreement in the use of the word *know*—provided our spontaneous, unguided reactions do agree.[40]

As a matter of fact, reactions often disagree in such instances. This is not surprising. In conceptual borderlands, dissimilarities balance similarities, and the dissimilarities suggest one verdict while the similarities suggest the contrary. And in the absence of any independent guidance from common word meanings in the language, opposed inclinations, preferences, or ideological allegiances cause some to stress similarities (for example, the familiar behavior and appearance of Twin-Earth water) and others to stress dissimilarities (for example, the different chemical structure). However, such lack of agreement is no misfortune. Nothing hinges on people's reactions to such borderline queries. Once we recognize the nature of the game being played, we can see that it is not worth playing.

Consider the linguistic games Wittgenstein cites, of assigning colors to vowels or calling days "fat" or "lean." ("Given the two ideas 'fat' and 'lean,' would you be rather inclined to say that Wednesday was fat and Tuesday lean, or the other way round?"[41]) And suppose that people all agreed in their reactions, either concerning some single day (compare: some single candidate sample of knowledge) or concerning all the days of the week (compare: all candidate instances of knowledge, however varied and bizarre). What significance would that have? Would it reveal for the first time what the words *fat* and *lean* mean? And would no one know what they meant until they had imagined all possible language-games and elicited people's reactions to them? So is it impossible to know the meaning of any word?[42]

Harman's remarks show affinity with the traditional, Tractarian style of thought rejected by the later Wittgenstein. The *Tractatus*, too, wandered in semantic limbo. Guided, at least to some extent, by usage, it did not define propositions as jet-reaction engines or names as pedigreed Alsatians. Yet it made no explicit appeal to usage, and freely departed from it. The *Tractatus* was not engaged in "linguistic analysis." Neither, however, was it engaged in simply describing the real while respecting standard terminology. In its failure clearly to distinguish between the conceptual and the real, and to articulate a procedure in light of this distinction, young Wittgenstein's thought was (in his later terminology) typically "metaphysical." So, it seems, was Harman's and others' like it.

In defense of the painstaking, seemingly more rigorous type of essentialistic thinking popular in our day, I have heard one practitioner reply that methodological clarity cannot be expected; whether in science or in philosophy, one must just muddle through. I am less pessimistic. Essentialistic urges lead to essentialistic darkness, in the manner Wittgenstein noted; but once people free themselves of essentialistic expectations and corresponding modes of investigation, they may undertake inquiries both meaningful and worthwile.

In my own practice I think, for example, of the work already cited in which I attempt an overview of the concept *true*, without formulating precise sufficient and necessary conditions of truth, and in which I assess the general validity of the norm implicit in the concept, without enunciating a comprehensive ethics of acceptable predication. Regardless of whether they are successful, both of these attempts, as attempts, look worthwhile. As noted above, mapping may be an intelligible, profitable enterprise even though it delineates no essences and achieves no absolute precision. The "ultimate" precision philosophers often aspire to makes no better sense in philosophy than it does in cartography.

These methodological reflections connect the present chapter, concerning particular concepts, with the preceding chapter's more comprehensive theories. The theorizing of Cajetan, Wittgenstein, Williams, and Dretske, with regard to analogy, propositions, language, and knowledge, does not derive from nor rely on general, essentialistic theories such as those enunciated in chapter 1 by Ross, Russell, Moore, Scheler, and Husserl. Cajetan does not say: "All words have a single, original meaning, hence *analogy* has a single, original meaning." Wittgenstein does not argue: "Words have uniform meanings, hence *proposition* has a uniform meaning, hence a general form of propositions exists and can be discovered." Quite the contrary; both attend explicitly to semantic variation. Similarly, Williams and Dretske, familiar with Wittgenstein's later work, do not suppose that close examination of usage will reveal a single entity called knowledge or a set of sufficient and necessary conditions for knowledge. It would not do so even if Kripke and Putnam were right about natural kinds, for knowledge is not a natural kind. Disputants like Williams and Dretske are equally uninterested, however, in Carnapian stipulation of senses. If Harman speaks for them, their aim is to discover the truth of the matter. What this means or how it is possible, they do not explain through recourse to any more comprehensive theory, under which the inquiry about knowledge is subsumed. There being no such connections with essentialistic theory, none are severed when the theory is eliminated. From all these samples it is evident, then, that inquiry can continue essentialistically concerning particular topics (truth, knowledge, meaning, reference, action, love, causation, etc.) despite the decline of general essentialistic theories documented in the last chapter.

The like holds at a deeper, less explicit level of practice. Essentialists not only reach essentialistic conclusions, general or particular; they also reason essentialistically, in ways that, to be valid, would require their words to have uniform, invariant meanings. From their ratiocinations, one would think the meanings were tesserae—colored bits of glass—whose hues do not vary wherever they may be placed in a mosaic; or that the reasoners were operating a calculus whose symbols each have a single, undeviating application. As we shall see, such essentialists in practice may be opposed to essentialism in theory. As in the case of Cajetan or the author of the *Tractatus,* their practice may remain strangely unaffected by their theory.

Chapter Three

CALCULUS AND MOSAIC

Since Reasoning, or Inference, the principal subject of logic, is an operation which usually takes place by means of words, and in complicated cases can take place in no other way; those who have not a thorough insight into the signification and purposes of words, will be under chances, amounting almost to certainty, of reasoning or inferring incorrectly.[1]

In the Socratic dialogs, one can sense how profoundly the essentialistic suppositions of Socrates and Plato affect their modes of inquiry and argumentation, both critically and constructively. Critically, Socrates rejects the varied instances of knowledge cited by Theaetetus; he did not ask for many things, he explains, but for one thing—knowledge. Constructively, assuming in the *Republic* that justice must be the same wherever it appears, he examines justice in society so as to see it "writ large" and thereby discern more clearly what it consists of for individuals. It is as though justice, or the word *justice*, were a colored bit of glass that might be placed here or there in different mosaics without affecting its hue: if red in a robe, it will be red in a sunset or a flower; if black in a boot, it will be black in a beard or a baldachino. Wherever one examines it, the result will be the same. If it is not—if one notes any variation of shade from one spot to another, one can be sure that the two bits are not the same. They cannot both be justice—or knowledge.

Such thinking persists. To illustrate: "Where an author mentions and discusses only types of interpersonal love, we try to discover what these types have in common. We assume that a proponent of a theory of love can be expected to provide identical answers to the questions: What is love among human beings? and What do the types of love among human beings mentioned have in common? If the answer to these two questions is not the same, the author is discussing more than one subject"[2]—he is not discussing the one thing, *love*. Implicit here is an invitation to speak and reason as though one were operating a calculus according to definite, essentialistic rules. If love is one thing, then the term *love* denotes one thing, and argumentation can proceed accordingly.

"Invariant-unit reasoning" might be a fitting label for such thinking, but "calculus-reasoning" is more suggestive. For it is characteristic of various calculi—propositional, predicate, mathematical, and others—to employ invariant units (the p's and q's of propositional logic, the phi's and psi's of predicate logic, and so forth), and to value their invariance as permitting valid reasoning without regard for context. Within such calculi, calculus-reasoning is appropriate; for there the units are invariant. It becomes inappropriate when the units are the concepts of any natural language.

Such reasoning crops up with surprising frequency even in the writings of avowed opponents of essentialism. An arresting example is George Pitcher's critique of the saying in *Investigations* §43: "For a *large* class of cases—though not for all—in which we employ the word 'meaning' it can be defined thus: the meaning of a word is its use in the language." According to Pitcher,

> Wittgenstein's identification is implausible on the face of it. In nonlinguistic areas, at any rate, things which have uses (e.g., tools, instruments) normally cannot sensibly be said to have meanings. Moreover, things which may sometimes have meanings—or (in case nothing non-linguistic can be said to *have* a meaning) things which may sometimes mean something—(e.g., black clouds on the horizon, footprints in the snow, the rising pitch of someone's voice) do not, except rarely, have uses. So one would not expect the meaning of a *word* to be the same thing as its use(s) in the language, and I think it can be shown that it is not.[3]

The facts Pitcher cites, here and later, do indicate how mistaken it would be to assert the universal identity of meaning and use. But, of course, Wittgenstein did not identify meaning and use. He identified in some contexts the meaning *of a word* with the use *of a word* in a language. So how do the facts cited make his definition look "implausible on the face of it"? For what reason would they make one "not expect the meaning of a *word* to be the same thing as its use(s) in the language"?

The only connection I can see is one Wittgenstein demolished in his study of general terms. If all meaning is of one sort and all use is of one sort, then the equivalence of meaning and use in any individual case would lead us to expect equivalence in all cases. And a lack of equivalence in other cases would lead us to expect non-equivalence in any particular case, for instance that of words and their meanings. But Wittgenstein has shown to Pitcher's satisfaction that everyday terms like *use* and *meaning* rarely, if ever, designate invariant essences. So is not a situation such as the one Pitcher describes precisely what we should expect? Is it so strange if only *one* member in each of two families bears a close resemblance to the other?[4]

Pitcher's reasoning exemplifies the form of essentialism scrutinized in this chapter. In his argument, he advances no general theory, like those in chapter 1: he does not suggest that all or most general terms, including *meaning* and *use*, designate essences. Nor does he espouse any particular essentialistic theory, akin to those in chapter 2: he does not allege, in the manner of Cajetan or Russell, that only one kind of meaning is genuine meaning or that one kind of use is bona fide use; he does not propose sufficient and necessary conditions for meaning or use, in the manner of Williams and Dretske. Were such claims advanced, he might reject them. Yet his mode of argumentation demands some such essentialistic supposition. Basic invariance, both of meaning and of use, supplies the missing premise of his critique.

Pitcher's practice, distinct from and opposed to his general theory, illustrates anew how impervious to direct refutation essentialism may be. At a deeper, more implicit level, still more pervasively than appeared from the last two chapters, essentialism may remain operative in people's thinking long after explicit essentialistic theories have been discredited. However, a single paradigm cannot reveal the full magnitude of the problem. To indicate the variety and prevalence of calculus-thinking like Pitcher's, the present chapter offers a focused sampling. Its samples come from the discussion of word meanings, a discussion that peaked in the years following publication of Wittgenstein's *Investigations*. Ample illustrations of essentialistic, calculus-like reasoning lie in the near vicinity of Pitcher's, indeed in discussions of the identical topic—the equation of the meanings of words with their uses.

Meaning and Use

Donald Gustafson's critique of Pitcher's calculus-reasoning itself provides further instances of calculus-reasoning. Gustafson contends that Pitcher was wrong to assume that Wittgenstein meant to identify word meaning and word-use. "Wittgenstein does not identify the use a word has in the language with the meaning of that word for the good reason that the very idea of such an identification is nonsense."[5] It would be like identifying veracity with eggnog or stupidity with a centipede. Things identified, rightly or wrongly, must be of the same type, and meaning and use are not. The first of these two premises Gustafson enunciates as follows:

> If someone proposed as a thesis that the meaning of a word is identical with the use of that word in the language, what could he mean? In order for an identification to be possible, something described or identified in one way must also be described or identified in another way. "That man on the corner by the mail box is the thief" is an identification of that man as the thief. A particular man is first identified as "that man ... etc." and then is said to be the same as the man who is the thief. This is a typical kind of identification. It demands two logically independent descriptions of one individual.
>
> Now if a philosopher sets out a theory which has the form of an identification (e.g., "material objects are identical with ..." or "mental events are identical with ...") and we think of what he is doing along the lines of a typical identification, then there must be some category or type to which the terms of the identity both belong. We normally resort to very, very generic types such as *thing* or *event*. If Wittgenstein is making a typical move of this sort by identifying the meaning of a word and the use of that word, we may reasonably ask what is the single type or category to which the meaning and the use both belong?[6]

Citing a single specimen of identification, Gustafson categorizes it as "typical." Two *typical*'s and one *normally* later, an essence has been distilled, by virtue of which any divergent attempts at identification can be counted as non-identifications. (How could any swan be black, since most are so evidently white?) Gustafson's conditional clauses ("if ... we think of what he is doing along the lines of a typical identification," "If Wittgenstein is making a typical move of this sort") seem to give more leeway, but his argument does not.

In support of his second premise, Gustafson observes that word meanings are found in dictionaries, and are there written formulas, not word-uses. Similarly, a child asking "What does this word mean?" and pointing to "pony" in a story book can be told that it means a small horse. She is given a defining formula, not a word-use. "These are typical cases in which we explain or tell what a word means. Whatever the use of a word in the language is, it is not something of the same type as a definition."[7] Hence neither is it of the same type as the meaning of a word, for the meaning is not only of the same type as the defining formula, but is identical with it.

If, as Gustafson asserts, the meanings found in dictionaries are formulae, not uses, and if this is evidently so, then it is plausible to suggest that *Investigations* §43 does not equate word meanings with word-uses. But what about these premises? To adapt a comparison from Wittgenstein, it is as though, from the fact that people ask for the value of things, and that answers are conveyed by phrases such as "thirty francs" or "fifty dollars," the inference were drawn that values are identical with coins, checks, or paper currency, hence are minted, printed, signed, folded in wallets, or tucked in people's pockets. This conclusion is patent nonsense, but the error of the reasoning that begets it is less evident. The fallacy becomes still less transparent when the reasoning concerns, not things and their monetary values, but words and their meanings. Then it is easy to suppose that if people look for meanings in the dictionary, and what the dictionary contains are formulae, the formulae must be the meanings—and not expressions or accounts of the meanings, by which they are conveyed.[8]

To see why such argumentation might be termed "calculus-reasoning" and how it relates to essentialism, consider what paradigms might nourish it and how it might arise. "I looked for my wallet and found it in the park," someone says. Surely the thing looked for and the thing found are the same. "I did not know the word's meaning," another person says, "but I found it in the dictionary." Here, too, we may assume, the thing not known and the thing found are the same. And, indeed, the meaning is found by finding certain words in the dictionary. However, this does not signify that the meaning found consists of words and syllables. Does one "read" the meaning, as well as the words? If so, is the reading just the same both times? And is the meaning "found" in the dictionary found there in the same sense that the words are, or is the meaning "contained" in the dictionary in the same sense that the defining formula is? The calculus-reasoner is not troubled by such questions. Reading is reading, finding is finding, containing is containing; and reasoning can click along accordingly, untroubled by the possibility of diverging semantic tracks.

In further refutation of Pitcher's understanding of *Investigations* §43, Gustafson cites several facts mentioned by Pitcher, among them this: "John Wisdom in a paper on Wittgenstein says that he advises that in philosophy 'Don't ask for the meaning, ask

for the use.'" This would be "'contradictory' advice," Gustafson contends, if Wittgenstein believed that meaning was use.[9] It would
indeed be inconsistent, I agree, if context had no effect on sense
and verbal bits could be moved about like counters, or tesserae in
a mosaic, unaffected by their settings. But if the words "Don't ask
for the meaning, ask for the use" meant, for example, "Don't
employ the word 'meaning,' which tends to mislead you, but
employ instead the less doctrinally freighted word 'use,'" or if they
meant, "Don't ask for the meaning as you conceive it (metaphysically or psychologically, ignoring the everyday employment of the
term *meaning*) but ask instead for the use (which is what you need
and what the word *meaning* typically denotes),"[10] the saying would
occasion no problem for Pitcher's reading of *Investigations* §43.
There, in that setting, Wittgenstein might indeed be suggesting
that on many occasions when we speak of word meanings, we are
speaking, in effect, of word-uses.[11]

Others' reasoning not only resembles Pitcher's (as does
Gustafson's) but reaches the same negative verdict. Bruce Wavell,
for example, is also critical of *Investigations* §43. "It has always
seemed strange to me," he remarks, "that Wittgenstein, who was
concerned to map the actual uses of words, never, so far as I know,
paid any attention to scientific dictionaries which, after all, record
the ways in which words are used by proficient speakers."[12] If we
do consult such dictionaries, we find, for instance, that "*Webster's
New World Dictionary* defines 'meaning' as follows:

1. What is meant; what is intended to be, or is in fact,
   signified, indicated, referred to or understood: signification, purport, import, sense or significance.
2. (Archaic) intention, purpose.

It then distinguishes in a synonymy between these kinds of meaning in a way which makes it clear that the word 'meaning' is the
general term and the terms 'referent,' 'sense,' 'import,' 'purport,'
'signification,' and 'significance' connote species of meaning."[13]
Wittgenstein, however, in §§40–43, "denies that reference is a
species of meaning, which is contrary to what the dictionary tells
us."

For Wavell, it makes little difference that Wittgenstein spoke
of the meanings of words, and not of meanings generally, or just of
many occasions on which we speak of words' meanings, and not of
all. If the dictionary lists all these senses for the word *meaning,*
then such are the word's senses in all instances and on all occasions, whether the meanings alluded to are the meanings of words

or of statements, glances, gestures, clapping, bird entrails, road signs, human history, or the universe. The illegitimacy of such an inference is patent, both in general and in this particular instance. Besides, it is difficult to locate any everyday locutions which support Wavell's initial premise that "reference [in the sense of thing referred to, not referring function] is a species of meaning." True, we readily say, "I meant him," but much less readily, if at all, "My meaning was him," or, "He was my meaning." But philosophers are often little troubled by such niceties. Even Max Black illustrates "the ways in which 'meaning' is actually used" by listing "typical occurrences of the verb 'to mean.'"[14]

When scrutinized, the cross-inferences often made between *mean* and *meaning* look extremely odd. Statements like "I see him" or "I see your point" do not incline us to identify seeing with its object. Neither do we pass from "The words express my feelings" to "The feelings are my expression." Why, then, do philosophers assume that if persons or words mean X, X is their meaning? How are we to explain the prevalence of reasoning like Pitcher's, cited above, which does not hesitate to draw inferences concerning the noun *meaning* from the verb *mean*: "Moreover, things which may sometimes have meanings—or (in case nothing non-linguistic can be said to *have* a meaning) things which may sometimes mean something—(e.g., black clouds on the horizon, footprints in the snow, the rising pitch of someone's voice) do not, except rarely, have uses. So one would not expect the meaning of a *word* to be the same thing as its use(s) in the language"? It appears that calculus-reasoning has no need of a single, recurring word as stimulus or basis for essentialistic suppositions; a single word-root will do.[15]

Or perhaps still less than that minimum. For consider this anomaly: Wittgenstein wrote the *Investigations* in German (§§40–43 speak of "*Bedeutung,*" not "meaning"); yet Wavell cites an English dictionary. The possibility that the two terms, the German and the English, may not be perfectly synonymous and that their differences, if any, may affect the validity of his refutation, does not trouble him. His use of Webster's rather than Trübner's may be a mere oversight; but then again, it may not. No momentary slip causes an author to write, for example, of Latin-speakers, French-speakers, English-speakers, and others: "Human beings have used the word 'love' for a very long time. In the Western World, particularly through the vehicle of the Christian tradition, the word has perhaps been more frequently used or, at least, thought, than in any other culture area—more frequently and in more senses. Yet how many persons in our culture have understood the *true* meaning of this word?"[16] Vindication for such thinking may be found in Aristotle: "Just as all men have not the same writing, so all men have not the same speech sounds, but the mental experiences, which these directly symbolize, are the same for all."[17] Interlinguistic essentialism, as well as intralinguistic, has figured prominently in Western thought.

For reasons which I shall refrain from critiquing, despite their latent essentialism, Wavell rewords Wittgenstein's formula to read, "A sense of a word is a use of the word in the language." Then he raises a further objection:

> If a sense of a word is one of its uses, then senses are logically tied to words. This implies that it is logically impossible for a person who cannot speak, understand speech, or understand any other form of communication to have a grasp of the senses of any words. Now, it would, of course, be logically impossible for such a person to know whether or not a sense is a sense of a particular word, but this does not imply that he could not have a grasp of the sense. J. Piaget found by observing the behavior of infants that they have concepts, albeit rudimentary ones, of the self, reality, space, time and causality *before they have learned to speak or understand others' speech,* concepts which they have acquired by interacting with their nonhuman environments. Since these concepts are the cores of what adults mean by the words "self," "reality," etc.—i.e., the cores of the senses of these words—the senses of words cannot be *identified* with their uses.[19]

For "core" read "essence," and you will see why I cite this argument; note the consequences of this essentialism, and you will see why I view the argument as an instance of calculus-reasoning. Once non-essentials have been set aside, the demonstration can proceed as follows: The nonverbal concept clearly is not the word's use; but the nonverbal concept *is* the word's sense (essentially); therefore the word's sense is not the word's use. Q.E.D. Wavell feels no need to consider whether and how words like *concept* and *sense* may alter their meanings when applied to words and when applied to nonverbal thinking.[20] Such differences can be treated as nonessential.

Like Wavell's first critique, an argument of Robert Brown's closely resembles Pitcher's; and like Wavell's second critique, Brown's argument suffers from more than one deficiency. There can be little doubt, however, that it betrays a similarly essentialistic, calculus-and-mosaic mentality. As the first of a series of objections to *Investigations* §43, Brown cites and apparently endorses the following "familiar argument":

> To claim that an expression has a use is to claim in addition to other claims that it can be purposefully employed. But I may have an odds-bodds collection of noises which I use indifferently to frighten away cats and sparrows, to pronounce over witches' brews when I tell stories to my children, and to interject when I trip on the rug. They differ from the "Ouch!" of pain and the "Oh, oh" of surprise in that I seldom make the same noises twice or in the same order. They serve my purpose even when it is only to baffle people. If doing these things with noises is using them, surely my purposeful utterance of these noises does not give them meaning in our language?[21]

This is a puzzling argument. It might have at least a semblance of validity, if it did not focus on just a single feature allegedly implied by Wittgenstein's formula. Only if that feature—purposeful employment—were identical with the use Wittgenstein referred to would Brown's counterevidence carry any weight. And even with regard to that single feature the argument supposes such perfect uniformity that if any purposeful employment merited the label "meaning," all would. Yet the argument itself points out differences, indeed insists on them. ("I seldom make the same noises twice or in the same order.")

Only two explanations of this anomaly suggest themselves, both essentialistic. Either Brown believes that, despite differences, all instances deserving to be called "purposeful employment" are essentially similar, hence would all merit the common label "meaning" if any did (compare Wavell's second argument, above). Or he assumes as self-evident that Wittgenstein intended an essential definition, stating necessary and sufficient conditions of word-meaninghood—or that only if so understood need his saying be taken seriously (the spotting of essences being the only worthwhile purpose a philosopher could have in making an assertion like that in §43)—and that the formula in fact fails to specify *sufficient* conditions, setting off meaningful use from non-meaningful.

In support of the latter type of critique, it might be argued that if no strict equivalence is intended in *Investigations* §43, then "to employ the term 'definition' [or 'define'] is misleading at a time

when under the influence of Frege and Russell most philosophers
think of a definition as a sentence stipulating or stating that two
expressions have the same sense."[22] However, Wittgenstein's term
is *erklären,* not *define.* And even the term *definition* functions
more flexibly and extends more broadly than this objection recognizes. Ostensive definitions, for example, neither pretend nor
achieve a matching of senses. Nor do many dictionary definitions.
Water, for instance, is identified as "the liquid that descends from
the clouds as rain, forms streams, lakes and seas, and is a major
constituent of all living matter."

However, the objection contains a grain of truth. To a degree, it
is self-verifying, attesting as it does the strength of expectations
begotten by thinking like Frege's and Russell's. For many of their
admirers and successors, essentialistic thinking appears paradigmatic; all-and-only definitions assume canonical status.

Second Series

Let us break here. Although some of the most arresting specimens of calculus-thinking still await their turn, readers may need
no further convincing. Having already sensed what I mean by "calculus-reasoning" and how abundant such reasoning is, they may
prefer to cut short the demonstration and pass to the next section.
Further sampling may prove tedious. However, it may, instead,
prove more satisfyingly full and convincing. Struggling on through
these speculative thickets, readers may be impressed, as I have
been, by just *how* common such reasoning is, and how diverse.
From the evidence presented by discussion of this single
topic—meaning and use—they may divine how variously, powerfully, and pervasively calculus-and-mosaic thinking affects inquiry
in other areas as well. So I shall now add a second series of examples to the first.

Apparently guided by unspoken assumptions about the precision and specificity any well-formed philosophical formula must
possess, Raziel Abelson subjects §43 to a familiar essentialistic
procedure: stripping the artichoke of its leaves in search of the
artichoke. How, he asks, is the "use" of an expression to be understood in Wittgenstein's saying? As "the utterance of [the expres-
sion] in certain appropriate situations"?[23] Surely not just that. As
"syntactical, or grammatical use, namely, the ways in which the
expression in question can be combined with other expressions to
form phrases and sentences"?[24] This, too, would clearly be an inad-

equate characterization of meaning. As "whatever could be truly said by means of the word"?[25] As the purpose for which the expression is uttered?[26] As "the kind of use that we have in mind when we say that an expression signifies, indicates, expresses, connotes, denotes or designates something"?[27] Abelson rejects each suggestion in turn, so that finally, with the artichoke's leaves heaped about him, he reports his failure to find anything equivalent to word meaning. He does not consider whether all these leaves (all these single suggestions), or several, disjunctively bunched together, might yield a different result. Maybe they would, maybe they wouldn't; my interest is in methodology.

Thomas Hill's approach resembles Abelson's. Having reviewed a variety of specific versions of the meaning-use equation and having found each one inadequate, Hill, too, looks elsewhere for a solution of the kind he seeks. "What has now to be undertaken," he announces, "is the crucial task of working out a clarification of the central concept of meaning itself. To this end I shall endeavor to present a set of sufficient and necessary conditions for the applicability of the substantive term 'meaning' that will be in accord with such characteristics of meaning situations as have been disclosed—or may be disclosed by further reference to examples—and that will at the same time be as illuminating as possible concerning the character of meanings, the major differences among kinds of meanings, and the common features—if any—of meanings."[28]

Absent from Hill's statement of intent, and from the argumentation that precedes and follows it, is any explicit reference to everyday usage as a guide to what characteristics qualify as sufficient or necessary conditions of "meaning." So a certain arbitrariness colors his eventual conclusion: "The requisite necessary and sufficient conditions may, I suggest, be formulated by saying that anything is a meaning if and only if it is an experience pattern either as intended by an agent in using a bearer to be apprehended by a respondent, as disposed to be so intended by one or more agents, as causally inferable from a bearer, or as implied by a bearer."[29] As Hill recognizes, this formula, with its initial focus on an "experience pattern" and its closing four-fold disjunction, represents a compromise between the actual heterogeneity of the concept *meaning* and the ideal homogeneity he would prefer to find in it. "Since a conjunctive set of sufficient and necessary conditions for a concept, or for the applicability of corresponding terms, is likely to be more revealing than a disjunctive set," he observes, "it would be desirable, if possible, to disclose such a conjunctive set for the concept of meaning."[30]

Why or in what sense a conjunctive set "is likely to be more revealing" than a disjunctive set, Hill does not elucidate. A likely explanation, in terms of scientific fruitfulness, appears when he surmises: "It may well be that the experience patterns in which meanings seem to consist and the other indicated factors in meaning situations are so related to one another that initial insights concerning the former contribute to the selection of those instances of the latter that are most relevant to meanings, and that these instances of the latter, once selected, contribute to the objective confirmation of hypotheses concerning meanings."[31]

I cite these words as typical of the motivation that guides much essentialistic reasoning. In brief critique I would suggest that for the purposes Hill indicates it makes no difference whether "experience patterns as satisfying meaning functions are equatable with meanings."[32] He can tag the experiences as he pleases and still form the same hypotheses. If, for pragmatic reasons, he prefers the label *meaning,* he can attend explicitly to the linguistic question, resort to Carnapian explication, and explain why he believes the restriction of *meaning* to "experience patterns" satisfies Carnap's four conditions. One may doubt whether such an attempt would prove feasible or profitable; but at least the impression would not be given that an essence of sorts had at last been discovered, and that the search for essences, with this worthwhile result to its credit, may legitimately guide our thinking. Hill's artichoke plucking, in his discussion of "Uses and Meanings," looks no better founded than Abelson's.

Citing Ryle rather than Wittgenstein, Abelson continues his critique: "The inadequacy of Ryle's 'use' theory of meaning is strikingly revealed when compared with Ryle's insistence that proper names have no meaning. For the fact stares us in the face that proper names have a use! How then can meaning be the same as use?" The answer stares the non-essentialist in the face: It may be that not just any and every kind of use is, or is called, "meaning." (Why, for instance, are proper names generally omitted from the dictionary, or listed separately?) And it may be that Ryle, like Wittgenstein, intended a mere identification, not a strict definition valid for all and only members of the class defined. It is conceivable that an anti-essentialist might philosophize non-essentialistically.

This refutation of Abelson's, from proper names, is a favorite argument. Jon Wheatley extends it: "Consider the theory that the meaning of a word is its use. Though Wittgenstein never explicitly espoused it, he came very close to doing so, and other philosophers of stature, e.g., Ryle, do espouse it. This theory suffers from two serious difficulties," the first of which is this: "Certain words that have no meanings have a use, e.g., names, 'slithy,' 'a.'"[34] At first glance, this objection looks odd. A statement about the meanings of words is not a statement about the meanings of words (if they may be so called) that do not have meanings. Wheatley's objection would make sense only if Wittgenstein or Ryle were not merely pointing in the direction of use rather than (say) mental contents; nor identifying word meanings with *some* uses, not others; but were playing the essentialistic game of all-and-only definition.

This assumption is gratuitous. It cannot be taken for granted that such is the game being played by anti-essentialists, or the game that they should be playing. In explanation and defense of Wittgenstein's strategy in §43 I have suggested, for example: "If someone rightly believes that the important thing about a word is its meaning, yet has confused or erroneous notions about meaning, he can be brought to follow the advice to look for the use only by being shown that meaning is use."[35] In §43 Wittgenstein need not be giving an essential definition, discriminating this sort of use—meaning-use—from all others. The frequency with which Wittgenstein has been read as replacing one essential definition with another, subject to the traditional conditions of validity for such an enterprise, reveals how inveterate is the essentialistic mind-set he opposed.[36]

Essentialism manifests its power through the calculus-reasoning even of professed opponents. For example, Friedrich Waismann, a competent expositor of Wittgenstein's anti-essentialism, argued as follows against *Investigations* §43: "The fact that one can perfectly well know 'what time is' without knowing all the idioms of language is a pointer which suggests that all is not well with the doctrine that 'the meaning of a word is the way in which it is used.'"[37] This refutation requires an essentialistic simplification either with regard to knowing or with regard to word meanings. Were knowing X equivalent to knowing the whole of X, the refutation would work. Were word meanings indivisible, invariant items that had to be known (learned, remembered, taught, etc.) whole or not at all, then, too, the argument might hold up.

The continuation of Waismann's argument suggests first one, then the other, of these two interpretations: "Indeed, if that [doctrine] was correct, it would only be natural to expect that the adding of *any* new phrase, when it occurs for the first time, such as 'time is money,' alters something in the meaning of that word; which is obviously far from the truth. Ask yourself whether you are prepared to say that in learning what a number is one has also to learn the use of such phrases as 'a number of people,' 'a small number,' 'a round number,' etc.? Would it be right to say that, if a child is unfamiliar with such expressions, he does not know what a number is? Such examples should make us hesitate to accept the formula 'meaning = use.'" Does the essentialism now reside in *meaning,* as the first sentence suggests, or in the new verb, *learn*? If someone says, "You can't learn German unless you learn the whole of it," is he supposing that German is just one thing (the whole) or that learning is just one thing (viz., learning the whole of whatever is said to be learned)?

It would be natural and reasonable for Waismann to suppose that Wittgenstein meant his formula to be, if not all-inclusive, at least broad enough to embrace standard constructions like those Waismann cited. Having thus understood the formula, he might have concluded that knowing the use or learning the use would require knowing or learning something far more varied and complex than people often, or typically, know or learn. But they do know or learn the meanings of words. Hence the meanings cannot be the uses in the language. It looks likely, then, that the key point at which essentialism crept into Waismann's refutation was in the unspoken premise that knowing or learning, whether of meanings or of uses, invariably consists in knowing or learning the whole of what is known or learned.

In a sense, this is of course true, as it is for other verbs. But in the nontautological sense required by the argument, it is far from being the case. In customary English (and in what other language was Waismann writing?) to know, learn, see, remember, hear, cite,.. . X does not entail knowing, learning, seeing, remembering, hearing, citing . . . the whole of X. There is nothing solecistic in saying that a person "spotted Manhattan on the horizon," when only a few tall buildings hove into view, or "quoted a speech with approval," when she quoted only parts of it, or "studied mathematics in high school," though the course comprised the merest introduction to the field. In the manner typical of essentialists, Waismann, an avowed anti-essentialist, nourished his thinking with too restricted a diet of examples. Forgetful of other paradigms, he put learning the meaning or use of a term on a par with learning a person's name, an address, the alphabet, or the sum of two plus two, rather than learning German, mathematics, or the lay of the land.

I shall not inflict on the reader all the critiques of *Investigations* §43 which resemble Waismann's; a pair should suffice.[38] Putnam argues: "To give the use of a term does not necessarily impart its full meaning. Thus one can give the use of the expression *agathe* (*h*)*emera* in Greek by saying that this expression is employed as a conventional greeting during the daylight hours, and especially during the afternoon; but one still does not know from what has been said that it means 'good day.'"[39] To indicate the flaw in this refutation of Wittgenstein's saying, one might insert the missing term in the first premise and make it read: "To give the use of a term, *partially* or *completely*, does not necessarily impart its full meaning." Therewith, the appearance of non-equivalence between meaning and use would dissipate.

However, this rejoinder would not be adequate, nor would it pinpoint the essentialistic element in Putnam's refutation. The decisive move of his argument comes, not with the omission of "partially or completely," but with the unnoted transition from "term" in the first sentence, to "expression" in the second sentence, to a brief yet complete utterance in the first illustration (the Greek greeting), to lengthier utterances in subsequent illustrations. There the meaning-use equation no longer looks as plausible as in *Investigations* §43. "Pass me the butter" and "Pass me that dish" may have the same use in a particular context, but do not have the same meaning; "The door is open" might be used, without change of meaning, one time to command someone to shut the door, another time to halt someone who is moving with the intention of opening the door. On the strength of such contrasts as these (for complete utterances), Putnam concludes (for individual terms): "*Use* corresponds to what we have called the 'pragmatic meaning components' for a particular term, whereas the cognitive meaning components are specified only when the 'place' of a term (i.e., its syntactical and semantical relations to other terms in the language) is made clear."[40] Wittgenstein's comparison of words with tools, employed in the construction of utterances, suggests how slow we should be to assume that whatever holds for utterances holds equally for their components. Insofar as utterances may be said to have uses, the uses may not be comparable to those of individual words. And in fact they are not.

Pitcher plays a further variation on Waismann's refutation. "If someone tells me (a non-Latin-speaker) that 'ultus' means revenge in Latin, I thereby know the meaning of that word, but I have no idea how or when to use it."[41] Consider both sides of this alleged nonequivalence. On the one hand, Pitcher might have said, "I thereby know the meaning of that word *to some extent*." On the other, though it may be true, in a sense, that he has no idea how or when to use the word (since he does not know the rest of the language), it is not true that he has no idea how or when the word is used. He knows, for instance, that it does not function as a verb or pronoun; he knows that it does not serve as the name for an animal, plant, or body of water; he knows what kind of thing it does designate. He just does not know the whole of the word's use. And not knowing the whole of the use but knowing the meaning, he concludes that the whole is not the meaning, hence that Wittgenstein's identification is mistaken. It is necessary to point out, again, that "knowing the meaning" need not mean knowing the whole meaning, and frequently does not.[42]

The variation might occur in the word *know* or in the word *meaning* or in both. Consider the expression "see stars." Here the "seeing" is not ordinary seeing, nor are the "stars" ordinary stars. However, this double variation in sense is so obvious that no one is likely to argue, calculus-wise, that the stars, if seen, must exist outside the viewer, or that the viewer, if he saw the stars, must have had his eyes open. The variation is evident, for one thing, because it affects the sense of both terms: a person may "see stars" in a dark room, in the daytime, or with his eyes closed; the "stars" have no spatio-temporal location, no weight, no matter, and so forth. For another thing, the shift of sense for both words is radical. By contrast, the fluctuations just considered, for *know, learn, meaning*, and the like, are not nearly so obvious; neither of these two reasons—plurality or radicality—makes them so.

First, in a specimen such as Pitcher cites (with regard to "knowing" the "meaning"), it is not evident where the shift of sense occurs (when and if it does); but it does seem clear that if it occurs in one term it does not occur in the other. "Knowing the meaning" might mean knowing the whole meaning, but knowing it partially; or knowing just part of the meaning, but knowing it wholly. It would not mean both. Second, knowing the meaning, whether wholly or partially, would still be knowing, in much the same sense of knowing; and the meaning, whether part or whole, would still be meaning, in much the same sense of meaning. The shift would be less radical than that between the seeing and the "seeing," or the stars and the "stars," when one person sees stars at night and another "sees stars" after falling downstairs.

This comparison between "knowing the meaning" and "seeing stars" serves several purposes. First, it reveals the error of less obvious calculus-reasoning, like Pitcher's, through the more evident error of imaginary but basically similar arguments. Second, it suggests how and why the error is less obvious, hence more insidious, in many real-life instances. Third, it demonstrates the need to look both right and left, as it were, before venturing arguments like Waismann's, Putnam's, and Pitcher's. Either of the relevant words—for instance, either *know* or *meaning*—might shift in a way that invalidates the refutation.

Samples from the Other Side

By now, readers may suspect that my purpose in this chapter is not the one announced—to suggest the nature, prevalence, and invalidity of calculus-thinking, through a single, typical sampling—but rather to defend Wittgenstein's beleaguered formula. So let me turn from refutations of *Investigations* §43 to defenses of the same saying, and demonstrate that what is sauce for the goose is likewise sauce for the gander—the gander, in this case, being first of all myself.

In answer to the varied, invalid objections to *Investigations* §43, I once sought to show the soundness of Wittgenstein's assertion by means of a simple argument pieced together from his remarks. "The meaning of a word," I suggested, "is whatever we learn or explain when we learn or explain the word's meaning; but what we then learn or explain is not an object, say, but the word's use in the language." Hence its meaning is its use in the language.[43] To those who already accept Wittgenstein's equation of meaning with use, this demonstration may appear unproblematic; but how might it win agreement from others?

Consider the first premise: "The meaning of a word is whatever we learn or explain when we learn or explain the word's meaning." I sanguinely trusted that readers would identify the meaning learned or explained with the meaning subsequently known, taught, remembered, forgotten, compared with other meanings, declared to be the same, and so forth—that is, with meaning generally. From the one case, all would be inferred. But could they be? Should they be? Not, it seems, without some surreptitious calculus-reasoning. Recognition that the meaning learned or explained is the word's use in the language might open minds to the possibility that the meaning taught, known, compared, and so forth is likewise the word's use in the language. Examination of other allusions to word meanings than those containing the term *learn* or *explain* might reveal that such was the case. But only through such independent scrutiny and subsequent comparison could this larger equivalence be established; it could not be inferred from one or two instances, via the unspoken premise that meanings are, of course, always the same thing (once a word-use, invariably a word-use).

Granted, through familiarity with the logic of our language we have an intuitive sense that if people learn a word meaning, the meaning they then know is the one they learned, and the one they later forget is the one they previously knew, and so forth. And such intuitive impressions are often accurate, as I believe they are in this instance. So I should not be too hard on my argument. However, consider this further difficulty. Previous discussion alerts us to the fact that what we learn when we "learn the meaning" of a word may in fact be only part of the meaning. The word *learn* guarantees no equivalence between what is learned and the referent of the object of the verb. *Learn* does not function calculus-wise: sometimes we learn the whole of what we learn (for example, a person's address), sometimes we do not (for example, German). But the first premise in my demonstration presumably signifies that the *whole* meaning of a word is whatever we learn or explain when we learn or explain a word's meaning. This might be (and in fact is) similar to saying that the whole of a house is whatever we see when we see a house. So as it stands my argument looks as shaky as this one: "The whole of a house is whatever we see whenever we see a house; but what we see when we view a house from outside is its exterior; therefore the exterior is the whole house." Concerning such an argument, little more need be said.

Demonstration through elimination, as in the negative part of my premise ("not an object, say"), may elicit similar misgivings. Consider, for example, two arguments conflated in *Investigations* §40. One, suggested by the number's final sentence, may be stated as follows: If the meaning of a name (for instance, *Mary*) were the object it referred to, the name would no longer have a meaning when the object ceased to exist (for instance, when Mary died); but names continue to have meaning after their referents cease to exist; therefore their meanings are not identical with their referents. I shall bypass the objection that proper names are not generally said to have meanings, and shall focus on the verb *have*. If I have a neighbor and my neighbor dies, I no longer have a neighbor; but if I have a favorite author and my favorite author dies, I do not cease to have a favorite author. The argument overlooks this latter possibility, yet it should not do so. It is obvious that when people die their names do not become meaningless, in whatever sense the names may be said to have meaning. So the more plausible version of the doctrine under attack would not identify the meanings of names with existing referents, as such, but with whatever referents the names have or had, whether those referents are dead or alive, existent or non-existent. Names might continue to have such meanings even after the objects ceased to exist, just as people may continue to have the same favorite authors after the authors die. "Have," in the present tense, need not entail the present existence of its object(s).

Wittgenstein's second argument, also present in *Investigations* §40, proves more resistant to criticism. It is correct to say that one's favorite author has died, or has gone out of existence, but not correct to say that the meaning of a name has died, or gone out of existence; hence the meaning of the name cannot be identical with the person who dies or the referent that goes out of existence. The verb *exist* looks more rigidly calculus-like in its functioning—less affected by verbal context—than does the verb *have*.

However, this appearance may result from a limited or inappropriate sampling; neighbors and favorite authors may resemble meanings too minimally to serve as reliable objects of comparison. So let us focus specifically on meanings, and consider whether Wittgenstein's rival identification, of meanings as uses, could pass the same test as the one he applies to object-meanings. Word-uses, too, can go out of existence, but we would hesitate to say that the corresponding meanings then cease to exist. They still appear in dictionaries, though listed as obsolete. So should we conclude that words' meanings are not their uses in the language, as Wittgenstein suggested? Is he hoisted with his own petard—*Investigations* §40 refuting *Investigations* §43? I think not. The argument in §40 is at fault, I would say, not the identification in §43. For the argument implicitly assimilates all cases, without regard for differences. It, too, proceeds as though language were a rigid, reliable calculus.

Why do I still have a favorite author when my favorite author dies but not a neighbor when my neighbor dies—even though the two may be the same person? Because being my favorite author depends on something in me (my preference), and that something continues after the person's death. Why are we (or at least why am I) similarly reluctant to say that a word-meaning ceases to exist when a word-use passes from currency? Perhaps for the similar reason that the use's being a meaning depends on something in us—say, in our knowing about it—and this knowledge continues, in our collective or individual memories, after the use ceases.

Though I find this explanation plausible, my present purpose does not require that it be accurate. As variations in cases may affect the behavior of *have*, so variations in cases may affect the behavior of *exist*. No better a priori reason guarantees rigid regularity in the one instance than in the other; and a posteriori there is no telling what surprises semantic browsing may turn up. Thus, my response to the imagined refutation of *Investigations* §43 may err in some respect, but that would have to be shown. The parallel between this argument and the one in *Investigations* §40 may be illusory, but that too would have to be shown. Hence even the stronger of Wittgenstein's arguments in §40 does not suffice as it stands. If intended as a strict refutation, it is too calculus-like in its assumptions.[44]

In his *Encyclopedia of Philosophy* article on meaning, William Alston takes a different tack to support meaning as use. It is tempting, he writes, to "hold that for any word to have a meaning is for it to name, designate, or refer to something other than itself. Variations of the theory differ over whether the meaning of a word is to be identified with (1) what it refers to or (2) the relation between the word and its referent."[45] The first variant, though common, "can be shown to be untenable because two expressions can have the same referent but different meanings." Here he cites Frege's familiar illustration, the expressions "the morning star" and "the evening star." "They refer to the same extralinguistic entity, the planet Venus, but they do not have the same meaning."

The theorist being refuted would doubtless retort that they do have the same meaning, since they have the same referent. But Alston continues, "If they did [have the same meaning], one could know that the morning star is the same entity as the evening star just by understanding the meanings of the terms (as with 'The thermometer in my study is the same object as the instrument for measuring temperature in my study'). But this is not the case. It was an astronomical discovery that the morning star and the evening star are the same." To this an adversary could readily reply that what Frege's example demonstrates is not the distinction between meaning and reference, but the possibility of two different expressions' having the same meaning without our knowing they do. "Man possesses the ability to construct languages capable of expressing every sense, without having any idea how each word has meaning or what its meaning is—just as people speak without knowing how the individual sounds are produced."[46]

If charitably read—that is, as neither surreptitiously relying on an argument implicit in the parenthetical comparison, nor begging the question in a manner that comparison suggests—Alston's reasoning resembles Waismann's. Alston assumes that to understand the meaning would be to understand not only what referent one expression has in the morning and the other has in the evening, but also that the two referents are identical. One would have to understand everything about the referent (as for Waismann one would have to learn every detail of usage).

But why make this supposition? If I see one side of a mountain on one trip and another side on another, is it impossible for me later to discover that both mountains were the same? Is that precluded by my having *seen* the mountain previously? Perhaps *understand* functions differently in this respect, excluding partial understanding of X as an instance of understanding X, or at least partial understanding of a meaning as an instance of understanding that meaning; but that would have to be shown. And the showing would have to prescind somehow from whether the meaning understood is or is not the referent. Otherwise, it would beg the question.

Signs of Something Larger

The preceding sample arguments may be compared and contrasted with Frege's reasoning on the same topic, which appears to conflict with *Investigations* §43:

> That we can form no idea of its content is . . . no reason for denying all meaning to a word, or for excluding it from our vocabulary. We are indeed only imposed on by the opposite view because we will, when asking for the meaning of a word, consider it in isolation, which leads us to accept an idea as the meaning. Accordingly, any word for which we can find no corresponding mental picture appears to have no content. But we ought always to keep before our eyes a complete proposition. Only in a proposition have the words really a meaning.[47]

Is it mistaken, then, to speak of a word's meaning, or use, in the language (as in §43), or of its meaning in a given ambience, or for a given person? Frege, too, seems to have nourished his thinking with too meagre a diet of examples, or dismissed all but his favored example, essentialistically, honoring that alone as what meaning (*Bedeutung*) "really is." For this restriction he does not offer any demonstration; one is forced to surmise what case he might make for it. The like holds for many another essentialistic claim unbacked by explicit argumentation. Why, for instance, did Cajetan restrict analogy to a single variety? Why, in like manner, did Russell limit proper names? Chapter 6 will suggest a variety of possible *reasons* for such thinking—misleading analogies, disregard for language, contagion, the influence of the will—and view them as more powerful than arguments. Yet doubtless a Cajetan, a

Russell, or a Frege, if challenged, would adduce some argument or other in support of his favored essence. And the chances are good that the argument would resemble those examined here. The essentialistic conclusion would rest on and reflect essentialistic reasoning.

Frege, for instance, might argue: "Either word meanings are, exclusively, ideas in the mind, or they are elements in propositions. But they are not ideas in the mind. Therefore they are—always and only—elements in propositions." Here the major premise does not hedge; it does not speak of just a "large class of cases," as *Investigations* §43 does. It does not make allowance for meanings in a language, meanings in the dictionary, meanings in an author, or the like; still less for the experiential meanings Wittgenstein also acknowledged.[48] It could not do so and still permit the Fregean always-and-only conclusion. As for the minor premise, this chapter's samples suggest what a disproof of idea-meanings might look like: it might resemble Pitcher's, Waismann's, and others' disproofs of use-meanings, or Alston's and Wittgenstein's disproofs of referent-meanings. It, too, might proceed calculus-wise.

These, of course, are mere surmisings; but the surmisings look plausible, and they have a point. They are meant to suggest, first, how large may loom the bulk of unspoken calculus-reasoning, in addition to (and perhaps in comparison with) the spoken. They suggest, further, that the effect on people's thinking may be equally great, whether the reasoning rises to the surface, as in Pitcher, Waismann, and the rest, or remains submerged, as in Frege. Hence this chapter's samples take on added significance. Numerous though they are, even on this single narrow topic, they speak for many more. Essentialism's full mass—the berg beneath the visible tip—extends deeper than general theories, deeper than particular theories, deeper even than explicit calculus-reasoning or analogs still to be considered. Small wonder that as successive essentialistic theories succumb to criticism, others arise from the depths to replace them.

Chapter Four

NETWORK-REASONING

> We are under the illusion that what is peculiar, profound,
> essential, in our investigation, resides in its trying to grasp the
> incomparable essence of language. That is, the order existing
> between the concepts of proposition, word, proof, truth, experi-
> ence, and so on. This order is a *super*-order between—so to
> speak—*super*-concepts.[1]

How prone is the mind to error, exclaims Descartes in the
Meditations, and how deceptive is language!

> We say that we see the same wax, if it is present, and
> not that we simply judge that it is the same from its
> having the same colour and figure. From this I should
> conclude that I knew the wax by means of vision and not
> simply by the intuition of the mind; unless by chance I
> remember that, when looking from a window and saying
> I see men who pass in the street, I really do not see
> them, but infer that what I see is men, just as I say that
> I see wax. And yet what do I see from the window but
> hats and coats which may cover automatic machines?
> Yet I judge these to be men.[2]

Descartes here warns against one instance of calculus-reasoning
while formulating what looks like another. We should not suppose
that the verb *see* (*videre*) always works the same way, he seems to
argue, or that we can always draw like inferences from its application. Witness what we say about men we "see" in the street when
we do not in fact see them but only their coats, gloves, shoes, and
broad-brimmed hats. To really see the men, apparently we would
have to glimpse some flesh—say a patch of hand or face. However,
even a whole hand or face does not constitute a whole man; and
the hand or face we glimpsed, if detached from a cadaver and
attached to an "automatic machine," might figure in a still more
elaborate charade than the one Descartes imagines. Like objection
might be made to a whole man, stripped naked, but viewed from
only one side; to a whole man, naked, viewed from all sides but
only exteriorly; to a whole man, naked and split open, without his
whole interior being revealed by the single split; and so on. This

dire progression, inspired by Descartes' initial restriction, might suggest that we never do see a human being—or any other corporeal object. The only way to see an object would be to take it apart and view it bit by visible bit—in which case we would not see the object but only the parts that once composed it.

Where, then, before reaching such an extravagant conclusion, should we arrest the destructive progression? Probably at the start. Descartes, aware though he was of varied usage, simply supposed that there was one correct, essential use of *see* (*videre*), without further reflection on what that use might be. As Waismann assumed that "learning X" must be learning the whole of X, so Descartes assumed that "seeing X" must be seeing, without intermediary, at least part of X. By this test, no one sees frogmen in action, or observes astronauts walking on the moon; they are too fully clad.

I shall not dwell on this example; I cite it to illustrate the unsurprising fact that calculus-reasoning of the kind sampled in the last chapter extends beyond arguments concerning meaning and use. The samples scrutinized there, on that single topic, represent a mere fraction of those I might have used. And most of my examples illustrate just one variety of calculus-reasoning. As in this passage from Descartes, with its implicit restriction of *see*, their essentialistic suppositions generally concern just a single concept (*meaning, use, identify, learn,* and so forth). Other calculus-reasoning betrays multiple essentialism.

Observe this argument of Waismann's: "What I have to say is simply this. Philosophic arguments are not deductive; therefore they are not rigorous; and therefore they don't prove anything. Yet they have force."[3] Here two explicit premises beget an explicit conclusion with the aid of two tacit premises. Whereas the spoken premises are not essentialistic, the unspoken ones are. The first "therefore" suggests that only deductive arguments are or can be "rigorous"; the second "therefore" suggests that only rigorous arguments do or can "prove" anything. Such is the essence of rigor; such is the essence of proof. The essentialism looks multiple.

Sometimes such multiplicity results from mere multiplication: two separate bits of calculus-reasoning, of a kind that more commonly occurs instance by instance, happen to coincide within a single argument. Here, however, the argument's notions—rigor and proof—interlock. Hence the sample points to a more complex variety of calculus-reasoning, where concepts are conceived as forming an essentialistic network and are manipulated accordingly.

A Problematic Paradigm

The thinking of G. P. Baker and P. M. S. Hacker, and of others they report on, illustrates this type of reasoning. "The concept of meaning," they write, "is complicated and many-faceted. It plays a role in a wide variety of contexts, both within and outside philosophy, and it interlocks with many other concepts."[4] After citing a random score of such connections—for meaning generally, for linguistic meaning, for the meaning of a word, for the meaning of a sentence—they conclude, puzzlingly: "The concept of meaning is intended to give the solution to a huge array of simultaneous equations."[5] It appears that the phrase "the concept of meaning" does not here signify "the meaning of the word *meaning*," but rather a theoretical account, or analysis, of meaning. This surmise is confirmed when the authors continue:

> The aim of a philosophical investigation of meaning is to reveal, or perhaps to introduce some order into this apparent chaos, i.e. to survey and organize the multiple applications of the concept of meaning and the welter of conceptual connections between meaning and other notions. An obvious technique is to begin with some simplification or schematization of the concept of meaning and then to progress by successive approximations towards a complete analysis of the concept. By treating one or a few conceptual connections as basic, we might well hope to exhibit the rest as their consequences. The ideal would be to produce an analysis of the concept of meaning that would manifestly be a solution to the whole set of "equations" into which this concept enters. All of the important internal relations between meaning and other notions (denotation, truth, evidence, explanation, communication, etc.) would flow from this analysis. Whether or not they are intended to be executions of this programme, most philosophical "theories of meaning" conform to it.[6]

A paradigm instance is the "Augustinian picture of language," which, according to Baker and Hacker, Wittgenstein identified as "the proto-picture underlying the development of the important modern philosophical theories of meaning"[7] and therefore took as his chief target in *Philosophical Investigations*. In response, suggest Baker and Hacker,

Wittgenstein reverses the traditional direction of fit between meaning and understanding. The Augustinian picture tailors the accounts of understanding, explanation, and communication to the conception that meaning consists in correlations of words with things. Inverting this procedure requires investigation of what it is to understand an expression, what it is to explain it, and what is involved in communication. The concept of meaning must be shaped according to these constraints. Clarification of the appropriate criteria of understanding will dissolve the philosophical problems for which the Augustinian picture of language, in more or less sophisticated forms, provides the solutions.[8]

Although the Wittgenstein who emerges from this exegesis may eschew all "theory," his thought, as Baker and Hacker approvingly propound it, looks highly systematic. And though language, the matrix of the enterprise, may not be a "calculus according to definite rules," it appears sufficiently calculus-like to permit systematic solution "to a huge array of simultaneous equations."

This view of Wittgenstein, of language, and of philosophical method gives one pause. It is not obviously mistaken, and is developed with impressive thoroughness, competence, and skill. Yet the chief term of comparison Wittgenstein himself suggested for his later work was not Augustine's simple, undeveloped picture of language but Wittgenstein's own former way of thinking. And in the same number that lends credence to Baker and Hacker's exegesis, Wittgenstein warns: "If you say that our languages only *approximate* to such calculi you are standing on the very brink of a misunderstanding."[9] Is natural language really sufficiently calculus-like to permit our working out "equations"? Do its concepts interlock systematically enough to permit our "treating one or a few conceptual connections as basic" and exhibiting "the rest as their consequences"? Is their relatedness one-directional, requiring that we start with one concept or cluster of concepts rather than another?

These are the queries that occupy the present chapter. The samples of calculus-reasoning dealt with till now concerned single expressions; there was little suggestion of a system of interconnecting concepts, or of a direction in their connectedness that required a definite direction in explication, analysis, or argumentation. The new samples in this chapter, tying in with the earlier ones, open these new perspectives. The chapter's first two sections shift from the model of language as a mosaic, formed of independent bits, to language as an interlacing network of concepts. A third section then considers the theme of directionality. As before, the samples start simple, then become more complex. At the end, returning to where I began, I shall consider Baker and Hacker's reading of Wittgenstein and their corresponding conception of philosophical method.

Language as an Interlocking Calculus

When Descartes simplifies the concept *see*, he effects no similar simplification of other concepts. And were he to treat other concepts in like manner, the resulting calculus might still resemble chess. The concepts might be strictly, essentialistically delimited, one by one, and interrelate only generally, via the rules of syntax. Suppose, however, that chess pieces' moves were codified not only in relation to the squares on the board and whatever pieces occupy them, but in relation to specific pieces. Suppose it were stated, for example, that only kings can take queens, only queens can take bishops, only bishops can take knights, and so forth. Spotting a missing bishop, one might legitimately infer that a queen had taken it; spotting a knight out of action, one might conclude that a bishop had made off with it. This new type of essence might legitimize this new type of inference. Analogous inferences, from concept to concept, frequently occur in speculative discourse and are deemed equally legitimate.

In *Language and Truth* I cite several instances, for example this passage from Moore:

> Now it may be said that "'You ought to go away' is true" also doesn't make sense; on the ground that a person who says the words "You ought to go away" is, if he's using them in the ordinary way, not *asserting* anything. The mere fact that an indicative form of expression is used does not shew that it makes sense to add before it "It's true that" or "It's false that." If a person who says "You oughtn't to do that" or "You oughtn't to have done that," is not *making any assertion*, then it will make no sense to say that what he said was true or was false.[10]

"Here," I comment, "Moore's thinking proceeds as essentialistically as before, without regard for the vagaries of usage; only now he links moral utterances' truth or falsehood with their status as assertions. If they are assertions, then they are true or false; if they are not assertions, they are not true or false. All (genuine, true, bona fide) assertions, it would seem, are essentially the same, with truth-falsehood pertaining to their single essence; and truth, conversely, is as rigidly restricted to (genuine, true, bona fide) assertions."[11]

Keith Graham's treatment of performatives, in double disagreement with John Austin, reveals a similar configuration. For Austin, few performatives, whether explicit (for example, "I apologize") or nonexplicit ("I am sorry"), are true or false. For Graham, all genuine performatives are true, since they possess the essential feature of "corresponding with the facts";[12] but no nonexplicit performatives are genuine performatives, since they lack the essential feature of "being used to create their own truth."[13] His essentialistic reasoning works both ways, tightly linking the concepts *performative* and *true*.

Usage favors Austin. For good reasons, revealed by reflection, some performatives are customarily characterized as true or false while the majority are not.[14] As for the term *performative*, not only is it Austin's creation, with the extension he gave it, but his talk of nonexplicit, or "primary," performatives as well as of explicit looks reasonable: using the noun to signal similarity and the modifier to signal dissimilarity, it conforms to standard, sound linguistic practice. Graham, however, sets little store by standard linguistic practice, for reasons chapter 7 will examine.

Norman Malcolm cites a further example: "Ayer gives the following 'proof' that if we are in pain we know it, namely, that one can tell lies about one's sensations. For 'to tell a lie is not just to make a false statement: it is to make a statement that one knows to be false; and this implies denying what one knows to be true.'"[15] For Ayer, *know* and *lie* hook up tightly, whereas Malcolm comments: "I should take this [possibility of lying about one's sensation] as a proof that telling a lie is not, in all cases, stating what one knows to be false. The word 'lying,' like the word 'game,' is applied over a broad range of diverse cases." Malcolm may err in this conclusion, but his very disagreement indicates the problem with a priori arguments like Ayer's. The concepts being manipulated may not be as uniform or as rigidly related as assumed.

The same moral can be drawn from another, equally typical confrontation. According to F. M. Chapman and Paul Henle, "'I have a book,' 'Ich habe ein Buch,' 'J'ai un livre,' are three different sentences, but constitute a single proposition because they express a single meaning."[16] Here the inference from single meaning to single proposition assumes a tight, essentialistic connection between the terms *meaning* and *proposition*. If the meaning is single, ipso facto the proposition is single. John Pollock takes a different view. Citing a sentence, "He is here," which, like Chapman and Henle's examples, contains indexical expressions, he argues: "Clearly, there is no one proposition which is always expressed by this sentence. If there were, we could ask whether this sentence, all by itself and independent of context, is true (i.e., expresses a true proposition). But that is absurd. The sentence 'He is here,' all by itself, is neither true nor false."[17] Neither is "I have a book," "Ich habe ein Buch," or "J'ai un livre." We might say of such a sentence "that instead of *its* expressing a proposition, a speaker using this sentence expresses a proposition."[18] However, "the *sentence* does not change meaning. Talk about the meaning of a sentence is independent of any context. For example, without saying anything about context, we can say that the English sentence 'He is here' has the same meaning as the German sentence 'Er ist hier.'"[19] Thus for Pollock *proposition* disconnects from *meaning* and connects with *true* and *false*. Since the sentence's truth varies, so, too, does the proposition; whereas for Chapman and Henle, since the meaning does not vary, neither does the proposition.

Were chess players to reach such an impasse, we might wonder if both players knew the rules of the game. Is one or the other right? Are both wrong? In chess, the rule book would have to decide. In philosophy, there is no rule book, just a shared language. That is the place to look, not only for a verdict in each instance—Moore, Ayer versus Malcolm, Chapman and Henle versus Pollock—but, more importantly, for a verdict on all such argumentation, linking concept with concept. Do natural languages constitute calculi of the kind required by such a priori reasoning? What, then, are its prospects of success?

First, the bright side. In order for such network calculations to be valid, few if any of the strong claims that have been made concerning the connectedness of language need be right. It need not be true—though it may well be—that, quite generally, words' meanings are affected or defined by other words with which they interact.[20] It need not be true that all, or almost all, such meanings "are intricately interwoven in relations of inclusion, exclusion, implication, contradiction, comparison, and contrast, with other meanings."[21] It need not be true that "a word can have meaning only by virtue of its oppositions to other words"[22] or that "in order to understand the meaning of a word, one must also understand a set of semantically related words."[23] The network need not be extensive or universal, nor need its connections be strong; *local, non-functional* interrelatedness may suffice to validate reasoning like Moore's, Ayer's, Chapman and Henle's, and Pollock's.

The sense of this double concession, regarding the extent and the strength of the requisite connections, can be clarified by means of John Lyons's comments on "semantic fields":

> As an illustration of this notion we may take (as substance) the field of colour and see how it is determined, or "informed," in English ... For simplicity, we will first of all consider only that part of the field which is covered by the words *red, orange, yellow, green* and *blue*. Each of these terms is referentially imprecise, but their relative position in this lexical system is fixed (and as a set they cover the greater part of the visible spectrum): *orange* lies between *red* and *yellow, yellow* between *orange* and *green*, and so on. It is part of the sense of each of these terms that they belong to this particular lexical system in English and that they contract relationships of contiguity (or, more precisely perhaps, "betweenness") relative to one another in the system.[24]

Given this interrelatedness, inferences are possible. If a color lies between orange and green, it is not red; if it lies between red and yellow, it is orange; if it lies between red and yellow, it does not lie between orange and green; and so forth. Similarly, if *assertion* and *true* and *false* are related as Moore supposed, then if moral utterances are not assertions, they are not true or false. If *know* and *lie* are related as Ayer supposed, then if people can lie about their pains, they can also know about them. And so forth. If these relations hold, within a given field, it does not matter how organized or unorganized other areas of the same language (or the whole of that language, or language generally) may be, or what relations hold there. *Localized* linkage suffices.

Lyons next notes:

> It might appear that the notion of sense is unnecessary here, and that an account of the reference of each of the colour-terms would be sufficient as a description of their meaning. Consider, however, the conditions under which one might come to learn, or be said to know, the reference of these words. The child learning English cannot first of all learn the reference of *green*, and then subsequently the reference of *blue* or *yellow*, so that at a particular time he could be said to know the reference of

one, but not the other. (It is true that he might learn,
ostensively, that *green* referred to the colour of grass, or
the leaves of a particular tree, or one of his mother's
dresses: but the reference of *green* is wider than any
particular instance of its application, and a knowledge
of its reference involves knowledge also of the boundaries of its reference.) It must be supposed that over a
certain period the child gradually learns the position of
green with respect to *blue* and *yellow,* of *yellow* with
respect to *green* and *orange,* and so on until he has
learnt the position of each of the colour-terms with
respect to its neighbour in the lexical system and the
approximate location of the boundaries of the area in
the continuum of the field covered by each term. His
knowledge of the meaning of the colour-terms necessarily involves therefore a knowledge of both their sense
and their reference.[25]

The modal terms in this argument—*cannot, could, must, necessarily*—have at best a weak sense. It may be, for example, that a child
learning the scope of *red* is told, "No, that's not red, it's pink," or
"No, that's not red, it's orange"; but it is conceivable the child
might simply be told, repeatedly, "No, that's not red," until it
learned the term's borderline. Still more clearly, once the term *red*
has been learned, it is not typically employed in dependence on
other color terms (as, by contrast, the term *watt* is often not only
learned and defined in relation to *volt* and *ampere,* but is frequently employed in relation to and in dependence on those terms, watts
being calculated from volts and amperes, and vice versa). However,
none of this matters: Regardless of whether the terms in question
are learned or employed in dependence on one another, the same
inferences hold with regard to color positions—as they may, perhaps, with regard to the truth of moral utterances, knowing one's
pains, meaning and propositions, truth and propositions, and so
forth.[26] The linkage need not be strong.
    So much for the bright side. Problems appear from the contrast
just drawn between words like *red* and words like *watt.* We often
learn the word *watt* by explicit definition, specifying a uniform content. We often use the word *watt* in a way that recalls the definition,
relating it to other words in its field. Hence no debates are likely to
arise with respect to watts, amperes, and volts analogous to the
debates just cited about knowledge, lies, meanings, and propositions. Compared to these latter terms, the senses of *watt, ampere,*

and *volt* are reflectively better known, sharper, and more uniform. They not only form an interlocking network, but are known to do so. And reasoning can proceed accordingly. Such terms, however, are the exception. When we use less rigid expressions, arguments like those cited may commit the double error of supposing uniform content and supposing reflective knowledge of it.

Take Moore. Reflection on usage would have to show whether utterances like "You ought to go away" are standardly termed assertions, hence are assertions. Reflection on usage would have to show whether assertions are restricted to true-false utterances, or vice versa. Since Moore too seldom engaged in such reflection, he often supposed restrictions or equivalences not backed by usage, hence often engaged in calculus-reasoning of the network as well as of the mosaic, concept-by-concept variety. In this instance, if he had attended to familiar forms of speech, he would have found people readily referring to "You ought to go away" or "You ought to stay home" as assertions. Had he given any weight to this evident fact of usage, he would have felt no inclination to argue as he did. He would not have made such utterances' status as assertions hinge on their being true-false.

Within this particular assessment lies a general challenge to network-reasoning. It can be stated thus: If a verdict is reached (for example, concerning utterances as assertions) by reasoning unbacked by inspection of usage, the verdict is unreliable; if it is preceded by such inspection (for example, of the concept *assertion*), the reasoning is not needed, since the answer is evident already from the inspection.

Frequently, neither of two rival solutions is backed by usage, or based on inspection of usage; hence neither is reliable or correct. Consider the points at issue between Chapman and Henle, on one side, and Pollock, on the other. Does *proposition* link with *true* or with *meaning*? Does a sentence containing an indexical expression (for instance, "I have a book") have one meaning or several? When contrasted with some other sentence ("The lilacs are in bloom") or compared with sentences of like meaning in other languages ("Ich habe ein Buch"), the sentence is likely to be judged to have one meaning. When considered on different occasions, where its reference and its truth vary, it is likely to be judged to have many meanings. Such talk about meanings, propositions, and the like occurs primarily in the discussions of philosophers and linguists; and the contrasting texts of Chapman, Henle, and Pollock suggest what one finds there. No consistent usage backs either side. Rather than argue or syllogize, therefore, it would be better either to stipulate a single sense, for practical purposes, or to accept the fact that, for example, it may be natural and reasonable to use the term *meaning* one way in one context and another way in another. In such an instance, all-or-nothing argumentation is worse than useless.

Applying the lesson to myself, I have not argued, calculus-wise, that network-reasoning can never succeed. Rather, the discussion to this point can be summarized as follows. Three characteristics, present in the preceding samples, elicit the categorization "network-reasoning": 1) deduction of one concept from another; 2) essentialistic, "one-thing-only" assumptions; 3) failure to check the assumptions against the language spoken. Argumentation that manifests these traits stands little chance of succeeding.

An Alternate Line of Critique

In his review of Wittgenstein's *Investigations*, Peter Strawson suggests an alternative, perhaps complementary, line of critique: "We are apt to think we have a clue to the general nature of the *proposition* in the idea of *whatever is true or false*. But one of these ideas cannot be used to elucidate the other: they move too closely together, they share each other's ambiguities [134-137]."[27] If, for instance, we wonder whether commands are true-false, we are likely to wonder whether they are propositions; if we wonder whether they are propositions, we are likely to wonder whether they are true-false (compare Moore, above).

Stating the difficulty this way might seem to presuppose the validity of the kind of inferences I have been questioning. It might suggest that were the verdict clear for one notion but not the other we could proceed to infer the less certain notion from the more certain. This we have reason to doubt. However, Strawson's words need not be taken this way. They may instead indicate a supplementary objection to network-reasoning: Even were such inferences valid, they might not be feasible, occasionally or even quite generally. Perhaps the instance Strawson cites and the obstacle he alleges are typical. Let us take a closer look at both.

Do the notions *proposition* and *whatever is true or false* share *all* of each other's ambiguities, and is that why mutual clarification is judged unfeasible? If they do share all their ambiguities, must they not be synonyms? (*City* shares one fuzzy border with *inhabited*, another with *place*, but could not share all fuzzy borders with either of them without being the same, or an equivalent, concept.) Yet surely *proposition* is not synonymous with *whatever is true or false* (think of true reports, true friends, false gold, false impressions, etc.). If, instead, they share only some ambiguities, might not at least partial clarification of one term by the other be possible (supposing that inferences from notion to notion were valid)? Must clarification always be complete? Is all-and-only definition the only kind of clarification worth mentioning? So is Strawson's objection implicitly essentialistic? To answer these queries, let us consult the numbers he cites from Wittgenstein's *Investigations*.

Number 136 looks most pertinent. There Wittgenstein remarks: "To say that a proposition is whatever can be true or false amounts to saying: we call something a proposition when *in our language* we apply the calculus of truth functions to it." Without endorsing this equivalence, he continues: "Now it looks as if the definition—a proposition is whatever can be true or false—determined what a proposition was, by saying: what fits the concept 'true,' or what the concept 'true' fits, is a proposition. So it is as if we had a concept of true and false, which we could use to determine what is and what is not a proposition." Wittgenstein repudiates this talk of "fitting": "The use of the words 'true' and 'false' may be among the constituent parts of [the language-game with *proposition*]; and if so it belongs to our concept 'proposition' but does not 'fit' it." However we describe it, though, might not this fact of usage (when and if established) serve in the manner suggested: might it not discriminate between what counts as a proposition and what does not? Might it not settle debates as to whether commands are propositions, or questions are, or performatives, tautologies, predictions, contradictions, and so forth? Might it not function as first premise in an argument like the following: "A proposition is [only] what can be true or false; but questions are not true or false; hence questions are not propositions"?

On inspection, such a demonstration appears otiose. Suppose we start with the second premise and ask how it is known that *questions* are not true or false. "What is a question?" asks Wittgenstein in *Investigations* §24. "Is it the statement that I do not know such-and-such, or the statement that I wish the other person would tell me...? Or is it the description of my mental state of uncertainty?" Any one of these construals points both to questions' being propositions and to their being true-false; hence there is no need to establish either status via the other ("Questions are true-false, therefore they are propositions," or, "Questions are propositions, therefore they are true-false"). An alternative, pragmatic construal, stressing the evocative, non-informative role of questions, casts equal doubt on questions' status as propositions and their status as true-false. So in either construal—the reportive or the pragmatic—network-reasoning looks unnecessary. It looks similarly useless with regard to commands, performatives, moral utterances, and so forth, as well as questions. The difficulty recurs repeatedly.

Indeed, one may ask if there is any instance, any set of circumstances, in which ordinary English-speakers would be less certain whether something was a proposition than whether it was true-false. If there is, would that not show that the two notions—*proposition* and *truth*—are less tightly linked than supposed? If there is not, would that not show that there is no need of one-way clarification? Falsity or futility—the dilemma's horns look sharp.

This specimen looks typical. It would seem that any tightly-knit concepts, and not just the pair Strawson cites, would "move too closely together" to permit elucidation of one by the other. However, this is merely an initial impression. Fuller testing will come from further examples and arguments, in discussion of the chapter's second main topic.

One-Directional Reasoning

Argumentation cannot proceed validly without regard for the terms it employs and their existing meanings (conventional or stipulated). The relation of term to term, or of meaning to meaning, cannot be deduced a priori; the terms' established uses must be consulted. But if, as many have held, concepts are multiply, complexly interrelated—if every word "is inextricably part of a language" and "its meaning is shown only in its use as part of a *system*"[28]—a problem arises for such consultation. "How can philosophical inquiry be conducted without a perpetual *petitio principii*?"[29]

> Philosophers' problems do not in general, if ever, arise out of troubles about single concepts, like that say of *pleasure* or that of *number*. They arise, rather, as the traffic-policeman's problems arise, when crowds of conceptual vehicles, of different sorts and moving in different directions meet at some conceptual crossroads. All or a lot of them have to be got under control conjointly. This is why, in its early stages, a philosophical dispute strikes scientists and mathematicians as so messy an affair. It *is* messy, for it is a traffic-block—a traffic-block which cannot be tidied up by the individual drivers driving their individual cars efficiently.[30]

One popular strategy for bringing order to the chaos is that of formalization. With formal logic providing the basic framework, substitute systems of concepts can be constructed in which the mutual relationships of the parts will have the same clarity and precision as in formal logic itself. Familiar, tangled usage can be bypassed.[31] I have already touched on this approach, insofar as it frequently betrays a lingering essentialism. Now we can turn to an alternate, informal solution that is often preferred. The task of philosophy may still be seen as analysis, but the analysis need not achieve global, simultaneous clarity. A focal point can be chosen from which light will spread to surrounding concepts. In the words of Baker and Hacker, "By treating one or a few conceptual connections as basic, we might well hope to exhibit the rest as their consequences."

This notion of directional analysis boasts venerable, essentialistic ancestry. For example, a long tradition has distinguished between an essence and a mere property, in the sense of "an attribute that does not form part of the essence of its subject but necessarily results from that essence as a formal effect."[32] The essence of humanity, say, is rational animality, and from this essence derives the property of mortality or the property of risibility. Still closer to our concerns is the less patently essentialistic doctrine that distinguishes between definable and indefinable concepts, and seeks ultimate clarity through the latter.

"It can be easily proved," wrote A. C. Ewing, characteristically,

> that there must be some terms which are indefinable in the sense of not being analysable, reducible to anything else. For if you define A by analysing it in terms of B and C, you must, for the definition to be intelligible, know what B and C are, and though you may analyse B and C also in terms of something else, you cannot go on in this way *ad infinitum*. If you are to analyse your concepts, sooner or later you must come to concepts which are just unanalysable. If so, it will not be a mark of human failure but an inevitable result of the logic of the concepts that we cannot define them.[33]

This doctrine requires that analysis be one-directional. "Primitive," "indefinable" notions can and must be used to clarify definable ones, whereas definable notions cannot be used to clarify primitive ones. For example, according to Moore, "how 'good' is to be defined, is the most fundamental question in all Ethics. That which is meant by 'good' is, in fact, except its converse 'bad,' the

only simple object of thought which is peculiar to Ethics. Its definition is, therefore, the most essential point in the definition of
Ethics."[34] Elucidation must begin there. Right and wrong, for
example, must be defined in terms of the good, and not vice versa.

As Wittgenstein observed, we must at least be able to describe
the use of the word *good*. And if we can do that, what more do we
wish? What is this "definition" that we aspire to, that we can
achieve for some words but not for others? The essentialistic
nature of the enterprise appears when Moore explains: "The most
important sense of 'definition' is that in which a definition states
what are the parts which invariably compose a certain whole; and
in this sense 'good' has no definition because it is simple and has
no parts. It is one of those innumerable objects of thought which
are themselves incapable of definition, because they are the ultimate terms by reference to which whatever *is* capable of definition
must be defined."[35]

At the time he wrote those words, Moore failed to note the possibility that such definition might be impossible, not because the
concepts or "objects of thought" are simple, but because they are
not invariably composed of some one set of "parts." Later he came
to recognize that "all of us very often both use and understand sentences in which the adjective 'good' occurs. But it seems to me very
certain that in different sentences we both use and understand
this word in a considerable number of different senses."[36] The
same holds for *right,* the supposed derivative of *good.* And in both
instances we can characterize the word's varied uses, its varied
senses. The great divide between definables and indefinables is an
essentialist illusion.

With assurance equal to Ewing's, Schlick proposed an analogous demonstration: "It is clear that in order to understand a verbal definition we must know the signification of the explaining
words beforehand, and that the only explanation which can work
without any previous knowledge is the ostensive definition. We
conclude that there is no way of understanding any meaning without ultimate reference to ostensive definitions."[37] But some terms
(*percentage, culture, meaning*) are not ostensively definable,
whereas others (*plate, fat, toe, turquoise*) are. Hence analysis must
go from the former to the latter, from the verbally definable back
to the ostensively definable.

The idea that ostensive definition gives the meaning of a word
without relying on other words or previous knowledge of language—that it permits us to exit from the web of words and make
direct contact with reality—does not stand scrutiny. Let us explain

the word *tove*, Wittgenstein suggested, by pointing to a pencil and saying, "This is tove." Without further assistance—further *verbal* assistance—such a definition could be interpreted to mean: "This is a pencil," "This is smooth," "This is wooden," "This is hard," "This is yellow," "This is straight," "This is mine," "This is short," "This is inexpensive," "This is used to write with," and so on *ad infinitum*. Although "This is tove" already amplifies the utterance "Tove," still fuller elucidation would be needed to make the definition work: "This *instrument* is called 'tove,'" "This *shape* is called 'tove,'" "This *material* is called 'tove,'" or the like.[38] The ostensive definition would have to use one or more of the generic terms that appear in verbal definitions (unless, for example, the terms immediately preceded the defining formula, as in "What instrument is called 'tove'?" or "What color is called 'tove'?"). Thus the great divide between verbal and nonverbal definitions looks as illusory as that between definables and indefinables.

Clarification is not forced in one direction. Even a word like *red* cannot be elucidated by mere pointing. Nor can it be explained by indicating any single shade of red and saying, "This is red," or even, "This color is red." More adequate would be the purely verbal definition, "Red is scarlet, crimson, rose, salmon, and the like"—provided the defining terms were understood. And of course they might be, just as the term *color* might be understood in the ostensive definition, "This color is red." Either type of definition, the ostensive or nonostensive, requires previous understanding of other words. Ostensive definition enjoys no special primacy.

Various paradigms—the Porphyrean "tree," Sheffer's stroke, truth tables—have fostered the notion of one-directional analysis. Of special interest as a possible source is the field of kinship terms—*brother, mother, uncle, aunt, niece, grandfather, grandparent*—studied by linguists. No one of these terms is more definable or indefinable than another. Some, however, can be non-disjunctively defined in terms of other members of the field (for instance, *father* as "male parent"), whereas others cannot (*parent* cannot be non-disjunctively defined by means of *father* or *mother*). And one term—*parent*—can be used to non-disjunctively define all the rest. Were such conceptual clusters common, one-directional analysis might frequently bring greater order and clarity than multi-directional analysis. "By treating one or a few conceptual connections as basic, we might well hope to exhibit the rest as their consequences."

However, tightly knit clusters of terms, simply definable in terms of one another, are relatively rare. Still rarer are those which, like the kinship cluster and unlike color terms, permit reductive, one-directional analysis. And hardly ever do such terms become the subject of speculative debate. The reason seems clear. The terms' relations being orderly and their definitions simple, their meanings occasion scant confusion or perplexity. Thus if thinkers feel the need to bring order into chaos or to clarify a set of crucial concepts, this very fact suggests that the concepts are not the sort that permit one-directional analysis.

By way of concrete illustration, consider the examples Joel Feinberg cites:

> Many legal concepts are complex and derivative; that is, capable of reduction to the simpler notions of which they are composed. Soon, however, this process of reduction must come to an end, as we discover those fundamental terms whose meaning cannot be elucidated by other legal terms without a vitiating circularity, and that are therefore capable of theoretically enlightening definition only, if at all, in terms from outside the law. Austin gave, as examples of such terms, "duty," "right," "liberty," "injury," "punishment," "redress"; others have suggested "person," "property," "possession," "corporation." H. L. A. Hart, in his article "Definition and Theory in Jurisprudence," has pointed out that efforts to define such terms have generated a "familiar triad" of theories. (The same is true of ethical theories that purport to define such terms as "ought" and "good.") Some writers (such as the Legal Realists) argue that the basic legal terms stand for some familiar kind of empirical fact, the behavior of judges, for example. These definitions have the effect of reducing the whole subject matter of law to the social sciences. Other theorists find that basic legal terms stand for irreducibly legal (nonempirical) entities. The Scandinavian school (Axel Hägerström, Karl Olivecrona, Alf Ross) holds that basic legal terms stand for no kind of entities, empirical or nonempirical; rather, they are "fictions" or "imaginary ideas."[39]

If kinship terms do not give rise to such altercations and legal terms do, it seems safe to surmise that the legal terms do not form such an orderly field, with each term definable in terms of the others, and all definable in terms of one.

For Feinberg as for Moore, derivative concepts are more complex, non-derivative concepts simpler. The former are "composed" of the latter, and it stands to reason that a whole has greater complexity than any one of its parts. Whatever complexity each part possesses resides in the whole, and the parts are multiple. If, then, the simpler is more readily grasped than the more complex, it would appear that, wherever possible, analysis should take a single direction: from the more complex to the more simple. It may also appear that any time a term gets defined, such is the direction taken. The term defined is more complex, the defining terms simpler. For do not the latter constitute, or denote, parts of the former?[40]

Since it motivates much one-directional analysis, this compositional conception merits scrutiny. Suppose orange were defined as the hue between red and yellow, or yellow were defined as the hue between orange and green: would the concepts *red* and *yellow* be simpler than the concept *orange* in the first definition, and the concepts *orange* and *green* be simpler than the concept *yellow* in the second, and would the concept *yellow* therefore be both simpler and more complex than itself? "But these definitions are circular!" Very well, then: If a father can be defined as a male parent, and a parent can be defined as one that either begets or brings forth offspring, does that prove that the concept *father* is richer and more complex than the concept *parent*? No, only an essentialistic definition, were one possible, would permit such an inference; for then the essence of parenthood, common to male and female parents, would be present, entire and undivided, in the definition of *parent*, together with the specific difference, "male." As it is, however, *father* does not mean: "male who begets or brings forth offspring." The concept's content is not disjunctive, hence need not be richer than the content of the concept *parent*. The contrary impression is another essentialistic illusion.

"Yet doubtless some concepts are simpler than others, and some more complex concepts can be analyzed in terms of simpler ones; so that sometimes, at least, one-directional analysis is clearly desirable." Here both premises are more problematic than traditional thinking would suggest. Moore viewed *yellow* as a "simple notion"; for the essence of yellow—the pure, invisible yellow present in all yellows—omitted all variations of hue, lightness, and saturation. However, once this essentialism dissipates, the concept's true complexity emerges. Not only do variations of hue, lightness, and saturation compose the concept, as its leaves compose an artichoke; but the complex criteria that serve to discriminate between being yellow and appearing yellow also belong to the concept. Something that appears yellow—under lights, to someone with defective vision, or to someone wearing yellow glasses—may not be yellow; for similar reasons, something that is yellow need not always appear yellow. We might also mention further, peripheral complexity—"yellow" races that are not yellow, "yellow" people who are cowardly, diseases called "yellows" since they cause yellowing in leaves, and so forth. And without accepting Lyons's analysis in all its details, we may nonetheless recognize an immense negative content complementing the positive, and as immediately conveyed as the positive. Any native speaker or hearer knows right away that an object or area that *is* yellow is *not* black or brown or mauve or cobalt or aquamarine or green or purple or . . . In so describing the content, I have intentionally refrained from saying that an object or area that is *completely* yellow is not any other color, since frequently, at least, the completeness of the coloring—relative or absolute—is implicit in the predication "yellow." There is no need to say, "That spot is *totally* yellow," nor generally any need to say, even of a monochrome car, "My car is *entirely* yellow." People would then suppose that the hubcaps, tires, and aerial, and perhaps the whole interior, had been painted yellow. What "My car is yellow" affirms is the predominant color; what it excludes is any other predominant color. Though these and similar nuances may pertain to color concepts generally, and not just to *yellow*, that doesn't mean they do not pertain to the concept *yellow*. I might go on to mention spectral characteristics. But enough. What complex notion, one may wonder, is more complex than this "simple" one?

Other supposedly simple concepts, such as *pain* or *toothache*, reveal similar complexity. This does not mean that no concepts are more or less complex than any others; but even the simplest are so very complex as to make little practical difference. The idea of passing, by the mere expedient of a definition, from complexity to simplicity and *thereby* to clarity looks illusory. If the defining terms are better known, reflectively or unreflectively, than the term defined, then even if they are more complex, they can serve to clarify it. If they are not better known, then even if they are simpler than the term defined, they are not likely to clarify it. And we cannot safely assume that simpler notions will be better known or more readily grasped; for even the simplest are exceedingly complex. Witness Moore's simplistic misconceptions concerning color concepts.

Philosophers often take a less pragmatic approach, viewing the direction of analysis as dictated, not by the practical exigencies of the moment, but by the "logic of the concepts." If the concepts *A* and *B* interrelate, and *A* "presupposes" *B* but *B* does not "presuppose" *A*, there is only one direction to take: *B* must serve to explicate *A* and not vice versa. Thus Bruce Aune writes: "The notion of a mental state presupposes the notion of a person already, and thus could not be used to analyze it."[41] And J. N. Findlay declares: "The reason why it is absurd to tell us *not* to attend to the meaning of expressions but to concentrate on their use, is perfectly simple: it is that the notion of use, as it ordinarily exists and is used, presupposes the notion of meaning (in its central and paradigmatic sense), and that it cannot therefore be used to elucidate the latter, and much less to replace or to do duty for it."[42]

Before assessing such claims, one must first understand them. How should we interpret the term "presuppose"? The only relevant sense, it would seem, is functional. If one expression could be understood and used only in reference to a second expression, the second could not be clarified by means of the first; for then it would have to clarify itself.

This sounds logical. Yet consider the example of functional dependence already cited. Webster defines a watt as "the absolute mks unit of power equal to the work done at the rate of one absolute joule per second or to the rate of work represented by a current of one ampere under a pressure of one volt and taken as the standard in the U.S.: 1/746 horsepower." Use of the term *watt* depends on, hence "presupposes," these others—*power, work, joule, ampere, volt,* and so forth. Yet Webster's turns around and defines *volt* in terms of *watt*. Is this not legitimate? Does not the term *watt* serve to "elucidate" *volt,* and vice versa? In what sense does it not?

Consider a simpler, comparable cluster of concepts, which the same dictionary handles differently. Avoiding any circularity, it defines a foot in terms of inches, inches in terms of a yard, and a yard in relation to a meter, then ends the semantic trail by describing the meter as "the basic metric unit of length." This procedure may be contrasted with defining a foot as twelve inches or one third of a yard, an inch as one twelfth of a foot or one thirty/sixth of a yard, and a yard as three feet or thirty-six inches—without any mention of meters. The circularity of such a collection might elicit the objection: "How can this enlighten anyone? Eventually, each term must be understood in terms of itself." But this is not so. Just as a person might be acquainted with yards and feet but not with meters, so a person (say a child, who has a ruler but not a yardstick) might be acquainted with inches and feet but not with yards. The child might look up the term *yard* and discover that three feet make a yard. Similarly, someone might be acquainted with voltmeters and volts, but not know how to calculate volts in relation to watts, or vice versa. He could learn how to do so by looking up *volt* or *watt* in the dictionary.

It appears that the lesson of such examples resembles the one noted in the last chapter, in critiquing thinkers like Waismann. Knowledge of concepts admits of degrees. Complete knowledge is unusual. Few people, for example, know that in the United States a yard equals 0.9144 of a meter. Few need to know it. Fewer still know or need to know how to calculate the meter—"the basic metric unit of length"—in reference to the wave-length of light emitted by krypton. A scientific dictionary would tell them; Webster's does not. Yet it does not thereby fail in its duty. Nor would it necessarily be remiss, or fall into vicious circularity, if it defined a yard in terms of feet and inches (even though the concept *yard* might be said to "presuppose" the concepts *foot* and *inch*), and defined feet and inches in terms of a yard. After all, why define *any* of these terms in relation to one another—why not define them all in relation to metric measures—if their mutual relationships can be taken for granted among those who consult the dictionary? What is appropriate and helpful in any definition or analysis depends on the recipients and their needs.

Typically, philosophical analysis does not aim at teaching unknown meanings, or unknown aspects of meanings, but at reflective awareness of meanings already known. So a second reason might legitimize the expedient of clarifying one concept by means of another that "presupposes" it. Not only might the connection with that particular term be something not yet known, even unreflectively, to the recipient; it might simply not be known reflectively.

Reasons of both kinds might be cited in defense of Wittgenstein's formula and in reply to Findlay's objection that "the notion of use, as it ordinarily exists and is used, presupposes the notion of meaning (in its central and paradigmatic sense)." "What I am saying," Findlay explains, "is simply that we cannot fully say, in a great many cases, how an expression is used, without saying what sort of things it is intended to refer to, or to bring to mind, and just how, or in what angle or light, it purports to refer to them, or to bring them to mind."[43] It may be noted, first of all, that none of this gets us to the *notion* of meaning (as distinct from its area of reference). Even if it did, the words "fully" and "in a great many cases" are significant. Further, if a person betrays little reflective awareness of how the term *meaning* is standardly applied—so little that he supposes the meaning of a word is, for example, the object it refers to—a clarifying reminder employing the term *use* may point in a different direction. And it may do so regardless of whether talk about use partially and/or occasionally depends on the concept *meaning*. A close association of *meaning* and *use* might even render the reminder more effective.

In sum, "One might say: an explanation serves to remove or to avert a misunderstanding—one, that is, that would occur but for the explanation; not every one that I can imagine."[44] Contrary insistence, that analysis always be total or conform to some single ideal, betrays a further form of essentialism.

Back to the Beginning

An underlying essentialism vitiates much talk about definables and indefinables, complex concepts and their simple parts; one-directional clusters are rare; and "presuppositions" do not force analysis in a single direction. Hence most claims concerning directional analysis are suspect. It does not follow, however, that no such claims stand up. The moment has come to assess Baker and Hacker's suggestions, cited at the start, with regard to Wittgenstein's strategy in the *Philosophical Investigations* and key issues he addresses there.

As readers of this chapter may recall, Baker and Hacker claim that "Wittgenstein reverses the traditional direction of fit between meaning and understanding." From the Augustinian starting point in meaning, a whole set of "equations" develops; from a contrary starting point, in understanding, a different set can unfold. "Clarifying the concept of a criterion cannot be done successfully prior to (independently of) a correct conception of meaning, and, conversely, this conception turns on the notion of criteria of understanding. Wittgenstein's philosophy is like a stone arch; each stone supports all of the others—or, at least, nothing stands up until everything is in place."[45] From this account it would appear that, despite Wittgenstein's protestations that he was merely "clearing up the ground of language," the *Investigations* is as theoretical and constructive, in its own way, as the *Tractatus*.

How, precisely, might the concept *understanding* place constraints on the concept *meaning*, rather than vice versa? Baker and Hacker cite the equation: "Meaning is what is understood when one understands an expression."[46] They do not demonstrate this equivalence, but seem to accept it as a matter of common sense, or a relatively noncontroversial intuition.[47] And indeed, even "Augustinians" might have little difficulty with it. What we understand, they might suggest, when we understand an expression, is what the expression refers to; that, then, is its meaning. To this reasoning and its result critics might object that there is more to understanding an expression than understanding its reference, and that expressions can be understood which have no reference. But these objections would be valid only if the equivalence Baker and Hacker propose is sufficiently exact, and does not serve merely as a general indication. An expression's meaning would have to be all that is understood when the expression is understood, and all that is understood when *any* expression is understood. Once, however, the formula is thus interpreted, the original intuition looks less certain. Is the equivalence really an exact one?

Exact enough, it would seem. However, this answer derives as much from the concept *meaning* as it does from the concept *understanding*. And what the concept *meaning* tells us is so directly evident that we have no need of indirect inference via the concept *understanding*. It is the use of *meaning* that tells us whether the meaning of a term extends beyond its reference and therefore coincides with all we understand when we understand an expression. It is the use of *meaning* that tells us whether the class of meaningful expressions (expressions which "have meaning") extends beyond expressions with reference and therefore coincides with the class of expressions we understand. Thus the concept *understanding* places no constraints on the concept *meaning*. If the use of the word *meaning* established no equivalence between the meaning of an expression and what we understand when we understand the expression, there would be no equivalence. If it does establish an equivalence, it does so on its own—or rather, it establishes its half of the equivalence, independently, just as *understand* establishes its half, independently. Each traces its own border and the borders happen to coincide. They do not *have* to coincide.

We reach a like result if, taking a different tack, we contest the Augustinian suggestion by denying that understanding an expression's reference forms even part of what it is to understand the expression's meaning. "Reference, as Frege understands it," Michael Dummett observes, "is not an ingredient in meaning at all: someone who does not know the reference of an expression does not show thereby that he does not understand, or only partially understands, the expression."[48] If veridical, this restriction on meaning, no less than the previous two extensions, derives, and must be learned, from the use of *meaning*, not from the use of *understand*. And if the borders of both words coincide in this manner rather than the other (excluding reference entirely, rather than augmenting it), the coincidence results, as before, from how each word is used, independently. Again, the borders do not have to coincide.

Wittgenstein wished "to bring words back from their metaphysical to their everyday use." But there is no guessing everyday use, no deducing it a priori. One must look and see. And what one sees about one concept permits no inferences about others. By the same token, what one sees about one concept cannot be undone by what one sees about others. If, for example, examination of games reveals no common essence guiding our use of *game*, we need not fear that subsequent examination of *play, rule, competition,* or the like will force us to revise our verdict. Only the use of *game* can show us the use of *game.*

Similarly, only the use of *language* can show us the use of *language*, only the use of *meaning* can show us the use of *meaning*, and so forth. Hence, if concepts in the sense of word-uses are the stones in question, it is misleading to say that in Wittgenstein's philosophy "each stone supports all of the others—or, at least, nothing stands up until everything is in place." If, instead, the stones are concepts in the sense of accounts, or conceptions, of word-uses or word referents, the difficulty remains. For if correct conceptions of meaning, thinking, understanding, and the like must agree with the uses of *mean, think, understand,* and the like, how can the conceptions form a more interdependent system than the uses do?

Granted, terms are employed in combination with others; hence examination of one term's use cannot totally prescind from other terms' uses. *Meaning,* for example, occurs in combination with *learn, know, explain, same, unclear, . . . Game* occurs in combination with *rule, win, play, match, score, . . .* However, *game* also occurs in combination with *his* and *off* ("His game was off"), *chess* and *difficult* ("Chess is a difficult game"), *last, three,* and *hour* ("The game lasted three hours"), and so forth—indeed with countless other expressions of the language ("fun and games," "threw the game," "missed the game," "final game," "thrilling game," etc.). The like holds for *meaning.* But it does not follow that reflective understanding of the concept *meaning* must wait on reflective understanding of every other concept in the language. Unreflective understanding may suffice—for example, unreflective understanding of *learn, know,* or *explain* may suffice when one asks what it is that one learns, knows, or explains when one learns, knows, or explains the meaning of a word (just as unreflective understanding of *chess, bridge, solitaire, polo,* and the like may suffice when one asks what, if anything, various games have in common).

What is true is that an erroneous notion of understanding is more likely to affect a person's conception of meaning than is, for instance, an erroneous notion of justice, photosynthesis, or evolution. For instance, conceive understanding as a mental act, and meanings may seem items in the mind. However, the reverse holds equally true. An erroneous notion of meaning may adversely affect a person's conception of understanding. Conceive meanings as items in the mind, and understanding may appear to be a mental act. Hence, whereas system-building seeks sure starting points, once for all, then works deductively from these, therapy needs to be more flexible. It can go either way, as the occasion demands—or both ways together. The inquiry may compel us "to travel over a wide field of thought criss-cross in every direction," as in Wittgenstein's later philosophy.[49]

A possible positive outcome—especially in an inquiry that aims at something more than therapy or critique—is a "picture of the landscape."[50] Such a panoramic picture will likely be more informative and enlightening than a theory—certainly than a theory which draws false dichotomies between definables and indefinables, verbal and nonverbal definitions, or simple and complex concepts; or which conceives language as a tightly interlocking calculus and argues accordingly. From this chapter and the last, such an overview does in fact emerge—a view that can be summarized in terms of our earlier comparison with chess. Language both differs from chess and resembles it: differs from it with respect to the strict uniformity of chess pieces' moves; resembles it with respect to the relative independence of their moves.

Chapter Five

OTHER WORLDS

Very often in perusing a philosophical discussion we are greeted by the imperative, "consider the following hypothetical situation." Formal argument seems to break off. What follows is a short or longish narrative, describing more or less bizarre occurrences. After the fictional events have been subjected to judgment by intuition, the argument resumes and some philosophically interesting conclusion is reached or refuted. I suspect that a number of philosophers never get through to these conclusions, because they refuse to follow the diversion into fantasy. The problem with remaining thus aloof from the current philosophical fashion is that since this is the current mode, one is cut off from contemporary debates. Indeed, in two areas of great current interest—post-Gettier epistemology and theories of personal identity— anyone who spurns fiction will find that he has virtually nothing to read.[1]

A passage from Friedrich Waismann links the previous chapter with this one. Waismann first cites a standard piece of argumentation:

When we say of someone that he "sees" or "hears" an aeroplane, or "descries," "detects" a lark in the sky, or again that he "tastes" or "smells" roast pork, we do not ascribe to him an activity. That "seeing" is not a sort of doing can be illustrated, e.g. by calling attention to the fact that we don't use the continuous present tense. We say "I see the clock," not "I am seeing the clock" . . . , whereas it is perfectly correct to say "I am looking at the clock, listening to its ticking," and so in the other cases. Again, while it is proper to say "I have forgotten to post the letter," no one would say "I have forgotten to see the letter-box." There is no sense in asking you, when you look at me, whether your seeing is easy or difficult, quick or slowish, careful or heedless, whether you see me deliberately and whether you have now finished seeing me. So, it is argued, perceiving is not a doing (an argument used by myself in lectures).[2]

This argumentation looks like a new, interesting version of net-work-reasoning. In this instance, in order to determine the exten-sion of doing, one does not consult the customary use of the verb *do*, but examines instead the application of other verbs, and from them deduces what does and does not count as doing. One does not inquire, for example, what answers might be given to the query "What are you doing?," but considers instead what *grammatical* forms verbs like *see* and *hear* take, and in what verbal combina-tions they appear. This strategy looks unsound. One might per-haps stipulate, for whatever reason, that nothing will count as an instance of doing unless it is designated by a verb that occurs, on occasion, in the continuous present tense. Or one might consult the customary use of *do* and discover that it excludes the referents of all verbs not so employed. But without such preliminary stipula-tion or consultation, one cannot validly argue in the manner Wais-mann indicates. No Platonic form of "Doing," transcending human discourse, permits us to ignore the verb *do* and discriminate gen-uine instances from non-genuine via grammatical clues.

Waismann, too, contests the argumentation he cites, but for a different reason:

> The point to be labored is that this argument is not con-clusive. Odd as it sounds, "I have finished seeing you" *may* be said, though only in very special circumstances. A man with impaired eyesight who, unable to take in the shape as a whole, has perhaps to scan the face bit by bit in search of some characteristic marks might say, and understandably, "Now I have finished seeing you." We too are occasionally in a not much better position, as when, in magnesium light, we look at some scene, and afterwards complain, "Too quick, I couldn't take it in."[3]

Waismann himself is ready to reason network-wise—to judge doing by seeing and seeing by taking in. What is more—and here is the point that now interests me—he is ready to assess seeing (or the concept *see*), not from standard instances, but from "very spe-cial circumstances." An imaginary, far-fetched case counts as coun-terevidence, although the argument criticized was, presumably, concerned with actual cases—actual cases of seeing, actual uses of the verb *see*. This makes Waismann's reasoning look still more dubious. Even if the actual use of *see* were relevant to doing, how would the hypothetical use of the verb be relevant to its actual use? Might not the peculiar performance Waismann imagines—scanning the face bit by bit in search of some characteristic marks—be a case of doing, whereas familiar, non-imaginary forms of seeing are not? Must all seeing be the same? If even one imagined instance of seeing qualifies as doing, must all?

I do not exclude, a priori, a possible vindication of Waismann's reasoning. I just wish to suggest, for purposes of illustration, how problematic it is—problematic in a typical, essentialistic fashion that evokes Wittgensteinian misgivings. The argument from fanciful to familiar cases would look less suspect if the concepts in question resembled tesserae in a mosaic, unaffected by their surroundings. Or, to borrow Wittgenstein's comparison, if the sense of each expression resembled "an atmosphere accompanying the word, which it carried with it into every kind of application."[4] However, the uses of a word vary from case to actual case (compare, for example, ordinary seeing with the kind of active aspect-seeing Wittgenstein described[5]); and in imaginary cases they might vary still more. The preceding two chapters examined reasoning which supposed invariance in actual situations; the present chapter examines reasoning which appears to suppose invariance not only in actual cases but also in imaginary, frequently far-fetched ones.

Real Concepts, Unreal Worlds

The following quotation from Keith Graham exemplifies more starkly the kind of essentialistic reasoning we shall target. The familiar sound of his remarks suggests the prevalence of such reasoning.

> A consideration of actual cases will provide us with the limits of application where this means the range of cases over which we do apply the concept in question, but not where "limits" is taken to mean the range over which we might, could or would be prepared to apply the concept. There are reasons for thinking that it will be useful to know the limits in the latter sense, and not just the former, if the rationale of a concept is to be given. As we pare away from the hypothetical situation more and more of the features normally present where the concept applies, then if we are still prepared to apply the concept we shall come nearer to finding out what, in the situation, actually gives the grounds for the concept's application, as opposed to being merely accidentally present features where it applies. In this way, a

consideration of fantastic cases may serve as an aid to the better understanding of actual cases.[6]

It will reveal what is essential, what not—supposing that the varied cases, actual and fantastic, do in fact conceal some single essence or "rationale." But why make that supposition? As I have noted elsewhere,

> One need not imagine fantastic cases to see how this method might work. Take the concept *chess*. Normally, people play chess face to face. Yet when they play by mail, we do not hesitate to call the game "chess." When they play in their heads, with perhaps only an imagined board and imagined pieces, we apply the same term with equal readiness. When a computer replaces one person, and not even an imagined board and imagined pieces figure in the playing, we still call the game "chess." And if we envision both human contestants thus dispensed with and one computer matched against another, then, too, we may be prepared to say that the computers are playing a game of "chess." Now, after paring away the board, the pieces, the rules for moving them, even the human beings who usually play the game, do we thus arrive at "what actually gives the grounds for the concept's application"? Not in the least. For as new, different situations arise, we are ready to spin fibre on fibre, as Wittgenstein put it, till finally there may be no overlap at all between the beginning and the end of the series. The final application may share no single feature with the initial, more typical examples.[7]

Jenny Teichman speaks of the "philosophically vicious and unreasonable" practice of "imagining or supposing that a concept is simple and univocal when in fact it isn't and then drawing metaphysical and/or moral conclusions." She contrasts this procedure with "the philosophically virtuous moves of (i) testing generalizations with imaginary but logically possible counter-examples, which is a special case of (ii) describing imaginary but logically possible states of affairs with a view to examining the entailments or implications of the descriptions."[8] Teichman believes this contrast merits more attention than it has received in philosophical writing and teaching. I agree, first because the vicious moves look so common; second because it is often difficult to distinguish between the vicious and the virtuous; third because little systematic guidance has been provided to facilitate such discrimination.

Counter-examples—real or imagined, realistic or fantastic—are philosophers' stock in trade; but which examples are valid counter-instances is far from evident. Consider an apparently simple case. In the treatment of attributives, many, including myself, have equated an expression like "tall X" with "an X taller than most X's" or "an X taller than the average X." Samuel Wheeler objects: "My problem with this analysis arises from the following sort of case: The population of acrobats consists [let us suppose] of 101 individuals, 51 of which are exactly seven feet tall, and 50 of which are exactly five feet tall. It seems to me that the 51 are tall acrobats, but they are not taller than most acrobats."[9] Wheeler, like Waismann, invokes imaginary circumstances; like Graham, he would decide the actual concept by consulting a non-actual application of the term. So I responded, in a footnote: "With Wittgenstein, I would answer that if we imagine certain general features of the world or some segment of it to be different from what we are used to, as here, our terms may indeed then have quite different meanings—or none at all. I am describing the meanings that *tall, big,* and the like typically have in the world as it actually is."[10]

This riposte stayed brief, as becomes a footnote. Thus it skirted a key issue: should concepts be defined in terms of present usage or of potential usage? Should the ink spot be described as it presently appears or as it may develop, given a porous blotter? Many have favored the latter approach. For example, in his critique of Norman Malcolm's *Dreaming,* Putnam wrote:

> Although this is a wholly empirical question on which I am admittedly guessing, I feel convinced that, as a matter of fact, a great many speakers would *automatically* produce discourses similar to Dement and Kleitman's given the data from which Dement and Kleitman worked. Moreover, and here I am not guessing, virtually a hundred per cent of all hearers will "pass" these discourses without detecting the slightest trace of linguistic oddity. This seems to me to be overwhelming evidence that the "uses" in question, whatever may be their status, are not "new." They were always in the language, not in the sense of having actually been produced, but in the sense that the linguistic habits that lead to their production, given certain scientific experiences, are and have been virtually universal among speakers of the language.[11]

The evidence Putnam cites does indeed look overwhelming, given his criterion of being "always in the language." Doubtless Wheeler's imagined use of *tall* would pass the same test. However, one might with equal legitimacy assert that a person's plummeting ten stories to his death is nothing new in his life; the movement was already present, not as something actually produced, but in the sense that the physical disposition that led to its production, given certain circumstances, had been with him from birth. His body being heavier than air, it could be predicted with great certainty that he would head downwards, if ever he stepped off a ten-story building.

To equate sameness with predictability, whether of movements, uses, or meanings, sounds Pickwickian. Perhaps predictability is one factor inclining us to class a use or meaning as unchanged; but Putnam himself cites a further criterion: "conformity to the lexical definition."[12] This criterion may override the other. Pain, for example, might lexically be defined as "an unpleasant or distressing sensation due to bodily injury or disorder." Hence few demur, I imagine, when they read in Wittgenstein's *Investigations*: "We do indeed say of an inanimate thing that it is in pain: when playing with dolls for example. But this use of the concept of pain is a secondary one."[13] Although this extension of *pain* to dolls looks as natural as the extensions Wheeler and Putnam cite, and perhaps as predictable, it does not conform to the "lexical definition." So the concept is "secondary"; the meaning has altered.

A child might retort that her doll had indeed suffered bodily injury—had fallen on its face, twisted its leg, or been punched in the stomach by a kitten. This response would illustrate my point still more clearly. For most people would agree that *face, leg,* and *stomach* no longer have their standard meanings when applied to a doll; yet the child's mode of speaking is predictable. Teach a child the standard use of bodily terms, give it a recognizable doll, and such are the things it will say about the doll.

Thomas Hill's viewpoint resembles Putnam's: "Since at any given stage of the development of an individual the range of circumstances actually encountered is limited, a very important test of the meanings of the terms in a person's vocabulary consists in the manner in which that person is prepared to apply these terms in possible, as well as actual, circumstances; and at a different level, the same sort of thing is true with respect to the terms in the vocabulary of any given group of language users."[14] When, for instance, "a child who understands the term 'man' has as yet encountered only members of his own race, possible encounters with persons of other races are highly relevant to the meaning of the term 'man' in his vocabulary in that if they should be instantiated he would be ready to apply [the term to] them."[15] Similarly, the English-speaking populace as a whole has not encountered human beings over sixteen feet tall, "but circumstances in which they might be encountered are relevant to the meaning of the term 'human' in that people are prepared to apply the term in case these circumstances occur."[16]

In like manner, a population of acrobats such as Wheeler describes might be relevant to the meaning of *tall*. However, what were we to say about chess before modern communications permitted playing chess by mail, or before the advent of artificial intelligence permitted matches between computers? Was an account of the concept *chess* that omitted these future developments inadequate? Was it wrong to mention board and pieces? Was it wrong to mention human beings? And does it follow that all our semantic renderings are similarly inadequate, since they fail to mention future eventualities and what we would say about them?

Even if concepts were prospectively determined and all prospective circumstances were foreseeable, a problem would remain. What we say can be observed and reported; what we *would* say, in imaginary and often fantastic circumstances, cannot. How, then, can we be sure what we would say? How reliable are such predictions? Hill's surmise about *human beings* looks safe enough; so does Wheeler's about *tall*. Were the humanoid beings that tall, that is what we would call them; were the acrobats so divided, that is how we would describe them. But concerning chess between computers, without board or pieces, one may have doubts. Could it really be asserted with assurance, before the event, that if such machines were invented and programmed a given way, their performance not only could but would be called "playing chess"?

The more fantastic the imaginary case (for example, "The author relates what happens when the fairies, in order to prevent Gulliver, Dictator of the human race, from stopping their supplies of milk, remove his brain cells and replace each of them by a fairy who performs exactly the same function"), the more uncertain prediction becomes. As Jerry Fodor rightly insists, "there is no reason to trust our intuitions about what we would say in situations in which some of our relatively secure beliefs have proved false; the ability to answer questions about what we would say in such circumstances is not implicit in our mastery of the rules of our language."[17]

> To suppose that a perfectly reliable feature fails to obtain is, by definition, to suppose that a proposition

which we now believe to express a law of nature or a
true empirical generalisation is false. However, the discovery that such a proposition is false may, in turn,
require the abandonment of other beliefs and, in the
extreme case, of whole theories. Since there is no general way to determine how many of our beliefs may need
to be altered as the result of such a discovery (since,
that is, the set of beliefs that it would be reasonable to
abandon should the belief that *P* prove false need not be
coextensive with the set of beliefs formally incompatible
with not *P*), there can be no general way to determine
how much of our way of talking such a discovery may
require us to revise.[18]

Even in those instances where "our mastery of the rules of our
language" allows a surer response, a pertinent query may be,
whether the rules in question are specific to the term discussed, or
more general. To illustrate: It may be unrealistic to assume that
people would consistently and accurately apply PRS (the principle
of relative similarity) in according or withholding a given appellation. But suppose they did. Could we then attribute the result to the
rules for using that particular expression? For example, did the
rules for *chess*, by themselves, warrant the term's extension to
chess played by computers, or did they do so together with the rules
for extending terms—for instance, PRS? If the latter, is there not a
risk of drawing illegitimate inferences from imaginary cases, and
attributing to present meanings what does not belong to them?

Think, by comparison, of translation. There too, a principle
analogous to PRS operates, permitting the replacement of an
expression of one language with an expression of another. Yet
translators are aware of, and often insist on, the non-equivalence
between the expression translated and the expression used to
translate it. Given this parallel, might we not legitimately insist,
in like fashion, on the non-equivalence between a non-extended
term and its imagined extension?

In any case, a crucial ambiguity needs to be noted when, for
instance, Hill remarks that "tests for the current meaning of the
expression will inevitably have to be determined not merely in
terms of how the expression has been used but more importantly
in terms of how it would be used given the requisite conditions."[19]
How much will be attributed to the influence of, or equated with,
the current meaning, and how much will be traced to more general
principles of predication? To attribute everything to the ink-blot

and nothing to the blotter evokes Wittgenstein's comparison: "as if
the sense were an atmosphere accompanying the word, which it
carried with it into every kind of application." Yet such essentialism appears implicit in reasoning like Wheeler's, citing imaginary
predications in imaginary settings to prove—or more frequently
disprove—the alleged meaning of some term.

One can see why essentialistic disproofs outnumber essentialistic proofs. If a positive exposition of some concept must conform
to all probable applications in all possible situations, the prospects
of success look exceedingly dim. Suppose we set aside figurative
sayings, secondary senses, language-games like assigning letter-
colors (for example, "For me the vowel *e* is yellow"[20]) or calling days
"lean" or "fat,"[21] and other vagaries that make the task of once-for-
all delineation of a concept appear hopeless. Even so, we must still
confront the alternative either of disjunctively listing all possible
cases, individually or by clusters, or of attempting to capture them
all by means of a single, non-disjunctive formula. The latter
option, though much preferred, does not look promising, either a
priori or a posteriori. A priori, there is no end to the fantastic scenarios that may be imagined, and no assurance that varying circumstances will not yield varying verdicts. A posteriori, such
attempts have in fact had a dismal record.

Previous discussions here, for instance chapter 2's perusal of
the debate concerning knowledge, lend credence to E. J. Borowski's
verdict on another such debate, and suggest how widely his negative judgment may apply:

> The use of hypothetical puzzle cases in the literature
> presupposes that there is a unique criterion to be found
> not only for all actual ascriptions of personal identity,
> but also able to determine all possible extensions of our
> usage. This presumption is without foundation, and in
> fact, it is possible to construct a puzzle case against any
> revised theory in which our intuitions would conflict
> with the theory. At best, puzzle cases can be used to
> undermine a theory, and never to support one, but this
> argument also shows that no unique criterion can ever
> be discovered.[22]

Wheeler's counter-example suggests a similar impossibility. If *tall*
cannot be equated with "taller than most" or "taller than the average," how can it be unpacked, once for all and relative to all present or potential applications? However, cases vary. So, rather
than prolong these general observations, I shall turn now to a sur-

vey of examples. Granted, we should not assume that a concept persists, unaltered, through all imagined extensions; that the extensions are attributable solely to the present meaning; that the extensions can be as surely predicted as the circumstances can be freely stipulated; that a single theory or defining formula might be distilled from them, even if they were predictable. Many other-world arguments, such as Waismann's and Wheeler's, may therefore be fallacious. But are they all? Varied case studies may help us sort out the vicious from the virtuous.

A Systematic Sampling

The series of examples through which I shall pass resemble one another, step by step, but differ greatly from one end of the series to the other. What they all have in common is, first, their conjuring up imaginary, improbable worlds or situations, and, second, their doing so in a way that evokes at least the spectre of essentialism. The recurring question will be whether the sense of some expression has been treated as though it were an atmosphere which accompanies the expression, unaltered, into every kind of application, no matter how bizarre.

Gettier's Counter-Examples

Edmund Gettier's landmark article, "Is Justified True Belief Knowledge?," consists principally of two imaginary cases presented as counter-evidence to the traditional view that S knows P if and only if: (1) P is true; (2) S believes P; and (3) S is justified in believing P, has adequate evidence for P, has the right to be sure that P is true, or the like. The two counter-cases are similar enough that I can cite just the first:

> Suppose that Smith and Jones have applied for a certain job. And suppose that Smith has strong evidence for the following conjunctive proposition:
>
> (d) Jones is the man who will get the job, and Jones has ten coins in his pocket.
>
> Smith's evidence for (d) might be that the president of the company assured him that Jones would in the end be selected, and that he, Smith, had counted the coins in Jones's pocket ten minutes ago. Proposition (d) entails:

(e) The man who will get the job has ten coins in his pocket.

Let us suppose that Smith sees the entailment from (d) to (e), and accepts (e) on the grounds of (d), for which he has strong evidence. In this case, Smith is clearly justified in believing that (e) is true.

But imagine, further, that unknown to Smith, he himself, not Jones, will get the job. And, also, unknown to Smith, he himself has ten coins in his pocket. Proposition (e) is then true, though proposition (d), from which Smith inferred (e), is false. In our example, then, all of the following are true: (*i*) (e) is true, (*ii*) Smith believes that (e) is true, and (*iii*) Smith is justified in believing that (e) is true. But it is equally clear that Smith does not *know* that (e) is true; for (e) is true in virtue of the number of coins in Smith's pocket, while Smith does not know how many coins are in Smith's pocket, and bases his belief in (e) on a count of the coins in Jones's pocket, whom he falsely believes to be the man who will get the job.[23]

In certain respects, Gettier's counter-case resembles Wheeler's. For one thing, both scenarios look possible, although far-fetched. It is conceivable, though not probable, that acrobats might be neatly divided in the manner Wheeler envisages, without violating any law of nature. It is equally conceivable, though not probable, that someone might entertain a composite belief like Smith's, might have just counted the coins in the other person's pocket, might happen to have the same number of coins in his own pocket, might happen to be the one who would get the job, and so forth. Second, despite the oddity of the two cases, the verdict on both looks equally sure. We would call the 51 seven-footers tall, although they formed the majority; Smith would not know (e), although his belief was justified. Third, in each instance, the verdict is proposed as evidence against the received position, on attributives or on knowledge. In view of this extensive parallel, then, should we reach the same negative judgment on Gettier's reasoning as on Wheeler's?

It may appear quixotic to raise suspicions of veiled essentialism against an argument whose purpose is to challenge an alleged essence of knowledge. However, listen to Patricia Kitcher's defense of Gettier's reasoning. In response to "Fodor's well-known critique of appeals to the anomalous," she writes:

I will argue that the presentation of unusual situations can support conclusions like this: the common, tacit pre-

sent view about what X is (or about what X's are) is/is
not that X is Y (is/is not that X's are Y's). In this formula, both "X" and "Y" may be replaced by simple or very
complex expressions. What I mean by "the common,
tacit view about what X is" is the set of beliefs about X
or X's which pervades and guides all our encounters
with X (or all, save a few unimportant exceptions), our
attitudes and actions concerning X.[24]

The cautionary phrase "save a few unimportant exceptions" need
not be taken too seriously. Kitcher sees no need to establish that
Gettier's cases are important ones or, despite their oddity, are
unexceptional. From any one such case, all can be judged. By
means of a single imaginary example, "Edmund Gettier demonstrated that our common, tacit view of knowledge is not that
knowledge is justified true belief."[25] This result is negative, but
Kitcher sees it as furthering a more positive enterprise: "The
search for what I call 'our common, tacit views' about, *inter alia*,
virtue, substance, beauty and knowledge is a peculiar and perenni-
al philosophical task."[26]

Were Gettier's viewpoint identical with Kitcher's, the charge of
essentialism might stick. However, no essentialistic suppositions
appear in his brief presentation. "Various attempts have been
made in recent years," he writes, "to state necessary and sufficient
conditions for someone's knowing a given proposition." The conditions as stated by Ayer, Chisholm, and others lay themselves open
to refutation by his examples. Hence their claims are untenable.
Gettier does not conclude: "Hence their claims must be revised."
He does not countenance the continued search for an essence of
knowledge or endorse the kind of underlying conviction that motivates this search. He expresses no support for the idea that a single, definable set of beliefs pervades and guides all our talk about
knowledge.[27]

Essentialism there may be on the part of those who have stated sufficient and necessary conditions of knowledge and who, in
the face of failures, persist in their quest, formulating ever more
complex defining conditions, like Ptolemaic astronomers, postulat-
ing ever more complex cycles and epicycles.[28] Indeed, the more
essentialistic his target, the better Gettier's argument succeeds
and the less it resembles Wheeler's. The more universal and absolute the proposed definition of knowledge, the less problematic is
Gettier's tactic of citing merely possible cases as evidence against
the definition.

Suppose we ask: How can Gettier assert with such assurance, "It is equally clear that Smith does not *know* that (e) is true; for (e) is true in virtue of the number of coins in Smith's pocket, while Smith does not know how many coins are in Smith's pocket, and bases his belief in (e) on a count of the coins in Jones's pocket, whom he falsely believes to be the man who will get the job"? Is this verdict "clear," as alleged, by virtue of an implicit fourth condition of knowledge? Or by virtue of PRS (taken as a necessary condition of truth)? Or of a spontaneous "intuition"? It may not matter. If the verdict looks the same in any likely supposition, Gettier need not choose. In responding to essentialistic claims, he may speak the language of essentialism and disregard the details which essentialists tend to disregard.

Robot Cats, Sleek Toads, Etc.

Gettier's argument has three strengths: 1) Though strange, his imagined cases are clearly possible, both logically and naturally; 2) his negative judgment on both cases elicits general agreement; 3) he need not explain the basis for this agreement. Within the larger family to which his argument belongs, this three-fold configuration is unusual. For one thing, imagined cases usually stretch plausibility much farther. Consider, for instance, the fantasy Stephen Schwartz cites: "One well-known example, to illustrate the fact that statements about natural kinds are almost always synthetic, is the example of the robot cats. It is conceivable that we could discover that all the cats were robots sent from Mars to spy on us. Since this is conceivable, statements such as 'cats are animals' are not analytic."[29]

Putnam, its source, spells out this robot-cat hypothesis:

> Suppose evolution has produced many things that come close to the cat but that it never actually produced the cat, and that the cat as we know it is and always was an artifact. Every movement of a cat, every twitch of a muscle, every meow, every flicker of an eyelid is thought out by a man in a control center on Mars and is then executed by the cat's body as the result of signals that emanate not from the cat's "brain" but from a highly miniaturized radio receiver located, let us say, in the cat's pineal gland. It seems to me that in this last case, once we discovered the fake, we should continue to call these robots that we have mistaken for animals and that we have employed as house pets "cats," but not "animals."[30]

Putnam's proposal raises the spectre of essentialism in more than one way. First, his essentialistic-sounding allusion to "the cat," rather than "cats," veils the fact that cats form a disparate class. This fact looks important for Putnam's argument. As he notes, "if *some* cats are animals in every sense of the word, while others are automata, ... I think we would all agree that these others were neither animals nor cats but only fake cats."[31] So how are we to understand the phrases "the cat" and "the cat as we know it": as covering all the things we call cats—house cats, feral cats, bobcats, fishing cats, golden cats, marbled cats, Andean cats, pampas cats, big cats (lions, tigers, jaguars, etc.)? Or just more or less domesticated cats? Or domesticated cats together with their immediate ancestors (for example, Egyptian cats)? Or domesticated cats plus those descended from them (feral cats)? Any interpretation that leaves out large numbers of cats vitiates the argument, for the reason Putnam indicates ("if *some* cats are animals ... while others are automata"). Yet any interpretation that takes in lynxes and bobcats, or lions and tigers, doubtless conflicts with Putnam's exclusion of all those "many things that come close to the cat." And to say that the class in question consists of all genuine cats, without regard for how we label them, is an essentialist move we have repeatedly seen reason to reject. If "all cats" means "all the things that really are cats"—although Putnam's fantasy imagines them so strangely altered—then his argument sins through circularity. In supposing the conceivability of such *cats*—in so describing the situation to be judged—it would presuppose the very thing it was meant to prove.

Second, as it may seem unnecessary to specify more precisely the class of creatures in question, so it may seem unnecessary to detail exactly how the Martian espionage operation functions. It may appear that for semantic purposes it suffices to sketchily state a set of conditions, then elicit a response. However, problems surface here, too—with regard to the "conceivability" of such science-fiction scenarios, and with regard to our ability to pass judgment on them.

Consider the hypothetical being George Seddon scrutinizes.[32] For Seddon, a carnivorous rabbit, though less bizarre than Putnam's feline spies, is not merely scientifically impossible, but logically impossible. Fill in the details—rabbits' digestive system, their birth rate, their teeth, feet, ears, scut—and you will see the suggestion's incoherence. A likely reaction to Seddon's critique would be that he does not evince a sufficiently Humean conception of logical possibility. He assumes, for example, that rabbits could not eat meat since they have no canines to tear it with; this "could," however, is not logical but physical. We might *imagine* the meat crumbling to shreds in the rabbits' mouths. We might *imagine* its proving quite digestible. We might *imagine* rabbits' birthrate dropping, their scut being invisible to their prey, their excreta still proving palatable after their change of diet, and so forth. But with each such supposition, more physical laws and regularities would be discarded, without our knowing just which ones were affected or how extensively. And the more numerous and extensive the modifications, the less sure we could be which of our concepts—*eat? chew? excreta? scut? rabbit?*—still applied. As Wittgenstein remarked, "if anyone believes that certain concepts are absolutely the correct ones, and that having different ones would mean not realizing something that we realize—then let him imagine certain very general facts of nature to be different from what we are used to, and the formation of concepts different from the usual ones will become intelligible to him."[33]

Putnam's suggestion raises similar problems. Are "Martians" possible, given the actual condition of Mars? Or should we conceive of the planet as basically altered? In that case, is it still Mars? If the planet is indeed the one our instruments and space probes have examined, are the Martians and their activities somehow imperceptible? In that case, are they still "Martians"? If we imagine some laws as abrogated to allow the Martians to live on Mars, and others as abrogated to make them imperceptible, are the two sets of laws the same? Closer to home, are we to imagine these "Martians" visiting the earth every time a kitten is conceived in order to implant the "highly miniaturized receiver"? Is that possible, naturally? Is such a receiver possible, naturally? Is it possible for the receivers to program, not only new cats, but also new receivers in the new cats? I needn't insist. It is evident that Putnam's cat hypothesis faces the same kinds of difficulties as does the carnivorous-rabbit hypothesis: first with regard to the laws affected, then with regard to the impact on our concepts and our judgments.

A puzzle presents itself here, for Putnam's argument and for others like it. If the details omitted would be relevant in real-life situations, why are they irrelevant in imagined situations? If they are relevant in imagined situations, how can we be expected to pass judgment without knowing the missing details?

To illustrate, suppose we follow Wittgenstein's suggestion and "imagine a game of chess translated according to certain rules into a series of actions which we do not ordinarily associate with a *game*—say into yells and stamping of feet."[34] Are the performers playing a game? Are they playing chess? Before answering either query would we not need to know more about the "certain rules" followed in the translation and about the overall role of the imagined activity in these people's lives—whether, for instance, they reserve the activity for special occasions (say a coronation or a victory celebration); whether only certain persons (soldiers, parents, rulers, priests, . . .) may take part; whether performers are punished or rewarded, praised or blamed, for "winning"; whether the yelling and stamping are done to the accompaniment of music, of clapping, of drums, of popping firecrackers, or in stony silence; whether spectators are permitted or all eyes must be averted; and so forth?

The contrary approach smacks of essentialism. Only selective traits are relevant, the rest can be ignored, and we need not concern ourselves about which are relevant, which not—any more than we need determine precisely what class of things we are talking about. What doubtless helps to explain Putnam's cavalier attitude toward particulars is his conviction (examined in chapter 1) that he already knows what constitutes the essence of a cat—namely, its hidden constitution. Cats are all and only those creatures that possess the same inner makeup as paradigm members of the class. Relevant traits are all and only those traits that pertain to this inner structure. Thus the only essential feature in Putnam's sketchy scenario is the miniature apparatus in the pineal gland. Other circumstances (such as the Martians and their spying) are mere stage-setting; they need not be described in more than cursory detail.

For Putnam, "what is not clear is which of the available decisions should be described as the decision to keep the meaning of either word ('cat' or 'animal') unchanged, and which decision should be described as the decision to change the meaning. I agree with Donnellan that this question has no clear sense."[35] William Goosens thinks otherwise, and his disagreement affects his treatment of a similar case. "Suppose the following circumstances arise," he suggests: "We discover that the warty-looking skin of toads is caused by a disease which not only debilitates toads but makes them lethargic and awkward. Moreover, we discover that only in the last thousand years have toads been struck by this disease. Moreover, for the first time, a gene arises carrying resistance to the disease. These resistant toads not only are sleek in appearance but have an agility and grace approaching that of otters."[36] The question is, what should we call them? Someone might reply, "For better or worse, it is just a part of the meaning of 'toad' that toads are awkward and have warty-looking skin; so these are not true toads." Goosens rejects this answer. Associated properties like lumpiness and awkwardness form no part of the meaning of *toad*. For no matter how many such traits we deleted, we would still (spinning fibre on fibre) apply the label *toad*. The properties of toads would change with each imagined scientific advance, till none of the supposedly defining traits remained.[37] Furthermore, "That the properties associated with 'toad' change under the impact of the new knowledge is *completely predictable, based on merely a knowledge of current usage*. But this predictability is exactly a criterion of constancy in meaning."[38]

In the course of time, the term might indeed be extended to new, different referents under the impact of new knowledge. Such extensions are common. However, this does not signify that the present standard traits—the lethargy, awkwardness, and warts—lie outside the present meaning, any more than the pre-extension traits of *chess*—people, boards, and pieces—lay outside *its* meaning. For Goosens's essentialistic inference to be valid, the phrase "a criterion of constancy of meaning" would have to signify "a sufficient condition of constancy of meaning"; and this invalidates his claim. As I have already argued, mere predictability is not a sufficient criterion for sameness of meaning.

Such an argument is not grounded in usage. Usage being what it is, one can be sure that, to reach such a result, Goosens conducted no survey of when and why people call a meaning changed or unchanged, new or old, different or the same. This essence is of his own creation. And as Putnam remarks, "presumably our question now is not which decision is changing the meaning in some future technical sense of 'meaning,' but what we can say in our present language."[39]

Cartesian Selves, Bracketed Worlds

Although far-fetched, Wheeler's and Gettier's imaginings—the 51-50 division of acrobats, the two candidates for promotion—look realistic in comparison with Putnam's robot cats and Goosens's frisky toads. In turn, these latter imaginings (of a plentiful genre sometimes dubbed "philosophical science fiction"), look realistic in comparison with the still more far-fetched suppositions one meets, for example, in Descartes.

The *Meditations*' three-step sequence is familiar: (1) Descartes's methodic doubt, "setting aside all that in which the least doubt could be supposed to exist," including all terrestrial or celestial bodies; (2) the *cogito,* by which he settles on his thinking self as the one indubitable thing; (3) his conclusion that his essence "consists solely in the fact that I am a thinking thing." Each of these moves holds essentialistic interest; each, in its own way, suggests that Descartes proceeded on the assumption that words' senses, like transcendent atmospheres, are unaffected by even the most radical suppositions. Or, perhaps more accurately, that he attended very little to such issues of linguistic methodology. Thus:

(1) When his methodic doubt brings Descartes to temporarily hypothesize that nothing exists in all the world besides his thinking self—no heaven, no earth, no minds, no bodies[40]—one may wonder why his readers, his writing instruments, the marks he makes, and the language to which they belong are exempted from the holocaust. Why set pen to paper or suppose that his words have any meaning—indeed that any such things as words exist—so long as this comprehensive doubt persists? Would it make sense to write: "Let us assume for the moment that you, to whom I am writing, do not exist, nor does my hand, nor does the writing, nor does the language I am writing in"? Would such an utterance be coherent? Would not the content of the act clash with the act? As Wittgenstein remarked, "If you are not certain of any fact, you cannot be certain of the meaning of your words either."[41]

The difficulty I am raising may appear simple-minded; but is it really quite clear why Cartesian methodic doubt permits what genuine doubt does not, and does this justification explain why the difficulty goes unmentioned? I can think of several explanations of Descartes's unconcern, but none looks more likely than the surmise that he simply did not notice the difficulty.[42]

Since Descartes does eventually reenter the world and recover the right to use language, the problem may seem purely stylistic: instead of expressing his methodic doubt in the present tense, thereby incurring apparent inconsistency, he might have used the past tense and recounted the doubts he previously entertained. However, the doubts would make no better sense from being reported later. While supposing himself not to have learned any language from any speech community, Descartes would nonetheless ruminate: "I consider that I possess no senses; I imagine that body, figure, extension, movement and place are but the fictions of my mind. What, then, can be esteemed as true?"[43] One might wonder wordlessly whether it was raining or leaves were falling on the roof, but such doubts as those stated in the *Meditations* would have to be formulated linguistically; and the existence of a language in which to formulate them would presuppose a linguistic community and its world. So the problem of incoherence will not go away, whether Descartes talks to himself in the present tense, or to others in the past tense.

It might be suggested that language appears to presuppose a linguistic community and its world only if one surreptitiously takes for granted what Cartesian doubt calls into question. If consistently developed, Descartes's methodic doubt would eliminate other persons and other things, but not thought-persons and thought-things, nor thought-world communication among them. (Compare the solution twentieth-century phenomenalists might offer, if similarly challenged.) Thus, incoherence should not be charged to Descartes, but to any reader who does not take the *Meditations'* stipulations seriously and adjust his or her thinking accordingly.

To this seemingly plausible defense I would reply that nothing in Descartes's writings indicates that he himself made such mind-world adjustments in his thinking, or that they could be carried through coherently. He simply passed from one world to the other and continued to use linguistic concepts without perceiving any problem—either for his employment of concepts generally or for his employment of specific concepts such as *I* and *think*.

(2) "I am thinking," wrote Descartes, "therefore I exist." "But what am I, now that I suppose that there is a certain genius which is extremely powerful, and, if I may say so, malicious, who employs all his powers in deceiving me? Can I affirm that I possess the least of all those things which I have just said pertain to the nature of body? I pause to consider, I revolve all these things in my mind, and I find none of which I can say that it pertains to me."[44] What, then, am I? Evidently, "a thing which thinks."[45] That is, "a thing which doubts, understands, [conceives], affirms, denies, wills, refuses, which also imagines and feels."[46]

Wittgensteinian misgivings have focused on whether it makes sense to suppose such acts as these to be performed by a bodiless being, indeed whether it makes sense to speak of such a bodiless being.[47] The indictment, as I see it, proceeds dialectically. First comes the claim that only of a full, corporeal human being, and what resembles one in appearance and activity, do we say that it thinks, has feelings, or the like;[48] and that even inner acts have need of outer criteria.[49] From this it is often inferred that disembodied human existence and disembodied mental acts, for instance in an afterlife, are logically, conceptually excluded.[50] In dialectical response it may then be noted that the degree of similarity required to make such claims both meaningful and true is not determined rigidly, concept by concept, but for instance by PRS. For statements describing such a being or such acts to be true, it suffices that the statements' use of terms resemble more closely the established use of those terms than it does the established use of rival, incompatible terms.[51] Finally, however, it must be pointed out that this response, which may validate talk of an afterlife or the like, will not work for Descartes. For we, who are corporeal and have acquired our concepts corporeally, may extend them to noncorporeal referents, whereas Descartes, through his methodic doubt, has rendered impossible (for the duration of the doubt) the acquisition of these or any other concepts. Wittgenstein's strictures on the solitary construction of a language, without any previous acquaintance with language, apply a fortiori to a Cartesian solitary ego describing itself as having thoughts, feelings, desires, and the rest. For at the stage of Descartes's itinerary where contact with his body and other bodies has not yet been regained, he is not just momentarily disembodied by his doubt, but has never, so far as he knows, possessed a body or had relations with other corporeal beings.

(3) Even if methodic doubt differed from genuine doubt, so that the doubter might freely continue to express himself linguistically after having doubted virtually everything that makes language possible, misgivings would remain with regard to the way Descartes infers the nature of actual selves from that of hypothetical, incorporeal selves. It would be bad enough to conclude from chess between computers that board and pieces are accidental features of chess between people, but at least that argument would originate with fact; Descartes's comparable reduction originates in sheer hypothesis. Once it is supposed that I, though thinking, have no body, then, to be sure, "to speak accurately I am not more than a thing which thinks."[52] But with what right can Descartes pass from this mere supposition to the conclusion that real-life human beings are essentially incorporeal?

For an essentialist the transition comes easily and naturally: assume a single essence of human selves, real or imagined, and it follows (readily though not rigorously) that if noncorporeal, thinking selves are conceivable, then thought, not corporeality, pertains to that single essence. "Just because I know certainly that I exist, and that meanwhile I do not remark that any other thing necessarily pertains to my nature or essence, excepting that I am a thinking thing, I rightly conclude that my essence consists solely in the fact that I am a thinking thing [or a substance whose whole essence or nature is to think]."[53] A paraphrase might run: "Just because I know certainly that I am playing chess with a computer, and that meanwhile I do not remark that any other thing necessarily pertains to our game, excepting the rules of chess, I rightly conclude that the essence of chess consists solely in the rules." Board and pieces and moves and human opponents drop out as nonessential, as do the body and its members in Descartes's kindred demonstration.

Anthony Kenny suggests that Descartes did not notice the difference between the premise "I do not remark that anything pertains to my essence but thinking" and the premise "I remark that nothing pertains to my essence but thinking." The first of these two premises, established in the *Second Meditation,* does not yield the desired conclusion; the second premise yields the conclusion, but has not been established. Hence Descartes's proof fails.[54] However, the transition can be made from the first premise to the second, assuring the conclusion, if we insert the further premise, explicitly stated by Descartes: "There is always one principal property of substance which constitutes its nature and essence, and on which all the others depend."[55] It then follows that thought, if established as essential to René Descartes, alone constitutes his essence.[56]

The question now becomes: How does Descartes think he has established, not only that he is a thinking thing, but that he is such essentially? Here the same implicit premise can be invoked, but with the emphasis shifted to there being an essence, rather than its consisting of a single trait. Thus Bernard Williams reconstructs Descartes's reasoning as follows:

(1) I have some essential property.
(2) Any property which I might lack is not my essential property.
(3) I might lack every property except thought.
Hence,
(4) Thought is my essential property.[57]

On the third premise, Williams comments: "(3) is the supposed result of the thought-experiment of the *Second Meditation,* converted into an objective possibility."[58] It emerges from Descartes's methodic doubt, in a way that looks objectionable. However,

> since it rests on the notion of an essential property, all that is necessary for (3) is that there should be *some* possible circumstances (not necessarily the present ones) in which I could exist without a body and without any other property except thought. If I could exist disembodied at all, with things perhaps seeming very different from the way they seem now,... that possibility by itself would be enough to show that thought is my essential property, if I have an essential property at all.[59]

This is the tack some have taken. Setting aside Cartesian doubt, Richard Swinburne writes:

> The crucial point that Descartes and others were presumably trying to make is not that (in the case of men) the living body is not part of the person, but that it is not essentially, only contingently, part of the person. The body is separable from the person and the person can continue even if the body is destroyed. Just as I continue to exist wholly and completely if you cut off my hair, so, the dualist holds, it is possible that I continue to exist if you destroy my body. The soul, by contrast, is the necessary core which must continue if I am to continue; it is the part of the person which is necessary for his continuing existence.[60]

Swinburne's defense of this position stresses the possibility of bodiless continuation, not the impossibility of soulless continuation. He develops in detail the supposition "of a man acquiring a new body,"[61] then the supposition "that a person who is a man might become disembodied,"[62] and infers "that continuing matter is not (logically) essential for the continuing existence of persons."[63] He does not mention the counter-possibility that the spiritual part of persons might be equally nonessential for continuing existence. He says not a word, for example, about comatose people and our reason(s) for calling them by their proper names. One can sense a likely explanation for this silence. Surely *something* must be essential to selfhood. And if it is not the body (as Swinburne's thought-experiments show), then it must be the soul. Given the assumption of an essence—a "necessary core"—the imaginary cases can do double duty, identifying the soul as essential and excluding the body.

Alvin Plantinga's reasoning is more overtly essentialistic. He recognizes that, as it stands, Descartes's argument does not establish that he is not a body or a material object. However, perhaps we can do better.

> Suppose, first of all, that I am a material object—that I am identical with some material object. Which material object am I? With which such object am I identical? The answer seems clear: I am the object that I refer to as "my body." So if there is any material object at all with which I am identical, I am identical with my body (which for ease of reference I shall name 'B'). But
>
> (56) It is possible that I exist at a time when B does not.

> For it certainly seems possible that I should acquire a
> new body—either by exchanging bodies with someone
> else, or by having B replaced in one fell swoop or piece
> by piece by another body—perhaps one made of some
> synthetic and more durable material. But then clearly it
> is possible that I acquire a new body and continue to
> exist when B is destroyed. Accordingly there is a time *t*
> at which it is possible that I exist and B does not. That
> is to say, there is a possible world *W* such that in *W* I
> exist at *t* and B does not exist at *t*. Hence I have the
> property *exists at t in W;* B lacks that property. By the
> Indiscernibility of Identicals, therefore, it follows that I
> am not identical with B. But then surely there is no
> material object at all with which I am identical.[64]

The Indiscernibility of Identicals[65] may hold for actual objects in
the actual world, but assuming that it holds over all possible worlds
gives evidence of the syndrome we are discussing. Even the slight-
est variation in an object's characteristics, between the actual world
and a possible world, challenges the principle's unrestricted applicability.[66] A response might be to distinguish between essential
traits of an object, for which the principle holds in all possible
worlds, and non-essential traits, for which it does not. Such a
response appears implicit in Plantinga's reasoning. Without it there
would be no difficulty in supposing, for example, that I am a body
(or a bodily human being) and that another body, in some other
world, might nonetheless be "me." So, too, my body of flesh might
dissolve, leaving a purely spiritual self, and my actual self might
nonetheless be bodily. Abandon the assumption of essences, and the
interrelationship of many-world objects may be governed by PRS or
the like, rather than by the Indiscernibility of Identicals. Other-
world Gorbachevs might, for example, be all other-world entities
that resemble the actual Gorbachev more closely than they do the
bearers of any rival names; or that resemble him more closely than
they do any other actual persons; or that resemble him more closely
in certain key respects; or . . . Various criteria are conceivable.

Kripke and Possible Worlds

Descartes envisaged a single alternative world, composed of a
single, noncorporeal self, and drew conclusions from this hypothesis, essentialistically. Possible-worlds theorizing extends to all conceivable worlds—Cartesian, science-fictional, or other—in ways
that repeatedly raise the issue of essentialism, not only in the

modal sense of necessity, but also in the one-thing-only, core-reality sense of this inquiry.

Kripke's writings provide illustration. I shall not repeat chapter 1's critique of the view he shared with Putnam, concerning natural kinds, relevant though that view and critique are to possible-worlds theorizing. More prominent in Kripke's writings is his kindred treatment of proper names.

For Kripke, "names are always rigid designators."[67] They stay with their referents regardless of what changes the referents undergo. In this they differ from definite descriptions. Nixon may get elected, Nixon may resign, but *Nixon* still designates him, whereas *the president of the United States* designates now one person, now another. A similar contrast holds for possible worlds. Thus,

> it seems that we cannot say "Nixon might have been a different man from the man he in fact was," unless, of course, we mean it metaphorically: He might have been a different *sort* of person (if you believe in free will and that people are not inherently corrupt). You might think the statement true in that sense, but Nixon could not have been in the other literal sense a different person from the person he, in fact, is, even though the thirty-seventh President of the United States might have been Humphrey. So the phrase "the thirty-seventh President" is nonrigid, but 'Nixon,' it would seem, is rigid.[68]

The name refers to the same individual in all possible worlds.[69]

As it stands, this account imposes no restrictions on the variability of Nixon from world to world. Nixon, to be sure, will always be Nixon, in all conceivable worlds; and *Nixon* will name him. But what criteria, if any, a person or organism or object must satisfy in order to count as Nixon, we have not been told. In the actual world, a tiny, innocent infant may become the present occupant of San Clemente, without change of identity; in other worlds variations might be still more radical. However, Kripke's "rigid designators" appear to be rigid not only in the sense that they rigidly refer to the same thing but also in the sense that what they refer to remains rigidly the same.

"Intuitively," writes Quine, "the idea would seem to be that a rigid designator picks out its object by its *essential* traits."[70] Kripke himself speaks of individuals' essential properties, even of their "essences." But the essential properties he suggests, such as origin or composition, are all necessary, not sufficient; and the readiness with which he equates having "essential properties" with having an "essence" suggests that by "essence" he may not mean "the property or set of properties necessary *and sufficient* for being that individual."[71]

However, Kripke repeatedly conveys an essentialistic impression when he contrasts the invariability of a name's referent with the variability of its history. For instance: "Most of the things commonly attributed to Aristotle are things that Aristotle might not have done at all. In a situation in which he didn't do them, we would describe that as a situation in which *Aristotle* didn't do them."[72] Similarly: "We are speaking of *Nixon* and asking what, in certain counterfactual situations, would have been true of *him*."[73] "We can point to the *man,* and ask what might have happened to *him,* had events been different."[74] The referent—the man—is the constant; all else is variable.

Kripke strengthens this impression of essential sameness, and highlights its significance, when he declares: "Those who have argued that to make sense of the notion of rigid designator, we must antecedently make sense of 'criteria of transworld identity' have precisely reversed the cart and the horse; it is *because* we can refer (rigidly) to Nixon, and stipulate that we are speaking of what might have happened to *him* (under certain circumstances), that 'transworld identifications' are unproblematic in such cases."[75] The core, transworld Nixon resolves all problems; or so it would seem. If, instead, the name *Nixon* imposed few limits—if, for example, it fixed only necessary conditions (not sufficient), of uncertain extent, for unstated, unsure reasons—this Copernican claim of Kripke's would not stand, indeed would not make obvious sense.

How much does a name's referent, once established, embrace? How much pertains to *him* or *her* or *it*? Kripke has a way of italicizing a proper name or pronoun, as though emphasizing that the designator leaves no doubt who is in question. And indeed it does not; we do know who is meant. But knowing who is meant offers no clue as to how much of Aristotle, Nixon, Gödel, or Moses—how large, varied, or definite a set of present, past, and future intrinsic or extrinsic properties—the designator carries with it into counterfactual, other-world discourse. Kripke's failure to clarify this question leaves a void at the heart of his writing on necessity and possible worlds, a void comparable to the emptiness at the heart of Moore's ethics, where the good defines all else but itself remains undefined and undefinable.[76]

A passage in "Naming and Necessity" helps clarify Kripke's silence. Momentarily, he raises the question whether, in addition to necessary conditions such as origin, there are "purely qualitative *sufficient* conditions for Nixonhood which we can spell out." "Should there be? Maybe there is some argument that there should be, but we can consider these questions about *necessary* conditions without going into any question about *sufficient* conditions."[77]

> Even if there were a purely qualitative set of necessary and sufficient conditions for being Nixon, the view I advocate would not demand that we find these conditions before we can ask whether Nixon might have won the election, nor does it demand that we restate the question in terms of such conditions. We can simply consider Nixon and ask what might have happened to him had various circumstances been different.[78]

"We can simply consider Nixon"—the simple, unproblematic Nixon; the referential Nixon, not the "qualitative," descriptive Nixon. The distinctive variety of essentialism suggested by this and earlier quotations might be termed "referential essentialism": the essences in question cannot be descriptively defined, any more than can Locke's "real" essences or Moore's indefinable essence of the good. They are simply what we *refer* to when we employ proper names.[79]

I hesitate to ascribe such a view to Kripke. Yet it has antecedents;[80] it harmonizes with many of his sayings; and it alone, so far as I can see, renders intelligible a silence that otherwise appears inexplicable, concerning the ontology of the objects that define possible worlds. What is more, it explains his thesis on identities.

From the rigidity of proper names Kripke infers the necessity of identity-statements employing them.[81] A statement like "Cicero is Tully," if true, is necessarily true. Why? Perhaps for the following reason. Assume that a single core essence endures through all changes in a referent; assume that any naming, at any moment in a referent's career, necessarily picks out that essence. It may now appear that if two names pick out the same referent, the identity, on that supposition, is necessary. It is not conceivable, for instance, that the person named "Steve" at birth and the person nicknamed "Butch" in college, if identical, might in some possible world fail to connect, with the infant taking an entirely different tack later on (different appearance, character, abilities, career, relationships, etc.) and the collegian deriving from radically different origins. Whatever contingent facts might vary, the core Steve and the core Butch would coincide.

In the original version of "Naming and Necessity," the reader is left to surmises like these. In the Preface to the later, book version, Kripke becomes more explicit about the connection between the rigidity of names and the necessity of identities employing them.[82] "It was clear," he explains, "from $(x) \Box (x = x)$ and Leibnitz's law [of the indiscernibility of identicals] that identity is an 'internal' relation: $(x) (y) (x = y \supset \Box x = y)$." From this latter premise, it follows ("roughly") that true identity statements between rigid designators are necessary. From this it follows, in turn, concerning proper names, "that *either* they are not rigid *or* true identities between them are necessary." But proper names are rigid; hence the identities are necessary.

Here, as in Plantinga's reasoning, the key move is the unhesitating extension of Leibniz's law from the actual world to all possible worlds. Steve and Butch are the same person; so they must be indiscernible. And they are, in this world, given their identity. It is true of Steve, for example, that he later was nicknamed Butch, and true of Butch that he was earlier named Steve. Each shares all predicates of the other. But what precludes the other-world divergence of Steve and Butch that I imagined? The answer, it seems, is the one already surmised. Each referent has an invariant core; each name picks out that core; so two names that pick out the same core establish a transcendent, all-worlds identity.[83]

Kripke's varied application of his identity thesis reveals a further aspect of his essentialism—his essentialism of names as well as of names' referents. In defense of Descartes's reasoning, he extends the theory of necessary identity not only to persons but also to their minds and bodies:

> Descartes, and others following him, argued that a person or mind is distinct from his body, since the mind could exist without the body. He might equally well have argued the same conclusion from the premise that the body could have existed without the mind. Now the one response which I regard as plainly inadmissible is the response which cheerfully accepts the Cartesian premise while denying the Cartesian conclusion. Let 'Descartes' be a name, or rigid designator, of a certain person, and let 'B' be a rigid designator of his body. Then if Descartes were indeed identical to B, the supposed identity, being an identity between two rigid designators, would be necessary, and Descartes could not exist without B and B could not exist without Descartes.[84]

Here, a counter-scenario challenging Kripke's claim proves more difficult to construct than it was for Steve and Butch. And the difficulty may appear to confirm both the validity of Kripke's reasoning and the accuracy of his conclusion. With regard to Steve and Butch, I could readily suppose, first, a double naming and, second, the identity of the persons named, then consider whether and why the identity might be necessary. With regard to the mind "Descartes" and the body "*B,*" both these preliminary steps look problematic.

First, the naming poses problems. We have familiar conventions for naming persons, but none for naming minds and bodies. To name a mind, shall we say simply, "This mind is Descartes"? Which mind? To elucidate, shall we point and say, "This mind"? The body gets in the way. So, to avoid the impression of pointing to a body, shall we have recourse to metaphysics and declare, "The mind that inhabits this body is Descartes"? But can a mind *inhabit* a body? At this point, the first difficulty starts to merge with the second; so let us move on to the problem of identity.

We have familiar conventions for the identity of persons, for instance of Steve and Butch, but none for the identity of bodies with minds or vice versa. Furthermore, it is difficult to make sense of such an identity, hence difficult to make sense of the hypothesis that a name (somehow) attached to a mind might designate the same entity as a name (somehow) attached to a body. So before testing the hypothesis that mind-body identities are as necessary as person-person identities allegedly are, we might have to elucidate matters no one has yet succeeded in illumining. No wonder Kripke's defense of Descartes looks impregnable.

Turn the same evidence round, however, and it presents a different visage. The problem of falsification becomes a problem of verification. The assumption that whatever names, however applied, to whatever referents (persons, minds, bodies, or what have you) yield the same result (rigid reference) and follow the same law (necessary identity) suggests Kripke's implicit essentialism, as well as its lack of foundation.

Retrospect

The failure of Waismann, Putnam, Goosens, Descartes, Swinburne, Plantinga, Kripke, and others mentioned in this chapter, to validate their essentialistic premises—implicit, explicit, or surmised—does not disprove the premises, any more than does the like failure of many other authors, cited in chapters 3 and 4; but it does invalidate the arguments. And chapters 1 and 2, in particular, suggest how dubious are essentialistic premises. Overall, therefore, the preceding chapters challenge as well as describe the varied, persistent phenomenon of essentialism. From the phenomenon's persistence, together with its error, the study's motivation also comes more clearly to view. In the realm of the mind, essentialism poses major grounds for concern. In the light of this conclusion, one naturally wonders how and why the phenomenon continually arises, and what, accordingly, can be done about it. These questions, touched on only in passing till now, need no longer be postponed.

Chapter Six

SOURCES OF ESSENTIALISM

The efficacy of the therapy rests upon enough philosophers
"seeing" the source of the trouble.[1]

A friend of Wittgenstein's recounts: "Kant said that a great
deal of philosophy reminded him of one person holding a sieve
while the other tried to milk the he-goat. Wittgenstein wanted
above all things to make an end of sieve holding and he-goat milking. I remember, after one particularly fatuous paper at the Moral
Sciences Club, Wittgenstein exclaiming: 'This sort of thing has got
to be stopped. Bad philosophers are like slum landlords. It's my job
to put them out of business.'"[2] "How very negative!" one may think.
"Surely there is more to philosophy than therapy or critique?"
Granted, but critique has always comprised a necessary aspect of
inquiry, whether philosophical or other. And amid all the varied
forms of sieve holding and he-goat milking, some are specially worthy of therapeutic scrutiny.

Essentialism merits attention for at least four reasons, all of
them now documented by this study. First, the preceding chapters
have shown the *pervasiveness* of essentialistic thought, in general
theories, particular theories, and the conduct of reasoning (atomic
calculus-reasoning, network-reasoning, and other-worlds theorizing). Second, these chapters have shown its *importance*, by revealing how significantly it affects our thinking about important matters: morality, natural kinds, language, knowledge, meaning, truth,
understanding, human nature, and so forth. Third, they have
shown its *error*, in instance after instance. Fourth, they have shown
its *persistence*. This last reason, added to the others, suggested the
need for a more thorough, sustained critique than had previously
appeared.

However, something more than critique is called for. Confront-
ed with such a powerful, persistent phenomenon, some readers are
bound to wonder: How has essentialism acquired such power? What
sources explain its persistence? Such queries may express misgivings as well as curiosity. If reasons, above all, shape philosophers'
thinking, and so many philosophers have thought essentialistically,
must not the reasons supporting their practice be stronger than I

have acknowledged? If, on the contrary, stated reasons and arguments have played a less decisive role than unstated, unrecognized influences, must not these influences be addressed if a cure is to be effected? Must not therapy deal with underlying causes and not just surface symptoms?

Here, as in the Introduction, a comparison with cancer seems apt. Like cancer, essentialism takes various forms. Like cancer, it has varied causes. For essentialism as for cancer, some causal factors can be stated with assurance, at least generally; often, however, the source or sources of a specific malignancy can only be surmised. *That* a person has a melanoma, may be clear; *how* he came to have it may be far from evident. Similarly, *that* a philosopher has, for example, engaged in calculus-reasoning may be clear; *how* he came to reason that way may be far less evident.

General etiology assists particular etiology, and vice versa. Each illumines the other. This chapter and the next take both tacks, the general and the particular, starting here with the general. As it can be stated with assurance that radiation, asbestos, vinyl chloride, tobacco smoke, and sunlight help to account for many cancers, so it can be stated with assurance that the following five factors contribute to the prevalence of essentialism.

A First Source: Language

The deceptive power of language (of standard English, German, Latin, French, etc., not of their misuses) has long been recognized. The following facts may help to explain it. First, any natural language is so fantastically complex that we would have trouble grasping its workings even if we scrutinized them. Yet scrutinize them we must, if we want to understand them. For we did not initially master language via grammatical, pragmatic, and semantic instruction, spelling out the rules of the game. Nor, as competent speakers or hearers, do we now typically attend to the linguistic medium of communication, but think, instead, of the matters we discuss by means of the medium (mortgages, square roots, life after death, the coming vacation). As a result, we have little reflective awareness of this instrument we employ with sureness and ease.[3] Unfortunately, any natural language is full of surface analogies capable of misleading those who lack such awareness.[4] Hence we are misled. And because language pervades our thinking, we are *continually* misled, in more ways than we imagine, and more seriously.

Essentialism, a prime example, permits close understanding of language's sleight of hand. The origins of essentialism illustrate, for example, the difference between misleading surface similarities in the form of some single expression and those in the forms of different expressions, and suggest how deception occurs in each instance. Let me begin with the first.

No surface parallel is closer, more evident, or more universal than that between instances of one and the same word in its repeated occurrences. Thus "it is sometimes almost impossible," Wittgenstein remarked, "for a child to believe that one word can have two meanings."[5] I can corroborate this observation from personal experience. However, something more than such anecdotal evidence can be adduced. The power of verbal sameness to suggest non-verbal sameness admits of demonstration. It can be exhibited in the laboratory, as it were.

One experiment goes as follows. Introduce a class to Wittgenstein's discussion of the concept *game* in *Investigations* §66, and indicate the significance of his negative result (as in chapter 1); then challenge the class to reverse his verdict by discovering a single essence—a single reality—that accounts for our applying the word *game* to all and only games. Some will suggest the possession of rules, others the purpose of entertainment. To each such suggestion, members of the class will object that other activities than games possess rules, other activities than games are meant to entertain, and so forth. But no one will notice that a single defining *formula*—"possession of rules," "purpose of entertaining"— does not demonstrate the presence of a single *reality*. Much less will anyone dream that a successful matching of a defining formula with the term to be defined, far from demonstrating the existence of a single essence, makes the existence of such an essence much less likely.[6] The unquestioning assumption of an essence will simply shift from *game*, where it is challenged, to *rule, purpose,* or *entertainment,* where it is not.

Still more revealing is the reaction of some to this objection. They have the impression that the inquiry is being gerrymandered, arbitrarily, when the point is made that rules, purposes, or entertainment, like games, may not be all of a piece, but may, for instance, reveal a family resemblance, as do games. What more can be desired than a single defining formula? How else might an essence be identified? Why assign the task of finding an essence if no answer can ever satisfy the request? The answer, naturally, is that no single formula assures, by itself, that an essence has been found; whether it does in fact isolate some single reality will have to be determined otherwise than by the verbal form. We shall have to look and see. The fact that this reminder is viewed as tricky and unfair reveals the power of mere surface appearances. From a single formula a single, invariant reality is inferred.

In an innocuous sense, verbal sameness does of course assure real sameness. Regardless of whether all blues have anything in common, all are the "same color," namely blue. Regardless of whether all games have anything in common, all are the "same kind of activity," namely games. But it does not follow that all blues are the same shade of blue or that all games are the same kind of games; nor does it follow that all shades of blue have something in common that makes them all blue (aside from the fact that they are called blue), or that all kinds of games have something in common that makes them all games (aside from the fact that they are all called games). To some these observations will appear obvious, to others they will not. My purpose in this paragraph is simply to suggest that the surface sameness of *same* may function much as the sameness of other terms does, and reinforce the impression that a single expression betokens a single reality. Blues are thought to have a single essence because all are "blue," but also because they are all the "same color." Games are thought to have a single essence because all are "games," but also because they are all the "same kind of activity."

Similar remarks apply to the expression "have in common." Wittgenstein invites us to compare the case in which I show someone figures of different shapes all painted the same color, and say: "What these have in common is called 'yellow ochre,'" and the case in which I show samples of different shades of blue and say: "The colour that is common to all these is what I call 'blue.'"[7] The phrasing ("have in common," "is common") is similar in both cases, but not the reference. Yellow ochre is a single shade, blues are not. If we do not notice the difference, or similar divergences elsewhere, we may mistake one sort of discovery for the other. Finding something "in common" to all and only the members of some class, we may too readily suppose that an essence has been identified. As the single defining formula may suggest essential sameness, so too may the fact that it indicates something "common" to all members of the class.

Evidence for such witchery appears in a typical passage where Russell explains the origin of the Platonic view he espoused. "Let us consider," he suggests, "such a notion as *justice*. If we ask ourselves what justice is, it is natural to proceed by considering this, that, and the other just act, with a view to discovering what they have in common. They must all, in some sense, partake of a common nature, which will be found in whatever is just and in nothing else."[8] If emphasis falls on the phrase "in some sense," this closing claim looks unobjectionable. All yellow ochres occupy one point in the spectrum, all blues fall within a broader range, all games reveal a family resemblance. They all, in some sense, partake of a common nature; for they all possess whatever it takes—however disjunctive or indefinite—to make them members of the single, named class. However, Russell's account clearly veers in an essentialistic direction when, with no better warrant than the recurring reference to something "common," he continues: "This common nature, in virtue of which they are all just, will be justice itself, the pure essence the admixture of which with facts of ordinary life produces the multiplicity of just acts."

This sampling of separate, reinforcing strands gives some intimation of the power of linguistic forms to beget essentialistic assumptions. Sometimes the etiology looks patent (e.g., someone asks: "Why would we use the same word if there weren't something common?"); sometimes it looks likely; and a mass of analogous evidence leaves little doubt that surface similarities work this way.[9] So I shall mention further likely strands, operating separately or in conjunction with those already noted. In addition to surface similarities between instances of the same expression (*game, same, have in common,* etc.), surface similarities between different expressions, or different types of expression, also come into play.

For example, given philosophers' penchant for generalization, the univocal, relatively sharply-focused terms in mathematics, physical science, and the like may suggest similar univocity and sharpness elsewhere. Or simpler, more definite concepts may exert a stronger paradigmatic pull than more complex, indefinite ones, and polarize thinking in their direction, making us suppose simplicity or definiteness where there is none. The fact that a relatively clear, unified account can be given of the concept *bachelor, rain,* or *circle* may beget the expectation that other concepts can be captured with similar neatness.

A more frequently cited influence appears in Wittgenstein's remark: "This roughly means, we are looking at words as though they all were proper names, and we then confuse the bearer of a name with the meaning of the name."[10] Proper names and general names can both serve as subjects, can both occur as objects, can both take modifiers, can both pick out referents—indeed, can both serve as subjects of the same predicate, can both occur as objects of the same verb or preposition, can both take the same modifier ("young Bob," "young man"), can both pick out the same referent. But typical proper names designate single, relatively invariant referents (mountains, rivers, pets, people); and this use stands out more clearly than the complex, varied application of general terms. Hence the simpler serves as paradigm in grasping the complex, and we readily suppose that general names, too, denote some single reality. "Proper names stand for particulars, while other substantives, adjectives, prepositions, and verbs stand for universals."[11] Thus, according to Aristotle, "'man' and every common name signifies not a certain *this*, but a quality or a relation or a mode (or something of the sort)."[12] *Socrates* designates a single man, *man* a single nature or essence.

Here, too, we can discern, not just a single influence, but a cluster of mutually reinforcing influences. The surface similarity between proper names and general names suggests that the latter function much as the former do.[13] The reference to both as "names" or "terms" may strengthen this impression.[14] And allusions like Aristotle's, in the singular, to the "quality," "nature," "property," "relation," "mode," or "thing" signified—allusions which need not indicate an essence and might function noncommittally—may pull the knot still tighter. Amplify the network of suggestive expressions to embrace allusions to "*the* concept *man*," "*the* idea of man," and the like, and the essentialistic implications of sheer grammar may appear ineluctable.

Mention of the singular draws attention to a complementary influence. As the sameness of the same word suggests sameness in its reference, so, too, the singular form, in contrast to the plural, may suggest a single reference. And as the sameness suggested does not amount merely to whatever sameness, maximal or minimal, the same word embraces, so, too, the unity suggested may not be merely whatever unity, maximal or minimal, the singular term happens to pick out. There can be little doubt, for example, that Socrates' negative response in the *Theaetetus* stems at least partly from the grammatical form of his initial query. Had he inquired "What are knowledges?" (odd in English, impossible in Greek without shifting the sense of the noun) rather than "What is knowledge?," he would less readily have retorted: "The question you were asked, Theaetetus, was not, what are the objects of knowledge, nor yet how many sorts of knowledge there are. We did not want to count them, but to find out what the thing itself—knowledge—is."[15] *The* thing, the *one* thing, indicated by the singular. Surely *knowledge* names some single essence or form. Surely it does not, for example, designate a "family."

A Second Source: Disregard for Language

Those who lack linguistic awareness are not conscious of being duped by language, hence see no need to acquire such awareness. They recognize that on most occasions there is little danger of bewitchment by language, hence little need to remove one's linguistic spectacles and examine them. What they do not recognize is that those who fail to reflect on language are thereby prevented from recognizing when and why such reflection does become necessary—why, for instance, speculative discourse requires constant vigilance whereas non-speculative discourse does not. They are thus caught in the vicious circle of seeing no reason to reflect on language, so not reflecting on it, so seeing no reason to reflect on it, ...[16]

Mere inadvertence differs from positive disregard, and there is no telling just how often essentialistic thinking results from the one rather than the other. However, a dismissive attitude towards language and language's relevance appears often enough to suggest that this attitude, too, figures significantly among the sources of essentialism.

Moore's discussion of the good, cited in chapter 1, illustrates the attitude. Observe the multiple movements—a zig, a zag, then a rapid zig-zag-zig (I have numbered them to facilitate observation)—by which Moore freed himself from the constraints of usage, and from merely verbal inquiry that might have distracted him from the "nature" or essence that concerned him:

> What, then, is good? How is good to be defined? Now it may be thought that this is a verbal question. A definition does indeed often mean the expressing of one word's meaning in other words. [1] But this is not the sort of definition I am asking for. Such a definition can never be of ultimate importance in any study except lexicography. If I wanted that kind of definition I should have to consider in the first place how people generally used the word "good"; but my business is not with its proper usage, as established by custom. [2] I should, indeed, be foolish, if I tried to use it for something which it did not usually denote: if, for instance, I were to announce that, whenever I used the word "good," I must be understood to be thinking of that object which is usually denoted by the word "table." I shall, therefore, use the word in the sense in which I think it is ordinarily used; [3] but at

> the same time I am not anxious to discuss whether I am
> right in thinking that it is so used. My business is solely
> with that object or idea, which I hold, rightly or wrongly,
> [4] that the word is generally used to stand for. [5] What
> I want to discover is the nature of that object or idea,
> and about this I am extremely anxious to arrive at an
> agreement.[17]

The precision with which Moore charts his course is illusory. If the object or idea that interests him is, by definition, whatever object or idea the word *good* standardly denotes, then he cannot ignore what the word does in fact denote, or whether it denotes anything at all. If the object of his interest is not thus defined, Moore owes his readers (and himself) an account of what does define it. Otherwise they cannot tell what he is looking for and whether he has found it.

What are the criteria of success in Moore's enterprise? Granted, if the word *good* regularly picks out some one entity, that entity might exist without the picking out, and without there being any such word as *good,* or any such language as English. But these possibilities do nothing to render Moore's undertaking intelligible. *Does* the word pick out any referent? Does it pick out a single referent? How can we know, unless we attend to the word's customary use?

Without the cavalier attitude toward language that Moore exemplifies, essentialism would not have been a force in Western thought. With it, the essentialism and calculus-reasoning that abound in Moore's works become predictable.[18] His discussion of colors, quoted earlier, provides a classic example; so does his treatment of moral rightness. "What I wish first to point out," Moore declares in *Principia Ethica,* "is that 'right' does and can mean nothing but 'cause of a good result,' and is thus identical with 'useful'; whence it follows that the end always will justify the means, and that no action which is not justified by its results can be right."[19] From essence to essence the inference passes, and thence to an "always" and a "no," as though by chain reaction; a finer instance of calculus-reasoning would be difficult to find.

"But how extraordinary it is," one thinks, "for Moore to assert that the word *can* have no other meaning than the one he specifies! Are not word meanings identical with, or at least dependent on, word-uses, and are not word-uses as varied and variable as the shapes of clouds that fill the sky?" No, not for the author of *Principia Ethica.* He did not view usage as varied, and he did not view meanings as dependent on usage. For Moore, in the full vigor of his early essentialism, the word *right* was used in only one way; and even if it were not—even if human speakers employed it variously—their usage would not affect the true meaning of the word.

Much contemporary thinking resembles Moore's in its disregard for usage, and in the calculus-reasoning this disregard fosters. Alan Donagan's recent work *Choice: The Essential Element in Human Action* can serve as illustration. At the start of one discussion we read: "Philosophers are largely agreed that doings are events (or happenings, or occurrences); but they are far from agreed about what events are. It is sometimes assumed that all events are changes. That is certainly a mistake. Socrates' staying in prison was an event that was also an action, a refraining from the escape his friends had arranged; but it was not a change."[20]

Anyone who acknowledges that the truth of statements depends on the meanings of the words the statements employ and that word meanings, in the absence of explicit stipulation, depend on current usage, might be surprised at the assurance with which Donagan declares, "That is certainly a mistake." Donagan himself recognizes "that colloquial usage permits us to deny that non-happenings of changes are events: to say that a dog's doing nothing in the night-time is not an incident, and to disparage standing and waiting as inaction." However, "it also permits us to follow the good example of Conan Doyle's Sherlock Holmes, and describe the persistence of a state of something as an incident—an event—as well as a change in one."[21] Since "colloquial usage" points in neither direction or both, Donagan feels free to maintain that the persistence of a state is an event, while others, with equal freedom—and apparently equal right—maintain the contrary.

Later, after describing a similar disagreement with Michael Bratman regarding the nature of intention, Donagan again adverts to the issue of standard usage. "In a celebrated paper," he recounts, "in which he recommended allowing the language we use for practical purposes in everyday life to have the first word on philosophical questions, Austin made much of the reported remarks of the prisoner, counsel and judge in the case *Regina* v. *Finney*."[22] According to Austin, the counsel and judge misused and misdescribed several terms of excuse, whereas the prisoner showed himself "an evident master of the Queen's English." From these contrasting judgments Donagan concludes:

> The moral is daunting. Philosophers who rely on what
> they are now not ashamed to call their "intuitions"

about the appropriateness or inappropriateness of a
word to a given context more often resemble judge and
counsel than they do the prisoner. The first word that
ordinary language should indeed be allowed to have is
hard to pick out from the learned flood of muddle and
inaccuracy. In trying to distinguish what uses of
"intend" and its cognates are accurate, a little philosophy may be a better guide than what we spontaneously
say when presented with examples.[23]

By "a little philosophy" Donagan does not mean that painstaking,
Austinian scrutiny of usage should replace facile, spontaneous
"intuiting." Linguistic scrutiny being difficult and fallible, he proposes, in effect, that we proceed to theorize without regard for
usage. Bratman draws the boundary of intention in one place;
Donagan draws it in another, and sees "no good reason" not to. His
digression on Austin forestalls any appeal to familiar forms of
speech; what the verdict of usage may be, or whether it yields any
verdict, need not concern a philosopher.

Various reasons account for this common attitude, but one
stands out above the rest: the confusion of language, the medium
of discourse, with discourse itself. "How people speak" and "What
they say" are taken interchangeably. As I have noted elsewhere,
this conflation takes many forms, and can be traced to varied causes.[24] Here I shall briefly suggest how it begets disregard for familiar word-uses.

First, the conflation obscures the most obvious advantage of
heeding such uses, namely effective communication, and all that
goes with it.[25] A language is an instrument. Its purpose is communication. Other things being equal, the more familiar the words or
meanings employed, the more effective the communication. Con-
flate meanings with theories, however, and this consideration
drops from view. For theories are not meanings. They are not
means of communication; they are what is communicated. Thus
theorists repeatedly declare, quite explicitly, that the least of their
concerns is whether their way of speaking conforms with familiar
usage. They have a theory, and according to this theory, the good
really is a simple, nondefinable property, or the persistence of a
state really is an event, regardless of how others may use the word
good or *event*. Reality interests them, not words.

Second, the medium-message conflation prompts disregard for
familiar word-uses not only negatively, by obscuring considerations relevant to language rather than to theory, but also positive-

ly, by highlighting considerations relevant to theory rather than
to language. As a medium of communication a language known to
all is preferable to one known only to the speaker. Its vogue is an
evident virtue. Popular beliefs, assumptions, or theories, on the
other hand, are more likely to be mistaken than are those of
experts, and are more likely to be "confused," "vacuous," or "inco-
herent" than are word meanings. Their vogue is not a virtue.
Hence, once meanings are confused with theories, and everyday
meanings with everyday opinions, the skepticism which the opinions often merit is transferred to the meanings. The results are
disastrous: ordinary meanings are ignored; no others are stipulated to replace them; babel ensues, under the guise of theoretical
advance.[26]

The medium-message conflation further fosters disregard for
familiar word-uses by creating a philosophical bogeyman, the Ordinary-Language Philosopher, and associating concern for known
uses with this disreputable figure. The Ordinary-Language Philosopher opposes both the creative extension of existing meanings and
the stipulation of new ones. Familiar forms of expression must be
maintained, come what may. In truth, such is seldom the issue. It is
one thing to extend terms creatively, to express some new reality or
vision of reality; it is quite another to express familiar realities in
unfamiliar yet supposedly nonpoetic, nonfigurative, more accurate
terms. It is one thing to stipulate new meanings for words, stating
one's reasons; it is quite another to disregard existing meanings and
stipulate no others in their stead. The issue is not new meanings
versus old. The issue is meanings, new or old, recognized as such,
versus meanings, new or old, treated as theories.

Essentialistic theories seldom meet the test of familiar usage,
on the one hand, nor make sense as implicit redefinitions, replacing current meanings, on the other. So, if the theories are to stand,
the claims of familiar usage must be ignored. This the medium-
message conflation not only permits but makes likely, given the
play of other causal factors.

A Third Source: The Will

Freedom to disregard usage is critical for those who would philosophize in the essentialistic manner. It permits them to eliminate rivals; it permits them to construct their own systems. If one
can simply declare what events are, what actions are, what inten-
tions are, and so forth, without regard for how these words are

used, one may proceed as Donagan does, with apodictic assurance. Such freedom is attractive; hence reason does not work alone: "The difficulty to be overcome," Wittgenstein once declared, "is not one of the understanding but of the will."[27]

Consider examples. Why did Cajetan restrict analogy to one type only, despite the counter-evidence staring him in the face? Because this one type is better, more excellent, he said, than the others, surpassing them "by dignity and name."[28] In other words, because it was his favorite. Also because, as McInerny characterized the cardinal's attitude, extension of the term *analogia* "has led to such an abuse of the term that impossible confusion has resulted."[29] Thus, no consultation of usage or examination of cases spawned Cajetan's essentialist doctrine; his preferences begot it.

Why, similarly, did Russell declare that "in the proper strict logical sense of the word" a name is not what we typically call a name, but the sign for some simple item within immediate awareness? In part, no doubt, because he was enamored of strictness and rigor, as he conceived them, and of logic. Because only by virtue of such rigor and strictness could philosophy be truly "scientific," as he maintained it should be.[30] Because he found excitement in the prospect that philosophical inquiry, if properly conducted, would generate such surprises. "The point of philosophy," he wrote, "is to start with something so simple as not to seem worth stating, and to end with something so paradoxical that no one will believe it."[31] People suppose that *Napoleon, Chicago, Vesuvius,* and *Mars* are proper names, but they are mistaken: strictly speaking, none of the expressions we call names are in fact names! How tame, by comparison, appears the Wittgensteinian practice of simply accepting the verdict of usage.[32]

Wittgenstein spoke of the influence of the "will," William James of "temperament." Many of James's evocations of the temperamental sources of "rationalism" and "intellectualism" apply equally to essentialism. For instance: "*Refinement* is what characterizes our intellectualist philosophies. They exquisitely satisfy that craving for a refined object of contemplation which is so powerful an appetite of the mind."[33] Plato's ideas, the Scholastics' essences, Frege's concepts,[34] Wittgenstein's general forms—all satisfied this craving. Again: "Your typical ultra-abstractionist fairly shudders at concreteness: other things equal, he positively prefers the pale and spectral. If the two universes were offered, he would always choose the skinny outline rather than the rich thicket of reality. It is so much purer, clearer, nobler."[35] As Wittgenstein eventually remarked of his earlier thinking, "The crystalline purity of logic was, of course, not a *result of investigation*: it was a requirement."[36]

Despite James's declared pluralism, he himself proffered a single, relatively uniform account of truth, an account that reflected his own pragmatic preferences. If truth could not always be copying, then doubtless it was never copying. What it was—always and only, from a pragmatic point of view—was utility.[37] "To 'agree' in the widest sense with a reality, *can only mean to be guided either straight up to it or into its surroundings, or to be put into such working touch with it as to handle either it or something connected with it better than if we disagreed.*"[38] Such a worthy thing seemed deserving of the honorific title "truth." Like other worthy things, it became enshrined in a persuasive definition.

Comparison of different will-guided, essentialistic definitions reveals a variety of patterns. Sometimes, as in James's case, the operative value gets stated in the definition (think, for example, of definitions of democracy, science, education, or philosophy). Sometimes, as for Cajetan, Russell, and young Wittgenstein, the operative values do not enter the definition (of analogy, names, propositions, language, or the like) but motivate and guide the defining. Sometimes the values beget a specific definition (of truth, democracy, philosophy, personhood, religion, and so forth); sometimes they operate more generally. James observed that, in his day, "a certain abstract monism, a certain emotional response to the character of oneness, as if it were a feature of the world not coordinate with its manyness, but vastly more excellent and eminent, is so prevalent in educated circles that we might almost call it a part of philosophic common sense."[39]

Yet essences owe their appeal to something more than personal temperament, individual preferences, or mystical affinities. As chapter 7 illustrates, essences may play a key role in an individual's intellectual agenda, or that of a whole school; they may appear crucial to large speculative projects (modal logic, objective ethics, a role for philosophy, drawing the limits of speech and thought, a theory of performatives, etc.). More generally, they may appear desirable, even indispensable, for *crisp communication, rigorous reasoning,* and *general understanding,* and may maintain a commensurate grip on the will, which aspires to all three benefits.

First, crisp communication. Deprecatory remarks concerning the confusing "ambiguity" of everyday concepts are commonplace. Indefinite concepts, it has been said, are no concepts at all;[40] if you cannot define your terms, you do not know what you are saying.[41] So, too, words should have single meanings.[42] (It is a disgrace to the human race, Russell declared, that it has chosen to employ the word *is* in two entirely different senses.[43]) Now, essences satisfy this double demand of definiteness and uniformity. Hence they are desired and, being desired, are stipulated or supposed. Wishful thinking about the way things should be reinforces impressions, received for instance from language, concerning the way things are.

Essentialistically sharp and uniform concepts look equally desirable for the sake of rigorous argumentation. Formerly, the Thomistic stress on analogous concepts roused Scotistic misgivings with regard to valid deductive reasoning. In our day, Wittgensteinian emphasis on family resemblance, Waismannian stress on open texture, and the like have occasioned similar doubts. And the preceding chapters may have aggravated them. Calculus-like reasoning, rigid and rigorous, has been standard philosophical procedure for refuting others' theories and establishing one's own. Yet, time and again, discussions here have shown such reasoning to be fallacious, and have traced its failure to essentialistic assumptions concerning the concepts employed. So perhaps without essences rigorous reasoning is doomed.

Apparently desirable for the sake of communication and effective argumentation, essences also gratify the desire for understanding. Understanding unifies, through principles, laws, and definitions; it clarifies, by drawing precise boundaries; it furnishes a comprehensive view, bringing order to myriad details.[44] Essences do all these things. They unify (analogy is *one* thing, names are *one* thing, knowledge is *one* thing); they clarify (just *this* counts as analogy, just *this* counts as a name, just *this* counts as knowledge); they furnish a comprehensive view (*all* analogy is such, *all* names are such, *all* knowledge is such); and they thereby bring order to the confusion of varied cases. Such virtues cannot help but be attractive, cannot help but entice the will.

A Fourth Source: Contagion

To account for the prevalence of measles, one would first cite the virus that causes it. But that would not suffice: one would need to add that the disease is highly contagious. The same holds for essentialism. The sorcery of language, disregard for language, the tug of the will—these go far to explain the genesis of essentialism, but they do not fully account for its prevalence. True, such factors can beget the malady in mere children; it does not have to be caught from others. But often it is. Oral and especially written communication are ready media of transmission.

The most evident sort of contagion works directly, within the same discipline. Socrates infects Plato, Plato infects Aristotle and various neo-Platonists, neo-Platonists infect Augustine, Augustine infects Augustinians, Aristotle infects Arab Aristotelians, all infect Aquinas, Aquinas infects Thomists, and so forth, with the result that for few thinkers is essentialism entirely original.

Indirect, interdisciplinary contagion works more subtly. Natural science, in particular, acts as a prestigious paradigm which philosophers strive to emulate. As we have seen, they offer essentialistic "explications," and propose them, not as verbal stipulations, but as theories. They treat the terms of everyday speech as "rigid designators" picking out whatever essences science assigns them. Like Copi, they agree with Aristotle that "definition is a scientific process" and that "the definition of a thing should state its essence." With Hill and others, they view essentialistic, non-disjunctive definition as scientifically more "fruitful."

Reflection on such samples suggests a paradox: the prestige of natural science, exciting emulation, tempts philosophers and others to adopt an approach seldom found in natural science. Scientific success, in physics, chemistry, physiology, and the like, requires scientific terminology. The precision and uniformity of scientific terminology stem partly from explicit stipulation and convention, partly from agreement in instruments, procedures, and results, without which the stipulations and conventions would not have precise or uniform senses. "Only in the stream of thought and life," wrote Wittgenstein, "do words have meaning";[45] and only in a scientific stream of thought and life do words have scientifically precise and uniform meaning. For the most part, however, philosophers, when engaged as philosophers, are immersed in no such stream. Nor can they readily duplicate the scientific deposit of centuries. Yet they wish to emulate science *now*. It is not surprising, then, that they sometimes take a shortcut. Lacking agreed terminology or agreed results, they present personal stipulations, redefining terms, as precise, uniform theories or statements of fact: only hidden structure establishes natural kinds, only explicit performatives are genuine performatives, only logical pictures are genuine propositions, only names for particulars are genuine proper names, and so forth.[46]

Mathematics and logic, with their penchant for invariant units, also exert an influence. Thus philosophers immersed in mathematics and/or logic—Plato, Aristotle, Descartes, Leibniz, Spinoza, Frege, Russell, Husserl, young Wittgenstein—have been notably essentialistic in their philosophical thinking. This is hardly surprising, for philosophers' minds are not hermetically compartmentalized. If they think with essentialistic precision and uniformity when engaged in logic or mathematics, they are likely to think similarly when engaged in philosophy—especially if they regard logic and mathematics as cognitive paradigms.

The four factors so far mentioned seldom work alone. And when they work together, they may function in new ways. In simple illustration: direct contagion begets loyalties as well as doctrines, and the loyalties add a new dimension to the influence of the will. Reverence for a master (Plato, Aristotle, Aquinas, Husserl,...) and/or commitment to a school (Platonism, Aristotelianism, Thomism, Husserlian phenomenology,...), when added to the influence of linguistic forms, disregard for language, and various enticements of the will, may render inherited essentialism virtually impregnable.

Essentialists are not the only ones affected in this manner, or in those suggested earlier; nor are they all affected equally. Even the most staunchly traditional may not place fidelity to master or school over the search for truth. Even the most avid for the unity, clarity, simplicity, and order of logic, mathematics, or science may not ignore counter-evidence. It can hardly be doubted, however, that essentialists, like others, are subject to the force of contagion. I am not here criticizing, but explaining.

A Fifth Source: Argument

David Pears has observed that "although realists are argumentative, it is difficult to answer the question why they maintain that universals exist. Any answer must be based on a selection from among the many reasons which they themselves proffer: and a good selection will be diagnostic; it will successfully explain the doctrine."[47] It may partially explain the doctrine, I would say, but all the explicit reasons that essentialists have adduced, collectively considered, do not come close to explaining their essentialistic thinking. Other sources than those I have suggested might be ferreted out, from psychoanalysis, intellectual history, social analysis, or the like;[48] but by now it should be evident that argument figures as just one among many contributing factors. Indeed, it may even be queried whether such arguments as essentialists offer deserve separate mention as a source of essentialistic thinking, or should themselves be explained by reference to factors such as those already mentioned.

Consider, for example, the revealing objection evoked by the notion of "family structure." Were concepts thus disjunctive, it is said, the words would have multiple meanings. But a word like *game* does not have one meaning when applied to poker, another when applied to chess, a third when applied to solitaire, and so forth. The meaning remains the same. Hence the family-resemblance analysis must be mistaken. I call this objection revealing because of its clear suggestion that for the objector "same meaning" implies essentialistically-uniform meaning, ruling out mere family resemblance. So perhaps the influence of expressions like "same meaning" should be added to the linguistic influences cited earlier: perhaps "same meaning," like "same color" or "same kind of activity," suggests uniformity.[49]

An equally plausible hypothesis is that forces such as those already noted beget an essentialistic conception of word meanings, and that this conception begets what amounts to a question-begging argument, basing its conclusion of uniformity on assumed uniformity wherever a term is said to have a single meaning. In either hypothesis, or in both combined, the ultimate explanation of the conclusion would be found, not in the argument, but elsewhere—in language, for example.

The same may be suggested for the familiar argument from abstractness. A word like *game* or *knowledge,* it was often pointed out, does not specify any particular game or any particular variety of knowledge. So if the word is to have any meaning at all, it must signify something distinct from all varieties or variations. In Ross's words (chapter 1), it must designate a "universal," "entirely different from sensible things." This argument, too, looks convincing only if one assumes the very thing to be established, namely that the word has no meaning—or no "single meaning"—unless it says the "same thing" every time. That is, unless it picks out some one essence, not a family resemblance or the like.

Again, consider Russell's argument in *The Problems of Philosophy.* Berkeley and Hume, he suggested, failed to notice the following refutation of their nominalistic views:

> If we wish to avoid the universals *whiteness* and *triangularity,* we shall choose some particular patch of white or some particular triangle, and say that anything is white or a triangle if it has the right sort of resemblance to our chosen particular. But then the resemblance required will have to be a universal. Since there are many white things, the resemblance must hold between

many pairs of particular white things; and this is the characteristic of a universal. It will be useless to say that there is a different resemblance for each pair, for then we shall have to say that these resemblances resemble each other, and thus at last we shall be forced to admit resemblance as a universal. The relation of resemblance, therefore, must be a true universal. And having been forced to admit this universal, we find that it is no longer worth while to invent difficult and unplausible theories to avoid the admission of such universals as whiteness and triangularity.[50]

An anti-essentialist reader of this refutation may find it curiously question-begging. Why must the resemblance between resemblances be any more uniform than that between whites or triangles? However, the argument becomes intelligible if read as follows. Some single thing must justify the use of a single term. For nominalists like Berkeley and Hume that one thing is a particular. But the first step of Russell's argument takes us beyond particular triangles, and the second passes beyond particular resemblances. Neither type of particular remains to explain the predication. Hence a universal—the alternative sort of single thing—is finally required.

In response, a critic might point out that three kinds of particulars, not two, are here in question—particular whites or triangles, particular resemblances between them, and particular resemblances between the resemblances. Thus the third category remains as a rival explanation at the last step in Russell's argumentation. Or the critic might question the underlying assumption that some single reality must justify the single term.

If all arguments resembled these question-begging ones, there might be no need to add argumentation as a separate source of essentialistic thinking: language, for example, might generate the thinking; arguments might merely reveal it. However, something more than linguistic bewitchment may account for the frequent objection: "Why would we use the same word for many different things unless they all had something in common?" This query may reveal nothing more than a gratuitously essentialistic understanding of the phrase "something in common," engendered in the manner previously surmised. However, it looks at least as likely that the objector cannot conceive any alternative pattern or patterns of use; or that, having conceived one, he or she does not see how language could possibly work that way.

"Signs would hardly be useful," wrote Frege, "if they did not serve the purpose of signifying the same thing repeatedly and in different contexts, while making evident that the same thing was meant."[51] These words might be given a non-essentialistic interpretation. However, by "same thing" Frege did not mean merely "thing(s) signified by the same sign."[52] And a long tradition has so conceived the functioning of language that it could not achieve its purpose non-essentialistically. Words conveyed ideas, the same in the hearer's mind as in the speaker's. And ideas were pictures, similitudes, representations. But image-representations could not conceivably be identical from person to person, since different minds are stocked with different paradigms. Only essentialistic representations, depicting something present in all instances no matter how varied, could serve as common currency.[53]

Communication apart, it was thought that even speakers would have to accompany their words with suitable representations; otherwise they would not be "thinking of what they said," but would be no better than parrots or talking machines. But no concrete representation—no single, specific image—mirrors the sense of a general term; and no speaker can mentally picture all imaginable instances while uttering each expression of a sentence. Hence it seemed that the only way to think what one said was to think it essentialistically, with a single representation per word, mirroring a single essence.

Belief in essences has also been linked with belief in truth as correspondence. Words do not resemble the realities we speak of, but thought may. And essentialistic concepts are more plausible truth-correlates than picture-images or other sensible representations. As James remarked, images may perhaps copy a clock-dial, but suppose we make some true assertion about the contents of the clock—say, about its works or about their elasticity. What image can represent elasticity? What image can depict works we have never observed?[54] Essentialistic concepts furnish a solution. We may not be able to *imagine* the unseen works, essentialists might explain; but, given an essence of works, we can form an abstract concept, or mental representation, of works in general, and can use this concept to make a truthful judgment without having to picture any particular works in detail.[55]

Such arguments have seldom been fully articulated. But all of their major premises—speech communicating ideas, thought accompanying speech, truth as correspondence—have enjoyed wide acceptance; suggestive fragments of argument appear here and there; and occasionally a representative thinker such as Locke has become quite explicit:

> First, It is impossible, that every particular thing should
> have a distinct peculiar name. For, the signification and
> use of words depending on that connexion which the
> mind makes between its ideas and the sounds it uses as
> signs of them, it is necessary, in the application of names
> to things, that the mind should have distinct ideas of the
> things, and retain also the particular name that belongs
> to every one, with its peculiar appropriation to that idea.
> But it is beyond the power of human capacity to frame
> and retain distinct ideas of all the particular things we
> meet with: every bird and beast men saw; every tree and
> plant that affected the senses, could not find a place in
> the most capacious understanding... Secondly, If it were
> possible, it would yet be useless; because it would not
> serve to the chief end of language. Men would in vain
> heap up names of particular things, that would not serve
> them to communicate their thoughts. Men learn names,
> and use them in talk with others, only that they may be
> understood: which is then only done when, by use or con-
> sent, the sound I make by the organs of speech, excites in
> another man's mind who hears it, the idea I apply it to in
> mine, when I speak it. This cannot be done by names
> applied to particular things; whereof I alone having the
> ideas in my mind, the names of them could not be signifi-
> cant or intelligible to another, who was not acquainted
> with all those very particular things which had fallen
> under my notice.[56]

For Locke, truth depends on such abstractive ideas, mirroring
essences.[57] For verbal truth depends on mental, and mental on
ideas: "When ideas are so put together, or separated in the mind,
as they or the things they stand for do agree or not, that is, as I
may call it, *mental truth.* But *truth of words* is something more;
and that is the affirming or denying of words one of another, as the
ideas they stand for agree or disagree."[58]

It would be unrealistic to trace doctrines like these solely to
essentialistic assumptions begotten by language, and to conclude
that the doctrines and the arguments they generate can be dismissed as purely derivative when tallying the sources of essentialism. It would be less implausible, however, to surmise that *language* was their source, as well as a source of essentialism, and
then to draw the same conclusion.

Wittgenstein offers evidence which could support this surmise.

For example, "what tempts us to think of the meaning of what we say as a process essentially of the kind which we have described is the analogy between the forms of expression:
'to say something,'
'to mean something,'
which seem to refer to two parallel processes."[59] A kindred analogy between "hear something" and "understand something" might suggest a similar pair of processes in the hearer. The double use of *think*—now for an activity, now for a mental state—might reinforce the impression that thinking what one says is a parallel process.

Much more of the same kind might be adduced. Still, whatever the outcome of this interesting exercise, it is clear that whether or not pro-essentialist argumentation derives entirely from other sources—language, disregard for language, the will—it reinforces those sources. The arguments fix more firmly a viewpoint unreflectively adopted. The viewpoint, it now appears, can be *proved*.

Arguments like those cited have passed out of vogue. David Pears cites one or two others (without offering textual evidence, or locating them historically);[60] and we have met a couple more (Putnam's from Twin-Earth fantasies, Hollinger's from science's alleged needs). For the most part, however, in the preceding chapters essences were simply supposed, explicitly or implicitly; they were not argued for. As a source of contemporary essentialism, argument appears to play a relatively minor role.[61]

Alternatives

To the preceding five-point analysis objection has been made that it ignores the positive sources of essentialism. Essentialists may be mistaken; but they, too, seek the truth. They, too, hunger for clarity and depth of understanding. They, too, realize how misleading are appearances, so probe beneath the surface. All this I take for granted. The question is, how and why the search for truth leads them where it does not lead others.

Essentialists would, of course, suggest that essences lead them to belief in essences. There is no need, for example, to surmise what surface linguistic similarities occasion the conviction that terms denote essences. A much simpler explanation is available: The terms do denote essences. Real sameness begets verbal sameness; verbal sameness does not beget belief in real sameness. This may not have been demonstrated, but neither has the contrary. I have not disproved the existence of essences. The critiques in preceding chapters might be valid, and there still might be essences. It would not be the first time that a sound view has been held for unsound reasons.

Thanks to the present chapter, I can now respond to this suggestion more fully than before. Chapters 1 to 5 did more than demonstrate the weakness of essentialistic arguments; they showed the weakness of essentialism, once its linguistic assumptions and requirements are laid bare. It is not realistic to suppose that the members of a natural-language community—children, poets, housewives, savants—employ their common stock of terms with essentialistic uniformity, precision, and rigidity. It is not realistic to suppose that they employ terms essentialistically without being able to identify, describe, or intuitively grasp the essences that guide them (as I, for instance, cannot do for any of the terms discussed in this study). If, however, no other explanation could be found for widespread, enduring belief in essences, the hypothesis of essences might retain some plausibility. The present chapter, by citing five sources of essentialism that do not require essences, has eliminated this argument. Hence essentialism is indeed implausible.

If essences looked likely, I would not need to seek far to account for belief in essences. If arguments for essentialism were more plentiful and less derivative than I have suggested—if they played the kind of role the quotation from Pears suggests—then, too, I might be spared the inquiries of this chapter and the next. For the comparison I drew at the start of this chapter would not stand. Individual cancers might be difficult to trace, but instances of essentialism would occasion little mystery: the arguments they concluded would typically reveal their provenance. As it is, the next chapter will confirm the slight significance of argument as a source of recent essentialism.

Chapter Seven

DIAGNOSES AND PROGNOSIS

This survey must extend over a wide domain, for the roots of
our ideas reach a long way.[1]

Wittgenstein's therapy is made palatable by the fact that he
himself at an earlier stage is the chief patient diagnosed. "Every
one of these sentences," he wrote on the flyleaf of Schlick's copy of
the *Tractatus,* "is the expression of an illness."[2] Unfortunately, I
have not been able to render the present work agreeable in the
same fashion. Though my own turn comes in chapter 3, most of my
criticism has been directed to others' thinking. And now I shall
have the temerity not only to criticize but also to diagnose. I shall
surmise the roots of individual thinkers' essentialistic views. I shall
venture to suggest how they came to think as they did—or do.

Several of those scrutinized are still alive. So it might seem that,
rather than resort to surmises based solely on written evidence, I
should sit down with at least these living thinkers and inquire of
them the sources of their essentialism. Were that possible, doubtless
it would correct many a false impression. People have an inner
understanding of how they themselves think and why. They know
the history of their own ideas in a way that others do not. However,
their understanding of the origin of their views varies directly with
the extent to which the views have resulted from reasoning. With
respect to other sources, they enjoy little if any advantage; indeed,
they may be blind to the true sources of their thinking. Asked to
account for their views, they are likely to proffer supporting arguments, not history. To cite subtle, non-probative influences would be
to call in question the strength or legitimacy of their positions.

So the last chapter's assessment, that recent essentialism typically does not result from discernible reasoning, acquires added
significance. Accurate etiology proves difficult not only for the
observer but also—perhaps especially—for the observed. Impressive paradigms in the history of thought suggest how little, on
occasion, even the arguments thinkers formulate may influence
their conclusions. And recent essentialists seldom adduce arguments for their essentialism. In none of the representative cases
examined in this chapter does argument play a notable role in support of the author's essentialistic views.

Though perhaps not disadvantaged, therefore, in comparison with the thinkers I shall study, I can claim no special expertise in the sort of intellectual etiology I shall attempt. Neither, perhaps, can anybody else. Wittgenstein offers some leads. But no treatise I know offers guidelines for inquiries like those undertaken in this chapter and the last. Individual studies that trace the history of an idea seldom attempt a thorough account of its likely causes. Thus, I have encountered no paradigm study that can serve as a model. Still, a close causal investigation into representative instances of essentialistic thinking seems worth venturing, not only as an experiment in a different sort of analysis, but for reasons such as chapter 6 suggested.

Etiology complements and checks critique such as that in chapters 1 to 5. To understand why a person said something is to understand it better and thereby avoid unsound criticism. In turn, micro-etiology complements and checks macro-etiology such as that in chapter 6. To understand how individual essentialists came to think as they did is to understand what factors account for essentialism generally and to understand their workings in rich and varied detail.

Also more realistically. Whereas causes of cancer—radiation, asbestos, vinyl chloride, tobacco smoke, sunlight—typically work singly, causes of essentialism seldom act alone. One function of the present chapter is to bring out this fact, as the last chapter's single-file discussion did not. Another of the chapter's functions is to suggest what factors and how many, in what ways, combine to generate essentialistic doctrines. The outcome will be a clearer overview of essentialism's origins.

Lest, however, I rouse unrealistic expectations, I should repeat what I said in the last chapter: for essentialism as for cancer, some causal factors can be stated with assurance, at least generally; often, however, the source or sources of a specific malignancy can only be surmised. Turning now to specific malignancies, I shall offer only plausible surmises.

In deciding how many authors to examine, I have had to compromise. On one hand, fewer case-studies would permit greater depth and thoroughness in each inquiry. On the other hand, more numerous case-studies would provide broader, more representative coverage. So, to make the sampling somewhat representative, I have drawn examples from each of the five preceding chapters of critique (general theories, particular theories, simple calculus-reasoning, network-reasoning, other-worlds reasoning); to permit some depth and thoroughness, I have limited the examples to one per chapter (Scheler, Wittgenstein, Pitcher, Graham, Kripke).

General Theories: Scheler

The prominence of the word *Wesen* in Scheler's works does not by itself signal the presence of essentialism. Rather, Scheler's essentialism surfaces when he states that a universal essence "comes to the fore in a plurality of otherwise different objects as an identical essence"; that "in certain circumstances a *single* deed or a *single* person is all that we need to grasp the *essence* of the value in question"; that the essence of red, for example, is given not only in the universal concept but also "in each perceivable nuance of this color."

Chapter 1 posed a dilemma for such views. If an essence of X is conceived as present in all and only those things customarily called X, how can the existence of such an essence be ascertained without examining what things are in fact called X and whether they reveal an identical essence? If, on the contrary, an essence of X is not conceived as present in all and only the things standardly called X, why and in what sense can it be termed the essence of *X*? When an author like Scheler offers no response to this dilemma, one may suspect that he has not noticed it and that this over-sight—this blindness to the methodological relevance of the lan-guage he employs—largely explains his essentialism.

To illustrate, Scheler says of the holy: "This modality is quite independent of all that has been considered 'holy' by different peo-ples at various times, such as holy things, powers, persons, institu-tions, and the like (i.e., from ideas of fetishism to the purest con-ceptions of God)."[3] On reflection, this proves puzzling. Have these varied judgements concerning the "holy," or the utterances that expressed them, all employed the single term *holy* (or *heilig*)? If not, have they employed a set of terms synonymous with that one, within each language or within the different languages spoken by the "different peoples"? Have these terms maintained an identical sense despite the shifting judgments they have figured in? Do shifts of sense concern Scheler as little as the fluctuation of judg-ments? If so—if the reality he refers to as the "holy" is indepen-dent of the terms people have employed and the senses they have given them—in what sense is that reality "the holy" ("*das Heilige*")? Why call it by that name?

Scheler saw the linguistic problem as one of communication, not of identification.[4] He knew what the holy was. He could spot it, by pure, wordless intuition. But he could not adequately define it. Otto was right: "This (the category of holiness) is perfectly *sui generis* and irreducible to any other; and therefore, like every abso-

lutely primary and elementary datum, while it admits of being discussed, it cannot be strictly defined."[5] "The indefinability of the X
under investigation (*per genus et differentia specifica*) is a sure
sign that in this X we have a genuine elementary essence which
underlies ultimate concepts but is itself 'inconceivable.' For 'to conceive' means to reduce the object of a concept in terms of other concepts."[6] Thus phenomenological discussion has as its sole aim "to
bring the reader (or listener) to see that which, by its essence, can
only be 'seen'; it is in view of this that all the propositions which
occur in [Husserl's *Logical Investigations*], all the conclusions, all
the provisional definitions which are introduced as they are needed, all the provisional descriptions, all the chains of argument and
proof, have simply the function of a 'pointer,' pointing to what is to
be brought to sight."[7]

This doctrine of indefinability offers causal clues. Those who
attempt to define are more likely to fix their attention on the link
between words and things. Looking in that direction, they are
more likely to spot the problem Scheler slighted—that of identification. If, in addition, they take the traditional view and connect
the existence of essences with the possibility of definition, difficulties of definition may cast doubt on the existence of essences.
Scheler, however, neither supposing the possibility of strict definition nor attempting it, was spared such doubts.

He did not even try to "fill in" the concepts he and others
employed. Ideally, it is true, "phenomenology has reached its goal
when every symbol and half-symbol is completely fulfilled through
the 'self-given,' including everything which functions in the natural
world-view and in science as a *form* of understanding (everything
'categorial')."[8] However, "*philosophical* cognition, by its essence, is
asymbolical. It seeks to know a being just as it is in itself, not in its
role of simply providing the filling for symbols applied to it."[9] "Certain[ly] philosophy, in trying to reach this goal, makes use of language, both as an instrument of discovery and as a means for
exhibiting results. However, philosophy never calls upon language
for help in determining its own object... The philosopher, by keeping up a resolute fight against the tendency to let the given be given
only in this form, discovers the *prelinguistically given* which is, as it
were, still untouched by language."[10] Subsequently, though, Scheler
should have noted, the same philosopher, producing marks or
sounds, starts to speak of X and Y and Z. He or she labels essences,
and borrows the labels from existing languages. At that instant, the
problem of identification arises.

Scheler's inattention to this problem may have a further explanation. "The phenomenological philosopher," he declared, "thirsting for the lived-experience of being, will above all seek to drink at the very *sources* in which the contents of the world reveal themselves. His reflective gaze rests only on that place where lived-experience and its objects, the world, touch one another."[11] Not on language; not on mere words. Such has been the standard response of those to whom the problem of identification is posed. Reality interests them, not verbiage.

Scheler had further reason to focus on phenomena. Not only is lived-experience distinct from the symbols that express it. Not only is it more important, hence worthy of closer scrutiny, than derivative symbols. But, as Herbert Spiegelberg observes, "the danger of symbolism lay in the tendency of symbols to displace and to conceal the phenomena."[12] Better, then, to bracket them from view. How foggy, by comparison, phenomenology would become, were it forced to attend to the complexities of language.

The intrusion of symbols might also obscure the *objectivity* of what is "immediately given." For Scheler this was a crucial consideration. Whereas Kant, in answer to Hume, resorted to subjective analysis, Scheler, in reaction to Kant, stressed the unmediated objectivity of phenomena. "The identity and difference of pure facts," he insisted, "must be completely independent of all the *symbols* with which it is possible for us to designate them and of the symbols which are used in presenting the facts of which they are parts."[13] Though these "pure facts" may need to be sifted symbolically, "the methodological role this 'thinking' plays would in no way be creative or synthesizing, as, for example, in Kant; it would be merely an unavoidable *means and tool* for bringing something to intuition..."[14]

So far, I have surmised that Scheler's attention may have been diverted from the problem of linguistic identification by his concern for objectivity, in opposition to Kant; by his fixation on reality, as opposed to mere words; and by his doctrine of indefinability, sparing him the doubts and difficulties attendant on traditional attempts at definition. However, there may be something more. Passages in *Vom Umsturz der Werte* suggest a role for essences akin to that of Platonic forms.[15]

"All signs," Scheler there asserts, "live in virtue of our stipulation and convention, both of which already *presuppose* agreement in *words* or equivalent forms of understanding. Not so for the word. The word presents itself as fulfilling a requirement from the *object itself*. We seek the 'right' word for the object, the one that—under the aspect it presents us at the moment—fits the object."[16] Reference to "the requirement from the *object itself*" occasions misgivings; surely we should add, "the requirement from the object itself, *given the word's present employment for such a phenomenon*—for instance, the use of the word *red* for this color, or of *scarlet* for this shade of red." Scheler, however, shows no inclination to introduce or recognize any such addition. "How we 'use' or 'employ' a word, or how a word is 'used' or 'employed' in a group—so-called 'linguistic usage'—has nothing to do with the word's *essence*. The word itself 'means,' 'signifies' something, 'has' its sense, that—no matter how vague—*prescribes* the word's *possible* application or use, or circumscribes the sphere of its possible application."[17]

We can now intuit, perhaps, how Scheler slipped between the horns of chapter 1's dilemma, and why he attended so little to standard or stipulated senses of the terms he employed. Reality itself would indicate what sounds or marks to make, what expressions to employ. However, if so, the mystery does not lift but merely shifts; for we cannot divine how nonverbal objects, on their own, might dictate word meanings or prescribe modes of speech. How, for example, might a specific phenomenon signal: "I, and I alone, should be called 'the holy'; all rivals or variants are impostors"? How and in what sense might this word, and not another, "fit" this phenomenon, and not another? The problem of identification remains.

The upshot of our probing is that Scheler enjoyed considerable leeway to be as essentialistic as he desired. Conventional usage would not stand in the way. What we have not yet discerned is why he availed himself of this leeway. Some light has been cast on his essentialistic freedom; none, as yet, on his essentialistic proclivities. For these, several explanations suggest themselves, in view of his ambience, interests, values, and aspirations.

The seed discernible in Scheler's doctoral thesis[18] developed in the ambience Giovanni Ferretti evokes:

> General reference to the phenomenological movement to which Scheler belonged and to the movement's founder who inspired him is not enough . . . More precise would be a reference to the Husserlian period of the *Logische Untersuchungen* and of the teaching at Göttingen that preceded *Ideen I*, which, by means of the theory of the intentionality of knowledge, of the intuition of essences, and recourse to the evidence of the immediately given as the ultimate and indubitable foundation of knowledge, furnished the general theoretical foundations of the two

> phenomenological circles of Munich and Göttingen in
> which Scheler took an active part, and permitted agree-
> ment on a programmatic platform shared by the editors
> of the *Jahrbuch für Philosophie und phänomenologische
> Forschung,* among whom Scheler figured. There result-
> ed the conception of phenomenology as the study of
> essences, given to immediate vision in the most varied
> areas of reality...[19]

In this development, it is not always clear just who influenced
whom. Husserl's and Scheler's essentialism came to sharpest,
fullest expression at the same moment. The parallel passages
quoted in chapter 1, asserting the possibility of single-case intuition of essences, appeared simultaneously, in Husserl's *Ideas*
(1913) and in Scheler's *Formalism* (1913-1916).

More readily surmised than the initiator of the doctrine is its
motivation. Scheler, like others, saw phenomenology as a correc-
tive to Kant, on the one hand, and to empirical science, on the
other. To fulfill this double role, it needed essences.[20] Scrutinizing
essences' connections and laws, phenomenology would be as general as either of its rivals for cognitive preeminence,[21] but richer and
more objective than Kant's subjective formalism, surer and more
basic than empirical science.[22]

On the Kantian connection, Quentin Lauer has written:

> Where both [Husserl and Scheler] refused to agree with
> Kant, however, was in his contention that cognition can
> be adequately explained in terms of formal a priori cate-
> gories (whether of understanding or of reason). It is not
> enough, they will say, that knowledge have its absolute-
> ly necessary a priori laws; the object of knowledge, too,
> if it is to be genuinely objective, must have its a priori
> laws. To speak of a priori necessity on the objective side,
> however, is to speak of an objective essence, which is to
> say, an a priori which is material as well as formal.
> Thus, as Husserl says, the mind is necessitated not only
> by the laws of its own functioning, which are psychologi-
> cal, and by the laws of thought, which are logical, but
> also by laws governing the object as such, which are
> ontological.[23]

Such an account, alluding to "laws governing the object as
such," connects with Scheler's assertions in *Vom Umsturz der
Werte,* concerning "the requirement from the *object itself,*" and

brings out their implications. As pure Forms, once contemplated, allowed the slave boy in the *Meno* to answer the inquiries put to him, without relying on logical or scientific laws (or, apparently, on the conceptual connections imparted when he learned Greek), so essences, when intuited, could provide answers more basic than any found in science and more satisfying than any found in Kant. There might, perhaps, be such a thing as an a priori study of particulars rather than of essences; but what a sorry figure such a piecemeal inquiry would cut, by itself, in comparison with the universal pronouncements of Kant or the laws of Newtonian science.

Philosophical unity as well as generality appealed to Scheler.[24] "The cultured person is one who has acquired in the world *a personal structure,* an inclusive concept of ideally mobile patterns superimposed on each other, in order to arrive at *one single* way to view the world, to think, comprehend, judge, and deal with the world and *any* of its fortuitous manifestations—patterns *anterior* to fortuitous experience, capable of utilizing and integrating this experience into the entity of their personal '*world.*' This is knowledge of culture."[25] "Knowledge of culture is *knowledge of essence,* derived and organized on the basis of *one,* or a few, good and striking examples of a phenomenon, a knowledge which has become form and rule of perception and 'category' of all fortuitous phenomena of similar future experience."[26]

Such evidence notwithstanding, I find it difficult to suppose that Scheler's belief in essences arose solely from a hankering for unity and generality. The doctrine must have possessed at least a semblance of verisimilitude. I shall therefore make one further suggestion. In addition to factors already touched on—disregard for language, contagion, the will—the influence of language may also be surmised, as in the case of Plato, or of Moore.

"Plato," it has been said, "seems first to have concerned himself with moral and aesthetic universals."[27] His theory of Forms was "first and foremost a framework for ethical certainty." It was not suggested by the Form of hair, mud, or dirt, nor even of man, fire, or water. The like might be said of Scheler. Ethical, evaluative, value-loaded concepts—love, knowledge, culture, religion, the noble, the good, the holy—predominate in his writings. These acted as paradigms. His essentialism was not suggested, say, by the essence of red. That concept served as an illustration, not an object of philosophical inquiry.

This focus has causal significance. For several reasons, value-concepts like *justice* and *love* are more plausible candidates for essences than neutral concepts like *red* and *horse.* For one thing, the suggestive abstract, singular form (see chapter 6) figures more prominently in evaluative terminology than in nonevaluative; talk of "justice" is commoner than talk of "horseness." For another thing, terms like *love* and *justice* are more prescriptive than are terms like *horse* and *red;* and unitary prescriptions do not conflict with reality as unitary descriptions may and often do. ("Such propositions will be true, regardless of whether the moral act contained in them has ever been realized in fact ..."[29]) Furthermore, unitary accounts of justice, courage, culture, and the like do not conflict with the standard application of the terms they use as readily as do unitary accounts of horses, reds, or human beings. The range of things called reds or horses is relatively fixed and uniform, permitting descriptive dictionary definitions, whereas value-concepts reveal far less consensus.

"Many philosophers," notes Chisholm, "disagree about ethics: they can't agree which things are good because they use different criteria of goodness and they can't work out a common criterion of goodness because they can't even reach a preliminary agreement about which things are good."[30] Hence Moore could maintain that the good is a single, simple, indefinable something. The very diversity, popular as well as professional, that precluded essentialistic uniformity made his essentialistic claim more plausible—for anyone, that is, who, like Moore and Scheler, fixed his gaze upon the good and not upon the vagaries of the term *good.* No standard, evident sense of the word conflicted with the claim.[31]

On the strength of chapter 6, I might surmise more general linguistic influences, operative in Scheler's thought as in others'. But I shall limit myself to the more evident possibilities I have cited. None of the suggested explanations looks sure. None looks adequate by itself. Collectively, however, these factors may go far toward explaining Scheler's essentialism. It appears unlikely that some elusive influence not here mentioned—a persuasive demonstration, say, nowhere stated in Scheler's writings—was principally responsible.

Particular Theories: Wittgenstein

Wittgenstein's Tractarian doctrines may be unique in the history of philosophy. In no other instance, one may surmise, have the roots of an author's essentialism been so fully and surely disclosed. Early notes reveal the *Tractatus*'s positions in process of formation; the *Tractatus* itself argues and explains them; and later writings diagnose what went wrong and why. Rarely, as a consequence, has it been possible to compare with such assurance the relative importance of explicit argumentation and subtler, non-demonstrative forces in deciding the direction of a philosopher's thought.

The *Tractatus* does not simply assume a general form of propositions, but presents an argument of sorts, in 4.5. Wittgenstein first explains that "to give the most general propositional form" is "to give a description of the propositions of *any* sign-language *whatsoever* in such a way that every possible sense can be expressed by a symbol satisfying the description, and every symbol satisfying the description can express a sense, provided that the meanings of the names are suitably chosen." Enlightened by such a form, one could anticipate the construction of any and every proposition,[32] and could see how a proposition is "able to communicate a *new* sense to us"[33] by means of "old expressions."[34] However, given such insight or such communicative ability, it would not follow that some single formula or single mode of construction accounted for the insight or the ability. One may therefore suspect that only someone otherwise convinced of the conclusion, or wedded in advance to a single explanation, would argue as Wittgenstein proceeded to: "The existence of a general propositional form is proved by the fact that there cannot be a proposition whose form could not have been foreseen (i.e. constructed)."[35]

Wittgenstein then added, abruptly: "The general form of a proposition is: This is how things stand." The link between 4.5's requirements and this specific general form had been indicated earlier, in 4.021: "A proposition is a picture of reality: for if I understand a proposition, I know the situation that it represents. And I understand the proposition without having had its sense explained to me." Suppose, though, that the proposition—the *Satz*—does not represent a situation? Suppose it functions differently? To this query, the *Tractatus* had no answer.

The weakness of its position can be seen from the rebuttal mounted from the start of the *Investigations*. To dissipate the "mental mist which seems to enshroud our ordinary use of language,"[36] Wittgenstein first imagines simple systems of communication whose formulae are constructed, foreseeably, from "old expressions," yet do not state "how things stand";[37] then passes to actual uses of speech—questioning, commanding, formulating hypotheses, making up stories, play-acting, telling jokes, guessing riddles, asking, thanking, cursing, greeting, praying—which fit no more comfortably within the Tractarian straitjacket.[38] How could the *Tractatus*—4.001, 4.01, 4.021, 4.5, 5, 6—be so myopic?

Wittgenstein drops a clue at the start of his long listing when he asks: "How many kinds of sentence [*Sätze*] are there? Say assertion, question, and command?"[39] The same triple sampling appears in notes that predate the *Tractatus*. "Assertion is merely psychological," they declare. "There are only unasserted propositions. Judgment, command and question all stand on the same level; but all have in common the propositional form, and that alone interests us. What interests logic are only the unasserted propositions."[40] As support for the theory of 4.5, this looks extremely flimsy; as explanation, it looks revealing.

Young Wittgenstein winnowed the logical kernel from the psychological chaff and tossed the chaff aside. Yet the kernel, it seems, was itself psychological. The words "Will you come tomorrow?" or "Come tomorrow" reveal no proposition, no picture of the world; but as "thought out" in a query or command they share a logical core: the proposition "You will come tomorrow," towards which the speaker assumes an inquisitive attitude one time, an imperative attitude the other. Such, it appears, was the viewpoint young Wittgenstein expressed.[41] "The worst enemy of our understanding," he remarked on a later occasion, "is here the idea, the picture, of a 'sense' of what we say, in our mind."[42]

Without such a picture, his youthful essentialism could not have survived. The verbal forms of language or discourse reveal no uniformity. Nor do the varied uses to which the forms are put. But so much lay hidden "in the medium of the understanding"[43] that essentialism could find refuge there. The wonders of thought, the centrality of mental "meaning," diverted attention from the behavioral aspects of speech.[44]

How effectively they did so is made clear by the same early quotation. In post-Austinian, post-*Investigations* times, one reads with astonishment, "Assertion is merely psychological." Is commanding, too, merely psychological? Is questioning? Or praying, cursing, greeting, thanking, giving instructions? "If I had to say what is the main mistake made by philosophers of the present generation, including Moore," Wittgenstein later observed, "I would say that it is that when language is looked at, what is looked at is a form of words and not the use made of the form of words."[45] He knew whereof he spoke.

Investigations §24 sharpens the focus: "What is a question?'— Is it the statement that I do not know such-and-such, or the statement that I wish the other person would tell me...? Or is it the description of my mental state of uncertainty?" Sooner or later, queries like these must have plagued the author of 4.5. How could a question be made to say, "This is how things stand"? How could it be made to fit 4.5's prescription? The query that concerns us here is why it had to fit that Procrustean bed. If young Wittgenstein's arguments were so weak, what influences worked, secretly and powerfully, to generate his essentialistic convictions? Between them, Wittgenstein's pre- and post-*Tractatus* writings provide numerous leads.

"A *picture* held us captive," *Investigations* §115 explains, with reference to 4.5. "And we could not get outside it, for it lay in our language and language seemed to repeat it to us inexorably." General terms beguile us. "We are inclined to think that there must be something in common to all games, say, and that this common property is the justification for applying the general term 'game' to the various games."[46] So thought Russell, Moore, and Frege.[47] So thought young Wittgenstein, with regard, for instance, to the terms *Satz* and *Sprache.* If the word is one, so is the reality.

With this instance perhaps in mind, *Investigations* §104 remarks, "We predicate of the thing what lies in the method of representing it"; then adds: "Impressed by the possibility of a comparison, we think we are perceiving a state of affairs of the highest generality." Such was the origin of the *Tractatus*'s picture theory of propositions and of language. An account of a trial, in which an accident was reenacted by means of dolls and tiny buses,[48] triggered the thought: "In the proposition a world is as it were put together experimentally."[49] Gripped by this revelation, Wittgenstein sketched two stick figures that might be used to assert, "A is fencing with B," then declared: "It must be possible to demonstrate everything essential by considering this case."[50]

"It is the characteristic thing about such a theory," Wittgenstein later commented, "that it looks at a special clearly intuitive case and says: '*That* shews how things are in every case; this case is the exemplar of *all* cases . . . The tendency to generalise the [clear] case seems to have a strict justification in logic: here one seems *completely* justified in inferring: 'If *one* proposition is a picture, then any proposition must be a picture, for they must all be of the same nature.'"[51] Why would we use the same name for all if they were not all basically similar?[52]

Such essentialism is self-confirming. Instilling a "contemptuous attitude towards the particular case,"[53] it makes "the philosopher dismiss as irrelevant the concrete cases, which alone could have helped him to understand the usage of the general term."[54] Failing to find a ready answer to his question ("What is language?," "What is a proposition?"), he may conclude that if the answer is not obvious, then obvious phenomena cannot be relevant to his problem; the answer must surely be something quite different, something concealed beneath the things we all observe.[55]

"'*The essence is hidden from us*': this is the form our problem now assumes," *Investigations* §92 comments. "We ask: '*What is* language?', '*What is* a proposition?' And the answer to these questions is to be given once for all; and independently of any future experience." The self-referential nature of this remark is unmistakable, for young Wittgenstein had written: "In giving the general form of a proposition you are explaining what kind of ways of putting together the symbols of things and relations will correspond to (be analogous to) the things having those relations in reality. In doing thus you are saying what is meant by saying that a proposition is true; and you must do it once for all."[56]

In passages like these, we detect the influence of theoretical aspirations as well as of words. "Our craving for generality," the *Blue Book* suggests,

> has another main source: our preoccupation with the method of science. I mean the method of reducing the explanation of natural phenomena to the smallest possible number of primitive natural laws; and, in mathematics, of unifying the treatment of different topics by using a generalization. Philosophers constantly see the method of science before their eyes, and are irresistibly tempted to ask and answer questions in the way science does. This tendency is the real source of metaphysics, and leads the philosopher into complete darkness.[57]

Russell preached scientific method in philosophy,[58] and young Wittgenstein concurred. He reduced all propositions and all uses of language to just one kind, subject to the smallest possible number of primitive laws: the truth-functional calculus. He unified the whole of logic by means of a single general form.[59] And not just the whole of logic. The *Investigations'* reminiscences evoke an all-embracing scheme: "Thought is surrounded by a halo.—Its essence, logic, presents an order, in fact the a priori order of the world: that is, the order of *possibilities*, which must be common to both world and thought."[60] "Thought, language, now appear to us as the unique correlate, picture, of the world. These concepts: proposition, language, thought, world, stand in line one behind the other, each equivalent to each."[61]

Once admit fuzzy diversity into each of these concepts—*proposition, language, thought, world*—and logic would no longer be all-embracing,[62] would no longer be transcendental,[63] would no longer mirror the world,[64] as Wittgenstein had supposed. The "great mirror" would be shattered, and a labyrinth,[65] a maze,[66] would replace it. Thus, the essentialistic formulae of the *Tractatus* answered the burning question of Wittgenstein's youth, as only essentialistic formulae could. "The great problem round which everything that I write turns is: Is there an order in the world *a priori*, and if so what does it consist in?"[67] An *a priori* order would be one that held regardless of what was the case, one required by sheer logic before all examination of contingent states of affairs. But that would be the order which founded the possibility of propositions as such, whether true or false. "My *whole* task," Wittgenstein concluded, "consists in explaining the nature of the proposition."[68]

The order he sought was, in his later characterization, "a *super*-order between—so to speak—*super*-concepts." For its rationale was not purely scientific. "The solutions of the problems of logic must be simple," Wittgenstein had declared, "since they set the standard of simplicity. Men have always had a presentiment that there must be a realm in which the answers to questions are symmetrically combined—*a priori*—to form a self-contained system. A realm subject to the law: *Simplex sigillum veri.*"[69] The alleged reason is feeble and the alleged sentiment dubious; but whatever others may have believed, this was clearly how Wittgenstein thought.

Earlier, in the *Notebooks*, he attempted no justification, but declared: "The solution to all my questions must be *extremely* simple."[70] Why? Whence this demand? A preference for the simple, stark, and unadorned characterized Wittgenstein's taste not only in philosophy but also in writing, furnishings, food, art, architecture, dress, speech, possessions, personal relations, and life generally. Hence his early essentialism can plausibly be traced, in large measure, to the factor William James stressed: temperament. Russell, too, aspired to be "scientific," but nothing in his thought matched the radical, essentialistic simplicity of the Tractarian structure, matching proposition, language, thought, and world, "each equivalent to each."

The *Tractatus*'s agenda was negative as well as positive, and the negative agenda had equal need of essences. "The aim of the book," the Preface explained, "is to set a limit to thought, or rather—not to thought, but to the expression of thoughts: for in order to be able to set a limit to thought, we should have to find both sides of the limit thinkable (i.e. we should have to be able to think what cannot be thought). It will will therefore only be in language that the limit can be set, and what lies on the other side of the limit will simply be nonsense."[71] The essences of language and of thought drew the desired borderline, via the essence of propositions, as their later replacements could not have. To say, "This and this alone is thought," would do the trick; to say, "This, that, and the other, and somewhat similar things, are thought,"[72] would not.

"This is not ignorance," Wittgenstein later maintained. "We do not know the boundaries because none have been drawn. To repeat, we can draw a boundary—for a special purpose."[73] What was the *Tractatus*'s purpose? Why did it have this new, negative need of essences, and produce them to order? Evidence points in different directions—some in a positivist direction, some in a Schopenhauerian, some in a Kantian. For present purposes, I shall just confirm the importance of the aim the Preface announced. Explaining his book in a letter, Wittgenstein wrote: "My work consists of two parts: the one presented here plus all that I have *not* written. And it is precisely this second part that is the important one."[74] According to a close friend at the time, "Positivism holds—and this is its essence—that what we can speak about is all that matters in life. *Whereas Wittgenstein passionately believes that all that really matters in human life is precisely what, in his view, we must be silent about.*"[75]

Passion, I suggest, played a more significant role in generating the *Tractatus*'s essentialistic theses than did sketchy subsequent arguments like those in 4.021 and 4.5. So did language. So did temperament. So did scientific aspirations. So, too, did the milieu in which young Wittgenstein did his philosophizing—a milieu much given, for example, to insisting on sharp distinctions.

"'What *exactly* do you mean?' was the phrase most frequently on our lips," recounts Keynes of the climate at Cambridge. "If it appeared under cross-examination that you did not mean *exactly* anything, you lay under a strong suspicion of meaning nothing whatever."[76] Thus Russell could write: "You can, for instance, say: 'There are a number of people in this room at this moment.' That is obviously in some sense undeniable. But when you come to try and define what this room is, and what it is for a person to be in a room, and how you are going to distinguish one person from another, and so forth, you find that what you have said is most fearfully vague and that you really do not know what you meant."[77] Logic and its concepts—*Satz, Wort, Sprache*—would have to be different. They would have to be "pure and clear-cut."[78] And they were, thanks to the *Tractatus*'s essences. With unity went definiteness: single forms traced sharp borders. Hence the forms' attractiveness.

Lacking clarity and rigor, familiar modes of speech could not serve as a standard. It is plausible to suppose that in his "scientific" youth Wittgenstein felt no more concern about the everyday use of *Satz* than he showed in giving his own, narrow sense to the words *Sinn* and *Bedeutung* and ignoring their broader sense in familiar usage. The restriction of *Satz* to truth-functional assertions of states of affairs, leaving out myriad utterances commonly called *Sätze*, would parallel his limitation of *Bedeutung* to referents, leaving logical, mathematical, and many other signs without any *Bedeutung;* it would parallel his restriction of *Sinn* to possible states of affairs, so that logical, mathematical, and many other statements had no *Sinn.* Justification of such moves may be implicit in *Tractatus* 3.323-3.325: if people commonly employ the term *Satz* in a vague, ambiguous manner to designate all sorts of things, the sooner we remedy the situation, the better.[79]

In this and other ways I have noted, Wittgenstein, like Scheler, was freed from the constraints of linguistic usage. Like Scheler, he was strongly, variously motivated to avail himself of this freedom in the essentialistic manner he came to regret. "When philosophers use a word—'knowledge,' 'being,' 'object,' 'I,' 'proposition,' 'name'—and try to grasp the *essence* of the thing," he later advised, "one must always ask oneself: is the word ever actually used in this way in the language-game which is its original home."[80] Clearly that was a question with which the author of the *Tractatus* did not trouble himself, in 4.001, 4.5, or kindred declarations.

Calculus-Reasoning: Pitcher

References to George Pitcher's *The Philosophy of Wittgenstein* recur through the text and notes of chapter 3. In the space of two pages, Pitcher: 1) argues, calculus-wise, that Wittgenstein's identification of word meaning and word-use is "implausible on the face of it," since tools, for example, have uses but do not have meanings; 2) argues similarly that meaning-use equivalence does not hold for words since it does not hold for proper names, which have uses but not meanings; 3) proposes a variant of Waismann's objection, supposing similar uniformity, in *know* as in *learn;* 4) assumes calculus-like linkage between *mean* and *meaning;* and 5), after noting §43's qualification ("for a *large* class of cases—though not for all"), essentializes Wittgenstein's position much as others have.[81] Here, then, is an author deserving diagnostic consideration.

The frequency of Pitcher's essentialistic moves suggests that they are not mere aberrations, but represent a habit of thought; and the abundance of similar moves cited in chapter 3 indicates that Pitcher's manner is not a personal idiosyncracy. Calculus-reasoning has enjoyed wide vogue as a standard form of supposedly rigorous argumentation. Its power as an influential paradigm can be judged from its persistence even in a philosopher like Pitcher, who repudiated essentialism.

"Whereas," he observed, "one had always quite uncritically, and most likely also unconsciously, taken it for granted that all things called by a general term had something—an essence—in common, he sees now that it is not necessarily so. At one stroke, that assumption has been revealed and destroyed. As it falls away, one's entire view of language, and indeed of the world, is quite altered."[82] But not necessarily one's accustomed style of argumentation.

Why, though, does calculus-reasoning appear with such special prominence in these specific pages of Pitcher's study? A further contrast offers a clue. The text of page 252 links *mean* and *meaning,* in the manner we have seen, citing what things mean in an argument about meanings: "Things which may sometimes have meanings—or (in case nothing nonlinguistic can be said to *have* a meaning) things which may sometimes mean something—(e.g., black clouds on the horizon, footprints in the snow, the rising pitch of someone's voice) do not, except rarely, have uses." Later on the page, a footnote unlinks the same two terms: "This is not to deny that proper names have connotation, nor that proper names can mean something to someone—but to admit these things is not to admit that they have meaning." How can we account for this discrepancy? It may be no coincidence that both moves serve Pitcher's argumentative purposes. His oversight in the text permits his argument from clouds, footprints, and the like to proceed; his carefulness in the note protects his argument from proper names. The will, one suspects, may have been at work.[83]

Pitcher *wanted* to refute §43, *wanted* his refutation to succeed. But why? Because, like J. N. Findlay in his *Wittgenstein: A Critique,* he wanted anything and everything Wittgenstein wrote to be wrong? Because, for some unknown reason, he wanted §43 to be wrong? Or because, having the impression that §43 was in fact wrong, he wished to show it was, by arguments? All three forms of influence are common, but as an explanation here, the third seems nearest the mark.

I do not mean to suggest that for Pitcher any argumentative stick was good enough to beat Wittgenstein's proposal with, or that he formulated arguments he knew were fallacious. The proposal looked wrong, and it looked wrong, at least in part, because the arguments looked good. Just why they did invites further explanation.

A natural suggestion concerning Waismann's defective argument, Pitcher's variant, and several other arguments in chapter 3 is that they result from "mere oversight," as do, for instance, various "fallacies of ambiguity" or "fallacies of equivocation." The author simply overlooked a shift of sense. This suggestion contains a kernel of truth, but calls for two comments: first, "mere oversight" does not adequately characterize even fallacies of ambiguity; second, "shift of sense" obscures an important difference between fallacies of ambiguity and even those calculus-fallacies of chapter 3 which most resemble them. Let me elaborate.

When someone sends a letter and forgets to attach a stamp, or writes a check and forgets to sign it, that may be a "mere oversight." But fallacies of ambiguity have a standard cause: likeness of expression veils a difference of sense. It is evident, for instance, why fallacies of four terms occur: it is because, phonetically or graphically, only three terms appear. Unpack the ambiguous expression, state its two senses, and no such error would occur. Textbooks need not warn against syllogisms that contain four *explicitly formulated* terms.

As the last chapter noted, surface similarity hiding sub-surface dissimilarity helps to account for essentialism, too, in theory and in practice. However, when logicians speak of fallacies of "ambiguity," in textbook or in real-life cases, they have relatively gross discrepancies in view. No one is likely to propose, or to be fooled by, an argument such as: "The end of a thing is its perfection; death is the end of life; hence, death is the perfection of life." The shift from "end" as goal to "end" as termination is too obvious. Even in real-life examples, the semantic differences are large enough to warrant talk of "ambiguity," "equivocation," or "different senses." One time *law* denotes a regularity, another time a command; one time *reason* denotes a cause, another time a motive; one time *natural* has a descriptive sense, another time an evaluative sense. In the past, shifts of this magnitude elicited talk of "analogy," whereas lesser variations were deemed compatible with "univocity," "sameness of sense," and underlying "essences." Chapter 3's samples are of this second variety; their shifts of sense are less notable. Even those most similar to typical fallacies of ambiguity call for different analytic terminology. Thus, with regard to Pitcher's Waismannian argument, chapter 3 noted that "knowing the meaning, whether wholly or partially, would still be knowing, in much the same sense of knowing; and the meaning, whether part or whole, would still be meaning, in much the same sense of meaning." The same holds for *use* as applied to tools and *use* as applied to words, in Pitcher's first argument, and for *use* as applied to words and *use* as applied to proper names, in his second argument.

These contrasts—considerable versus slight, obvious versus subtle—evoke causal conjectures. Generally speaking, the less considerable a semantic difference is, the less obvious it is. The less obvious it is, the likelier it is to be overlooked. The more likely it is to be overlooked, the likelier it is to occasion fallacious reasoning. Since, however, the differences ignored by calculus-reasoning such as I have cited are still less obvious than those that account for fallacies of ambiguity, such calculus-reasoning is still likelier than fallacies of ambiguity (frequent though the latter may be). Chapter 3 supports this hypothesis. So do further reflections on the sources of Pitcher's reasoning.

Another verbal influence may help to account for slips occasioned by verbs like *learn* and *know*. "In customary English," chapter 3 observed, "to know, learn, see, remember, hear, cite,... X does not entail knowing, learning, seeing, remembering, hearing, citing ... the whole of X." Sometimes these verbs are employed all-inclusively, sometimes not. This difference, I suggested, escaped Waismann's and Pitcher's notice when, in their critiques of §43, they assumed comprehensive learning or knowing. Perhaps, I now add, their oversight was assisted by the fact—if fact it is—that most verbs reveal no such part-whole fluctuation. Perhaps they assumed a comprehensive use, not only because verbs like *know* and *learn* have comprehensive applications as well as noncomprehensive, but because *carry, bring, send, give, lift, fire,* and countless other verbs have nothing but comprehensive, total-object uses. A person who carries a box or an insurance policy carries the whole of it; a person who sends a letter or an apology sends the whole of it; a person who fires a cannon or an employee fires the whole cannon or employee; and so forth. (I purposely mix the verbs' objects to make the suggestion still more plausible.) If comprehensive use is the rule and noncomprehensive use the exception, Waismann's and Pitcher's oversights become more intelligible. They would hardly have made the assumptions they did, had noncomprehensive use been the rule rather than the exception.

But is comprehensive use the rule? Consider *carry*. Granted, even when two men carry a table, each carries the whole table, though not by himself. If, however, a man "carries his lunch to work," does that preclude his adding so much as salt from the table or water from the faucet? If a woman, come spring, "carries out her potted plants,".must she carry out every last one of them? *Carry*, too, shows part-whole flexibility. Similar exceptions can be found for *bring, send, give, lift, fire*. The lady who "gave her fortune to charity" doubtless kept a few dollars for herself; the boss who "fired his critics" fired just those who worked for him.

Perhaps, then, the hypothesis should be made to read: "Whole-object *uses* far outnumber part-object uses," rather than: "Consistently whole-object *verbs* far outnumber verbs that switch." Thus altered, the hypothesis becomes more plausible, yet loses little of its explanatory power. In either supposition, the weak or the strong, a further dimension of verbal witchery supplements the simple fact that the single verb *learn* or *know* hides two different uses.

However, it does make a difference which conjecture is correct. The more numerous consistent verbs are, the more feasible are calculus-like arguments employing them; the more feasible the arguments, the more common; the more common, the stronger their influence. Given abundant consistent verbs, an explanation for such reasoning could be found in frequent like-sounding argumentation that was reassuringly valid.

To be sure, arguments relying on this particular type of consistency in this particular class of words (transitive verbs) represent a fraction of all demonstrations. The illustration, however, stands for something larger. If words in general—verbs, nouns, adjectives, adverbs—were quite regular, calculus-like argumentation would be more feasible and therefore more common. Being more common and more valid, it would foster the tendency to so argue even when employing less reliably regular terms. Paradoxically, fallacious calculus-reasoning like that in chapter 3 would be both less likely and more likely: less likely because the words employed would more frequently lend themselves to calculus-like employment; more likely because reasoners would be less alert to the danger, being influenced by a greater mass of valid calculus-reasoning and by acquaintance with a language that made such reasoning look safe.

As it is, thinkers like those in chapter 3 show little awareness of the dangers that confront them. The reason, I suggest, is not that language is highly regular, nor that they all believe it is regular, but that they do not attend to language sufficiently. Had Pitcher, for example, asked himself in his first argument, "Is *use* employed so uniformly that if word-uses were meanings tool-uses would be too?," no doubt he would have given the right answer and would not have argued as he did. Had he asked himself a similar question in the course of his second argument, concerning the "use" of words and of proper names, he would have abandoned that argument as well. Had he turned his attention to the verb *know* in the third argument, rather than simply using it, and asked himself whether its customary use was regular enough to support his argumentation, the chances are good that this argument, too, would have succumbed.

Chapter 6 considered various reasons for inattention to words, without specific reference to the calculus-reasoning Pitcher exemplifies. The preceding discussion suggests a more focused hypothesis. We might suppose that meaning-shifts belong to one or the other of the following three categories: (1) too big and obvious to be dangerous; (2) big enough to affect the validity of arguments, subtle enough to be dangerous; (3) slight enough to escape notice yet too slight to affect the validity of arguments; so not dangerous. To judge from the standard prophylaxis provided by logic texts, the middle zone, which alone looks dangerous, is one where terms are "ambiguous," "analogous," "shift their senses," or "have more than one sense." Lesser variations are cause for less concern; so long as a term retains the "same sense" and is not used "ambiguously," it is not likely to affect an argument's validity.

Pitcher's arguments, the arguments of chapter 3, and those of subsequent chapters all attest how mistaken this impression is. They also furnish evidence, in addition to standard logic-text treatments, that the impression is widespread. If I termed it a majority opinion, there would be more difficulty with the second term (*opinion*) than with the first (*majority*).

This distinction is important. If formulated as an opinion, the impression would be questioned and put to the test, and once tested, would be rejected. Slight semantic shifts can, indeed, make a big difference; they can invalidate important arguments. The less people are aware of this fact, the more likely they are to formulate such arguments. In fact, the general inattention fostered by this impression may have more causal significance than the individual, specific tricks of language I have cited above. However, whatever the relative importance of the specific and the general, both help to explain reasoning like Pitcher's.

Network-Reasoning: Graham

Chapter 4 cited Keith Graham's treatment of performatives and truth as an example of "network-reasoning." For Graham, regardless of what familiar usage may suggest, all and only those utterances are true which "correspond to the facts," as performatives may.[84] Regardless of how Austin and others employ the term *performative,* all and only those utterances which bring about the truth of the content they express as a consequence of people's so regarding them, are genuine performatives.[85] Graham links the two concepts—*true* and *performative*—essentialistically.

Baker and Hacker's linking of meaning and understanding figures more prominently in chapter 4 than Graham's linking of truth and performatives. However, the reasons for Graham's essentializing rise more clearly to the surface, and nicely complement the etiology revealed or surmised in preceding sections of this chapter. Whereas Scheler and young Wittgenstein ignored the standard employment of their essentialistic labels, Graham attended to customary usage and spurned it. So I shall focus on these two questions: Why did he take such a cavalier attitude toward familiar terminology, and why did he spurn it in favor of essences?

The reply to the first question, briefly put, is that he saw no other reason for respecting current word-uses than the reason Austin suggested, and that he repudiated that reason, as he understood it.[86] In a famous passage, Austin had written:

> Our common stock of words embodies all the distinctions men have found worth drawing, and the connexions they have found worth marking, in the lifetimes of many generations: these surely are likely to be more numerous, more sound, since they have stood up to the long test of the survival of the fittest, and more subtle, at least in all ordinary and reasonably practical matters, than any that you or I are likely to think up in our arm-chairs of an afternoon—the most favoured alternative method.[87]

"In short," comments Graham, "the concepts we already operate with have a claim to superiority, for otherwise they would not have survived but would have been replaced by more adequate ones."[88] "As far as I can discover, the only general argument Austin ever puts forward in favour of such conservatism is this neo-Darwinian one. It is therefore crucial to his case, and we shall see that unfortunately it is a very bad argument."[89] No other argument—no other virtue of semantic conservatism—occurs to Graham. Hence existing, accepted ways of talking must be put to exactly the same tests as innovative ways. Only a faulty evolutionary argument like Austin's could exempt them.[90]

Graham's blindness to the communicative virtues of familiarity is striking, both in general and on particular occasions. In one place he writes: "It should be noted that the scope of 'we' in this talk of *what we should say when* must be something like all, or most, competent native English-speakers. It could hardly be thought to hold any philosophical interest that I and a few other people in a room gave a particular reply to the question 'What should we say when . . . ?' unless this did hold some such wider implication."[91] For Austin, as read by Graham, the interest comes from the evolution of the language, in the whole population. But the same facts hold a significance which Graham never adverts to: this is the community we must communicate with; this is the idiom people know. The implication for effective communication is clear. And the relevance of effective communication for a language is equally clear—provided we do not confuse the language with what is communicated by its means, as Graham does.

This confusion, which runs through his book,[92] appears with special clarity when he writes (the emphasis is mine): "There is this permanent possibility of conflict both between different *languages* or *conceptual systems* and within one conceptual system. When such conflicts cry out for resolution, the conservatism which the neo-Darwinian argument is used to justify will be worse than useless, for there is nothing at all to be said for the preservation of incompatible *theories*."[93] Elsewhere he insists: "We may have many reasons, good or bad, for saying or not saying something, and it is our reasons, rather than our not saying something, which are of paramount importance."[94] Take "saying something" in the sense of making a claim, and this assertion is true; take "saying something" in the sense of employing an idiom, and the assertion is false. Graham does not advert to this distinction. Neither does he attend to the fact that our saying or not saying something, in the sense of customarily employing or not employing a certain form of speech, is of paramount importance for effective communication. He is far, therefore, from adopting a positive presumption in favor of existing usage. If anything, his bias favors revision.[95]

By itself, even such bias would not open the way to essentialism. Nothing but meaning-stipulations or Carnapian explications might result, all recognized, identified, and argued as such. A person who suggests, "Let us restrict the term X to all and only things that share property Y," betrays no essentialism; a person who affirms, "All and only those things which share property Y are X's," may, depending on the property Y. The latter mode of speech is Graham's, and stems, as often, from the conflation of medium and message.

At this point, such a conflation assumes double significance. First, it blocks recognition of familiar usage's advantages. Second, it blocks recognition that, if customary usage must be revised, the revision should take the form of a meaning-stipulation and not a theory. In these and other ways (chapter 6), the medium-message conflation leads to the proliferation of theories. These need not be essentialistic. Though the conflation is a key factor permitting essentialism, it is not immediately evident how it might predispose to essentialism. Thus, though it is clear by now why Graham took such a cavalier attitude towards familiar usage, it is not yet clear why he spurned familiar usage in favor of essences.

Graham is as explicit on this score as on his attitude toward familiar usage: his preference is for unity and simplicity. Thanks to his conflation of meaning and theory, this preference gets equated with a preference for "theoretical economy."

> A narrow theory is preferable *for theoretical reasons.* One such reason is that it meets the demands of theoretical economy. Occam's razor bids us not to multiply theoretical entities beyond necessity, and the narrow theory obeys this injunction by not multiplying the senses of a word or sentence beyond necessity. In aiming to associate just one sense with some verbal form it aims for theoretical simplicity, in contrast to a wide theory which will postulate a change in the meaning of a given verbal form whenever there is a change in any of a large number of factors governing its total import.[96]

Suppose we apply this viewpoint to a word like *deep,* with its multiple variations, for deep water, deep blue, deep sorrow, deep meaning, deep voices, and so forth. Have these senses proliferated "beyond necessity"? Certainly beyond any "theoretical" necessity. Yet one senses that this very proliferation of senses speaks in their favor. If human beings have found it natural to extend terms in this manner, human beings will find it natural to use them and understand them in this manner. The instrument will be well fitted to the user's hand.

This illustration may seem inappropriate for discussion of high-class concepts like *true,* but it raises a general issue. The majority of general terms reveal multiple senses, and variations within each sense. Is this a defect of ordinary language or a merit? Does it facilitate communication or impede it? Would efficiency be better served by a different term for each sense or by the existing multiplicity? Would it be better served by a still more abundant terminology, with a different term for each variation within each sense? Certainly communication would not be facilitated by replacing our color terms, say, by terms for each shade of each color (each shade, not only of red, but of crimson, rose, magenta, scarlet, and the rest). Where does the optimum balance lie?

Questions like those above do not interest Graham. His interest is in theory, not in communication. For he views concepts as theories, not as instruments of communication. Thus in his case, as in others', the medium-message conflation not only opens the door to essentialism but invites it in. Surely a simple, unified *theory* is preferable to a complex, disjunctive one.

Graham gives "a second theoretical reason in favour of a narrow theory":

> One task for any theory of meaning is to explain how we manage at all to use the sounds and marks of language to talk about a world quite separate from them. And one aspect in particular of this process calls for explanation—what I call the essential generality or re-applicability of language . . . To postulate a sense associated with a given verbal form is to suggest a route from language to the world. And to postulate *one* such sense leads us to abstract from all the particular circumstances in which that verbal form is used, to move away from superficial features up to a higher level of generality in extracting what is common to all those circumstances, and thus to show how we can use the verbal form in innumerable different situations and be understood. In contrast, if the meaning of sentences like these is constantly changing according to circumstances, then it becomes more of a mystery how we can use them and be understood at all.[97]

Were essentialistic uniformity the rule rather than the (questionable) exception, language would indeed be a less puzzling phenomenon. Were *deep,* for example, used only for depth in feet, meters, fathoms, or the like, and not for the depth of colors, feelings, meanings, voices, or notes, the term's "re-applicability" and its utility in speaking about a separate world (only oceans, wells, and the like, not colors, feelings, voices, notes, etc.) would be more readily intelligible. The simple is simpler to grasp. But such an example clearly indicates that language does not obey a law of "theoretical economy." It does not obey any theoretical law, for its purpose is practical not theoretical. Whereas theories tend to unify, language tends to diversify. Its concepts spread. A concept that did not spread—that retained a single, invariant sense in all circumstances—would be as unusual as a drop of ink or water that, dropped on a blotter, retained its initial pinpoint shape. Graham's readiness to postulate and seek "what is common" may reflect, again, his conflation of language and theory and his inattention to language as language—that is, as medium not message.

Varied interests, needs, analogies, connections, and associations influence the application of terms in ways that diversify them. Graham's tendency, when he encounters the resulting multiplicity and heterogeneity in a term of theoretical interest, is to suppose that the populace has erred en masse. The varied interests, needs, analogies, connections, and associations that influence speakers carry little weight with him. Theoretical needs for simplicity and uniformity dominate. Whatever is theoretically preferable is alone correct. People were mistaken to call whales fish. People are mistaken to withhold the word *true* from performatives. People are mistaken in their conceptual systems as well as in their individual utterances.

Graham's extension of *true* and *false* to conceptual frameworks as well as to statements looks important for his essentialism as a whole, since it systematically blurs the distinction between medium and message. His justification is revealing: "Given the criteria used in evaluating them, a choice between different frameworks is anything but arbitrary. But more than that, it is governed by just the same sort of considerations as enter into deciding the truth or falsity of many statements made *within* a framework."[98] In either type of decision, a person may "need to explain the meaning and the point of the terms he uses, show how they connect with other terms, and show how they embody a mode of organisation and interpretation which is plausible, coherent, adequate, fruitful, etc., in relation to the data they apply to."[99] He will not simply accept familiar expressions and meanings and, focusing his attention on the data, determine if the expressions apply; nor will he adopt a new terminology, then determine if the new expressions apply. No, *datur tertium*: one may muddle medium and message, systematically. Assimilate individual judgments with framework choices, as Graham does, and framework choices will look as deserving of the labels *true* and *false* as individual judgments are.

Graham here speaks of how terms "connect with" other terms. Elsewhere he advises that, if analysis reveals no compelling grounds for using or not using a given concept, we shall have to base our decision on, among other things, whether the concept "fits in well with" other concepts we employ.[100] This injunction may be understood pragmatically or theoretically. Pragmatically, a language resembles a tool kit. Its general terms resemble socket wrenches, some large, some small, and each useful within its own range of generality. Essentialistic revisions often weaken a language pragmatically, by making a term more general or more specific and thereby depriving the language of an instrument at the level of generality the term previously occupied while creating useless duplication at the new level.[101] If love, for example, is equated with any attraction, whether between people or between stars, two terms now do the work of one and none does the work of *love*. If love is restricted rather than extended—if, for example, it is equated with Christian agape—the result is the same: needless duplication at one level, a gaping hole at another.

Such might be the meaning of terms' "fitting in well" with others. Significantly, nothing of the kind appears in Graham's discussions. His focus remains theoretical. Consider, for example, the reasons he alleges for confining the term *performative* to utterances which bring about the truth of the content they express as a consequence of people's so regarding them. This position, he acknowledges, "may seem bizarre. It was Austin who coined the term 'performative,' introduced it by way of examples, explained their nature and finally abandoned the notion, or at least the belief that performatives could be contrasted with other utterances in a straightforward way. I have disagreed with his characterisation and denied that many of his examples are really performative at all. How can this be?"[102] Graham's point is that "once the term is introduced to apply to very special examples it is better to confine its application to other cases which share in this specialness, and find some other term for the similarity between these original examples and many other, more 'normal' statements . . . Otherwise, we run the risk of obscuring or overlooking what is very special in the nature of utterances like 'I bet you it will rain' and 'I leave my watch to my brother.'"[103]

Austin might have replied both theoretically and pragmatically to this theory-focused argument, in ways that would reveal the essentialistic thrust of Graham's theorizing and the blindness to linguistic pragmatics that partially accounts for it. Theoretically, Austin might have pointed out that some similarities would be obscured and some highlighted whether one restricted the term *performative* or extended it.[104] Restricting the term would highlight the similarities between explicit performatives; extending it would highlight the similarities between explicit performatives and inexplicit or "primary" performatives. Pragmatically, another term could be found to bring out either set of neglected similarities. A standard, effective alternative is to extend a general term to signal similarities and append a modifier to signal dissimilarities.[105] One may speak of a "*flying* machine," a "*video*-game," a "*complex* number"—or of "*primary* performatives."

Pragmatically or theoretically, then, Austin's way of speaking looks defensible. But no essences result from it. What appealed to Graham was the impression that he had discovered the hidden secret—the sharply defining essence—of performatives. Going by standard usage, Austin had denied that most performatives are true or false. Rejecting the verdict of standard usage, Graham argued that all genuine performatives—the ones he recognized as such—are true or false. Thus refined, the two concepts—*true* and *performative*—meshed nicely. They formed an essentialistic network.

As Graham's practice shows, essentializing can take either direction: it can narrow concepts (as for *performative*) or extend them (as for *true*). This is predictable. An essence must be common to all and only the members of some class. If the word's customary use conflicts with "all," the concept can be restricted; if the word's customary use conflicts with "only," the concept can be extended. Networking needs may also dictate direction. An essence of performatives may require restriction of the concept *performative* and extension of the concept *true*. For an essence to result from such contraction or expansion, concepts must be seen as theories, and conceptual revisions as innovative views of reality.

Therewith, the process becomes self-confirming. "We are familiar by now with the idea," writes Graham, "that if an analysis is sufficiently powerful, explanatory, etc., then this can itself be used as an argument against employing that concept in some situation which is not consonant with the analysis—even if, prior to formulating the analysis, people would be disposed to."[106] Austin, for example, was inclined to use the term *performative* more broadly than Graham; but Graham's "analysis" shows itself to be "powerful" by allowing him to deal with borderline cases,[107] and shows itself to be "explanatory" by allowing him to connect performatives with truth, thereby revealing the true "nature" of performatives.[108] The analysis "shows in a clear and non-obvious way how performatives work."[109]

In fact, Graham's account possesses none of these virtues. It indicates nothing new about the nature or working of performatives,[110] but if anything obscures their function, which typically is not to report or describe themselves.[111] And it reveals no differences previously concealed when, in deciding borderline cases, it declares these utterances to be genuine performatives, those not. The same demarcation could be effected, and often has been, without restricting the concept *performative* or extending the concept *true*. People could continue to speak of "explicit" performatives (for example, "I apologize") and "inexplicit" or "primary" performatives (for example, "I am sorry") for the same reasons as before.[112] Only the conflation of language and theory makes Graham's moves look momentous. Verbal shifts are viewed as substantive, and are therefore assessed by inappropriate standards.

In retrospect, it appears that the medium-message conflation played a triple role—permitting, inviting, confirming—in Graham's essentialistic networking. Its influence was decisive.[113]

Other-Worlds Reasoning: Kripke

"We do not begin," writes Kripke, "with worlds (which are supposed somehow to be real, and whose qualities, but not whose objects, are perceptible to us), and then ask about criteria of transworld identification; on the contrary, we begin with the objects, which we *have*, and can identify, in the actual world. We can then ask whether certain things might have been true of the objects."[114] Holding these pieces firmly in our fingers, we can ask what squares they might be moved to on the board, what pieces they might take, what pieces they might be taken by, while remaining their fixed, invariant, unmistakable selves. Such is the impression often given by Kripke's discussion of individual identity, as rigidly determined by names. Whence this essentialistic rigidity? Whence this sameness of all names, for persons, bodies, minds, or tables, attested for example by Kripke's "principle of the necessity of identities using rigid designators"?[115]

Kripke's repeated contrast between other-world objects and those "which we *have*, and can identify, in the actual world" suggests a first hypothesis. It has been observed that in Kripke's doctrine "the difference between speaking *with respect* to some possible world, and speaking *in* such a world, is crucial."[116] This saying may be truer than intended. The distinction prevents misunderstandings and invalid objections, it is true, but it may also generate confusion. In the world in which we speak, reference may seem perfectly definite. ("We can point to the *man*, and ask what might have happened to *him* had events been different."[117]) Since the speaker-world determines the meaning and reference of the terms we employ, this definiteness may appear to carry over to other, possible worlds. ("We are speaking of *Nixon* and asking what, in certain counterfactual situations, would have been true of *him*."[118]) But this is an illusion. Knowing precisely who or what we are speaking of among actual referents does not imply knowing who or what would count as the same referent in counterfactual discourse.

The sense-reference distinction, especially as viewed by Kripke, may work a like effect. A designator's reference, he insists, is not fixed by its sense. To indicate sense is one thing; to indicate reference is another. True, a description may serve to fix a name's reference; but the name is not synonymous with the description. Thoughts like these may deflect attention from the fact that the referent does possess properties; that indicating what referent a name picks out is not equivalent to indicating what, precisely, that referent comprises (with respect to past, present, or future properties, necessary or contingent, intrinsic or extrinsic); that the questions left behind as problems of intension remain to be dealt with as problems of extension. The result may be an impression of referential simplicity and definiteness, and a theoretical void such as chapter 5 noted in Kripke's doctrine.

Wittgenstein's self-diagnosis signals other, complementary possibilities in Kripke's case. "The basic evil of Russell's logic, as also of mine in the *Tractatus*," Wittgenstein wrote, "is that what a proposition is is illustrated by a few commonplace examples, and then pre-supposed as understood in full generality."[119] Kripke, too, illustrates his view by means of a few examples—examples that often favor an essentialistic conception of names and their referents—and on the strength of these examples characterizes all names. Though the names of Venus vary (*Hesperus, Phosphorus, Evening Star, Morning Star*), the planet itself does not alter in shape, size, color, composition, or orbit round the sun. Other Kripkean referents—pi, the number 9, the square root of 81, the length one meter—are still less prone to fluctuation. If all names' referents resembled these, a comparison with invariant chess-pieces, moving from square to square, might be appropriate.

Contrast these paradigms with the case imagined in chapter 5. To challenge Kripke's principle of necessary identity, I had to imagine considerable variation in the same referent (from the person named Steve in infancy to the same person nicknamed Butch in college), and for that I had need of the temporal dimension. The planet Venus reveals no comparable development or alteration, at least within the time available for human naming. Pi, the number

9, the square root of 81, and the length one meter, not being temporal, preclude all variation. Take these paradigms, therefore, as revealing the nature of names, and identities using names are likely to look necessary.

However, why not simply take them as typical, or as typical with regard to necessary identity? Perhaps because necessity as well as universality would then be lost. If the identity of Steve and Butch, or Tully and Cicero, in possible worlds depended on when or how the two names were imposed (e.g., simultaneously or years apart) and not on the very nature of names and naming, the identity might sometimes be necessary, sometimes not. Indeed, in a basic sense it would always be contingent.

So the questions become: Why might necessity look desirable? Why might universality? Why did Kripke make no effort to test his principle by possible counter-cases? Why did he mount no argument to show their impossibility, or at least their improbability? On occasion Kripke disclaims any intention to formulate a "theory"; he is merely presenting a better "picture." Yet such is not his attitude vis-à-vis identity. All names, he maintains, are rigid designators; hence the principle of necessary identity applies to all names; hence Descartes's critics are wrong. No need to examine in detail how the name *Descartes* might be attached to a mind, or the name *B* to a body, or what the results of such labeling might be. So, again, how can we explain Kripke's readiness to universalize?

"Part of the point of the thesis of terminable analysis," it has been said, "is that explanation of meaning can come to a definitive end."[120] Kripke's conception looked similarly attractive. As in an earlier notion of ostensive definition, so also here, "explanation is . . . conceived to terminate in a final, unambiguous and definitive rule"[121]—a simple, rigid designator.

In addition, such a doctrine had theoretical significance. "It is a consequence of my conception of names as 'rigid designators'," Kripke remarked, "that codesignative proper names are interchangeable *salva veritate* in all contexts of (metaphysical) necessity and possibility; further, that replacement of a proper name by a codesignative name leaves the modal value of any sentence unchanged."[122] This consequence probably seemed an advantage. As Wittgenstein's picture theory assured bivalence and bivalence assured the universal applicability of truth-table logic, so Kripke's rigid designation assured necessary identity and necessary identity assured, or made possible, the universal applicability of modal logic.[123] No need to bother about possible exceptions. No need to add provisos or disclaimers.

Such consequences may have appeared attractive, whether for certain purposes (e.g., resolving the mind-body debate),[124] or more generally. Midway in his philosophical development, Wittgenstein confessed: "I fight continually—whether successfully or not I do not know—against the tendency in my own mind to set up (construct) rules in philosophy, and to make assumptions (hypotheses) instead of simply seeing what is there."[125] One senses a similar tension in Kripke's thinking. His principle of necessary identity looks like a theory. So does his claim that names, unlike descriptions, are all rigid designators. Yet he remarks that if that is what it is, "I'm sure it's wrong too."[126]

Kripke's resistance to theory might have proved more efficacious had he perceived more clearly why philosophical theories tend to be mistaken. He concedes that he has, in a way, proposed a theory of reference. However, "my characterization has been far less specific than a real set of necessary and sufficient conditions for reference would be.... So other conditions must be satisfied in order to make this into a really rigorous theory of reference."[127] He suspects that "one might never reach a set of necessary and sufficient conditions," but is not sure.[128] His skepticism is less decisive than Ayer's in chapter 2 and his hopes somewhat higher; yet the prospects of success are basically the same for a "theory" of reference as for a "theory" of knowledge. Factually, the relationships between speakers, words, and objects reveal no single pattern. Semantically, the uses of the word *reference* neither reveal a single pattern nor draw a sharp border.[129] Nor do associated expressions—*speak, say, mean, talk about*, etc.—that might be enlisted to state a theory.

If, however, speculative inquiry ignores these facts and, unconcerned about the meanings of the expressions it employs, leaves the meanings of *reference, referent,* and other key terms indefinite (undetermined either by standard usage or by stipulation), a way may be found to state a "really rigorous theory of reference." Implicit redefinition may parade as explicit theory. In this semantic no-man's-land Kripke, though wary, still appears too willing to wander.

His stance with respect to language can be sensed in the following passage: "Can we imagine a situation in which it would have happened that this very woman [the Queen of England] came out of Mr. and Mrs. Truman? They might have had a child resembling her in many properties. Perhaps in some possible world Mr. and Mrs. Truman even had a child who actually became the Queen of England and was even passed off as the child of other parents. This still would not be a situation in which *this very woman* whom we call Elizabeth the Second was the child of Mr. and Mrs. Truman, or so it seems to me."[130]

Kripke's "it seems to me" resembles the "intuitions" critiqued in chapters 1 and 2.[131] It signals the familiar combination so crucial to essentialistic thinking: lack of firm backing in any standard or stipulated use of the terms employed (fairly obvious in this instance), and lack of concern for such backing. The truth or acceptability of statements seems not to depend in any discernible manner on the meanings of the statements' constituent expressions.

Overview

In chapter 6 we noted five sources of essentialism. In this chapter's five case-studies, we have spotted or surmised all five at work. We have seen them operate together, never singly. In no case was it plausible to single out one factor and suggest: This and this alone accounts for the present instance of essentialistic thinking. We have also achieved some insight into this fact.

In particular, we have noticed the basic complementarity of factors that elicit essentialism and factors that permit it. The eliciting factors are multiple and varied—language, contagion, argument, will; the permitting factors are chiefly one—inattention to existing uses of the terms employed, repeatedly reflecting or suggesting (in at least four of the five cases) disregard for such uses. Here, then, it seems, is the single most important factor of the five: disregard for established word-uses.

Hence essentialism figures within a larger syndrome. I remarked in the Introduction that "the Wittgensteinian view of existing languages as composed of shifting, indefinite, heterogeneous concepts has far-reaching implications—more far-reaching, I believe, than is generally recognized." It has implications for essentialism, which stems largely from disregard for current idiom. And essentialism has more varied forms than are generally recognized. Moreover, essentialism pervades not only philosophy but other disciplines as well, for example theology, where the same five causal factors operate. The implications are, however, still broader. Even when thinkers neither formulate essentialistic doctrines nor indulge in essentialistic reasoning, they may and repeatedly do manifest the same disregard for mere terminology. Word meanings, whether standard or stipulated, do not concern them.

This study might therefore seem incomplete. If I believe that disregard for existing word-uses is as important and as unfortunate as suggested, I should demonstrate its importance and its error more thoroughly and systematically than I have in the preceding chapters. However, this project I have already undertaken in a previous work, *Language and Truth*. What remains to be done here, now that I have both critiqued and diagnosed the phenomenon of essentialism, is to estimate the chances for effective therapy and prophylaxis. Essentialism, I said at the start, has been a prominent feature of Western thought. Its history has been so long and its influence so great that its current status merits scrutiny. So do its future prospects.

The findings of this chapter and the last suggest that essentialism will not soon disappear. For one thing, its causes are too varied. A single-cause malady may have a single remedy; multiple causes complicate both cure and prevention. Polio and measles could effectively be dealt with; the "common cold," with myriad sources, cannot. The like may hold for essentialism.

Consider just the will. Scheler's project differed notably from Graham's, and both differed notably from young Wittgenstein's. Even if a remedy could be found for all the varied agendas that seduce the will essentialistically, a temperamental preference for unity and simplicity might persist. And even if the will could be weaned from all essentialistic biases, essentialism might still be contracted through conceptual contagion, and language might continue to work its essentialistic witchery.

Even considered singly, the sources of essentialism look intractable. Temperament cannot be argued out of existence. Mathematics and science, so essentialistically seductive, are here to stay. Given our need to simplify and unify experience, and our repeated successes, the unifying tendency will not go away. And as Wittgenstein discovered when he attempted to construct an ideally perspicuous notation, no language which humans might actually use would lack surface analogies that might deceive the inattentive. In particular, none can be conceived which lacks analogies that might delude us essentialistically. Outside pure logic and formal semantics, we have need of general terms whose appearance is more uniform than their sense or reference.

So my prognosis resembles Kant's in his "Transcendental Dialectic":

> Here we have to do with a *natural* and inevitable *illusion* . . . —not one in which a bungler might entangle himself through lack of knowledge, or one which some sophist has artificially invented to confuse thinking people, but one inseparable from human reason, and which,

even after its deceptiveness has been exposed, will not
cease to play tricks with reason and continually entrap
it into momentary aberrations ever and again calling for
correction.[132]

Hence the ultimate hopelessness of Kant's efforts and at the same
time their possible utility. In his view, transcendental illusion
would not cease "even after it has been detected and its invalidity
clearly revealed by transcendental criticism."[133] A fortiori, it would
not disappear if the alleged invalidity was not generally acknowledged and the transcendental criticism was itself criticized. Such
was the outcome of Kant's efforts, and such, a fortiori, will be the
outcome of mine. In particular, I am under no illusion that my
defense of the norm of linguistic correspondence, in *Language and
Truth,* will have any notable impact within the philosophical community or beyond. And as long as thinkers feel free to ignore
established word meanings, standard or stipulated, the influences
I have catalogued will have their way; essentialistic thinking will
spring up like potato sprouts in a dark cellar. There is slight
prospect, then, that my efforts here will soon lose their relevance.

Or their utility. Although Wittgenstein did not put an end to
essentialistic he-goat milking, business does seem to have fallen
off, thanks to his efforts. Possibly its decline will be furthered by
this expansion of his thinking. Whereas Wittgenstein's critique of
essentialism was fragmented, mine has been more systematic.
Whereas he focused on essentialistic theories, I have attended
more to essentialistic practice. Whereas he became wary of causal
explanations, I have added etiology to critique.

This addition, I recognize, is problematic. Causal surmises
such as those in this chapter are, on the whole, less sure than critiques such as those in chapters 1 to 5. I am more certain, for
example, about the error of Pitcher's attack on *Investigations* §43
than I am about its source. Furthermore, the critiques in those
chapters have more evident therapeutic relevance than do the
causal hypotheses advanced in this one. The challenge in chapter 3
might make Pitcher reconsider his position, whereas the etiologi-
cal ruminations of this chapter would not. Still, etiology may have
therapeutic as well as prophylactic value.

Again, Pitcher may serve as illustration. The critiques aimed
at his errors in chapter 3 might remedy those errors but would
not remove the habit of thought that begot them. The chapter's
many critiques, aimed at similar errors, might go farther in that
direction. But the chances for prevention are improved by the eti-

ological discovery that slips like those in chapter 3 arise from semantic shifts more subtle than the ones logic texts warn against. That discovery sounds a general alert. Outside the exact sciences, *any* attempt at calculus-like demonstration should be viewed with caution.

In medicine, etiology has occasional relevance for cure but fundamental significance for prevention. If the etiology of essentialism had comparable importance, my five chapters of critique and only two of etiology would strike an improper balance. However, physical pathology differs from conceptual. No one needs convincing that cancer, typhoid, or tuberculosis is unfortunate. That is obvious to all. The conviction precedes and motivates both treatment and prevention. Intellectual pathology, however, reveals no comparable split. There, to prove the need is to provide both cure and prophylaxis. Thus, to show that an instance of essentialism is unfortunate, since mistaken, is to furnish the principal remedy for that instance. And to demonstrate that essentialism in general is unfortunate, since mistaken, is to furnish the principal remedy, both therapeutic and preventive, for essentialism in general. Essentialism may never entirely vanish from human thought; but measures may be taken, as here, to minimize its recurrence.

NOTES

Introduction

1. Wittgenstein, *Philosophical Investigations*, §116.

2. Ibid., §120.

3. Shimony, "The Status and Nature of Essences," p. 38.

4. Agassi and Sagal, "The Problem of Universals," p. 293.

5. Wittgenstein, *Philosophical Investigations*, §109.

6. Ibid., §124.

7. Ibid., §126.

Chapter 1: The Decline of Explicit Essentialism

1. Kennick, "Philosophy as Grammar," pp. 152–53, quoting from Donagan, "Universals and Metaphysical Realism," p. 212.

2. Ross, *Plato's Theory of Ideas*, p. 225.

3. Russell, *The Problems of Philosophy*, p. 94.

4. Ibid., p. 91.

5. Ibid., p. 93.

6. Ibid., p. 94.

7. Moore, *Commonplace Book*, p. 19.

8. Ibid., p. 21.

9. Moore, *Principia Ethica*, p. 10.

10. Ibid.

11. Ibid., p. 7.

12. For instance, his references to Plato, his argument for universals (see chapter 6), and his talk of abstraction (e.g., *Problems of Philosophy*, p. 101).

13. Scheler, *Formalism in Ethics*, p. 14. Compare von Hildebrand, *What Is Philosophy?*, pp. 110–14 (e.g., "When we see a triangle for the first time, we grasp not only this concrete triangle,

but also the genus 'triangle'"); Sokolowski, "What is Moral Action?", p. 18 ("I wish to clarify, philosophically, what a moral action is. The best way to proceed in this venture would be to exhibit a moral performance and to reflect on it").

14. Scheler, *Formalism in Ethics,* pp. 48–49. Cf. ibid., p. 488, and idem, *Selected Philosophical Essays,* p. 251; idem, *Man's Place in Nature,* p. 50; idem, *Philosophical Perspectives,* pp. 6–7; idem, *Späte Schriften,* pp. 41, 79, 245–46, 248, 251.

15. Husserl, *Ideas,* p. 53. The same doctrine still appears in Husserl's posthumous *Experience and Judgment,* pp. 340–42.

16. Husserl, *Ideas,* p. 59.

17. Ibid., p. 57. Cf. Solomon, "Sense and Essence," pp. 381–84.

18. Compare Cairns's account of the Husserlian viewpoint, where the neglect of the linguistic dimension is more starkly revealed: "An individual thing is intended to [*sic*] not merely in its individuality, as having individual parts and standing in individual relationships to other individual things. It is also intended to and may be explicitly seized upon *as* an individual (an instance of that *category*), as an instance of a *specific sort* of individuals, as having parts of *specific sorts,* etc. Furthermore, these 'categories' and 'specific sorts' may be not only thus cointended to but also directly paid attention to for their own sakes and grasped in their original self-givenness on the basis of a clear perceiving or phantasying of at least possible instances. Thus, for example, a thing may be intended to and clearly given as a possible, and perhaps an actual, instance of *color in general,* as having a quality that is an individual instance of *brightness in general,* and as standing in an individual relationship, that is an instance of *similarity in general,* to other individual instances of color. And color, brightness, similarity—these general kinds—may themselves be presented and seized upon. Indeed, it is only on the basis of the original givenness and seizedness of the kind as well as the individual that one can judge 'with original insight': This is an instance of color; this has a brightness; this is similar to that in brightness; this instance of color belongs to this instance of surface; etc. And only when one has thus judged with original insight can one seize upon, as originally self-given, the state of affairs itself: that this is a color, that it is bright, etc." ("An Approach to Husserlian Phenomenology," pp. 38–39; emphasis in the original). Current uses of the terms Cairns here employs (*color, brightness, similarity*) are treated as irrele-

vant. The nature of color, brightness, and similarity, in general, can be known directly from experience, without linguistic intermediary.

19. Cf. e.g. Solomon, "Sense and Essence," p. 394: "I do not wish to leave an impression that Husserl maintained, much less argued, that the grasping of essences can dispense with any consideration of language in which thoughts are expressed. Rather, his position on this matter seems to be ambivalent (not to say confused) concerning the rule [*sic*] of language in the essences to be examined."

20. Moore, *Principia Ethica*, p. 5.

21. Ibid., p. 6.

22. Ibid.

23. Wittgenstein, *Zettel*, §458.

24. Much the same move has been made by traditional essentialists when they have distinguished between nominal and real (or essential) definitions, and have seen the distinction as excusing them from concern about usage when they discussed and proposed definitions of the latter variety.

25. Moore, *Principia Ethica*, p. 6.

26. Wittgenstein, *Philosophical Investigations*, §116.

27. Ibid., §577.

28. Ibid., §66.

29. Ibid., §72.

30. Ibid., §66.

31. Ibid.

32. Ibid., §67.

33. Hallett, *Logic for the Labyrinth*, pp. 30–31.

34. See Hallett, *Language and Truth*, pp. 26–27.

35. For fuller discussion of this result, see chapter 2.

36. Moore, *Some Main Problems of Philosophy*, p. 301.

37. Wittgenstein, *Philosophical Investigations*, §371.

38. See Hallett, *Logic for the Labyrinth*, pp. 32–33.

39. McGreal, "An Analysis of Philosophical Method," p. 517.

40. Margolis, "Mr. Weitz," p. 92.

41. For extended illustrations, see chapter 2.

42. Achinstein, "Rudolf Carnap," p. 518.

43. Carnap, "Replies and Systematic Expositions," p. 933.

44. Ibid., p. 936.

45. Carnap, *Meaning and Necessity,* p. 8.

46. Carnap, *Logical Foundations of Probability,* p. 7.

47. Ibid.

48. See, e.g., Clarke, *Language and Natural Theology,* pp. 98–99, 103ff.

49. See, e.g., Dorrough, *Prolegomenon,* and Walton, *On Defining Death,* p. 17, and chapters 5 and 6.

50. Concerning, e.g., the brief account in Gorovitz, et al., *Philosophical Analysis,* p. 139, see Hallett, *Language and Truth,* p. 3.

51. Achinstein, "Rudolf Carnap," p. 524.

52. Carnap implicitly acknowledges grounds for this first complaint when he writes: "The explicatum (in my sense) is in many cases the result of an analysis of the explicandum (and this has motivated my choice of the terms); in other cases, however, it deviates deliberately from the explicandum but still takes its place in some way" (*Logical Foundations of Probability,* p. 3).

53. Ibid., p. 7.

54. See Hallett, *Language and Truth,* pp. 126–28, 146; Achinstein, "Rudolf Carnap," p. 531.

55. Carnap slightly mitigates this impression when he remarks, concerning the fourth condition, that "in general, simplicity comes into consideration only in a case where there is a question of choice among several concepts which achieve the same and seem to be equally fruitful" (*Logical Foundations of Probability,* p. 7).

56. Ibid., pp. 3–4.

57. Cf. Bunge, "The Complexity of Simplicity," pp. 113–35, and Bennett, "Analytic-Synthetic," p. 166.

58. Cf. Griffin, "Einstein's Simplicism," pp. 1048–49.

59. Carnap, *Logical Foundations of Probability*, pp. 4–5.

60. Hanna, "An Explication of 'Explication,'" p. 30.

61. Ibid., p. 33.

62. Ibid.

63. Ibid., pp. 33–34.

64. Ibid., p. 36.

65. Ibid., p. 28. This same basic confusion between linguistic usage and theoretical practice (however called) becomes especially evident on pages 41–42; e.g: "The objection to the correspondence condition as applied to an arbitrary explication appears to be based on the correspondence condition applied to the term 'explication' itself: the correspondence condition is too restrictive because it does not *correspond* to actual practice in explicating vague terms" (p. 41).

66. Ibid., p. 30.

67. Putnam, *Mind, Language and Reality*, p. 231. Cf. Kripke, "Naming and Necessity," p. 269, and "Identity and Necessity," p. 79.

68. Putnam, *Mind, Language and Reality*, p. 233.

69. Putnam, "Is Semantics Possible?", p. 102.

70. Putnam, *Mind, Language and Reality*, p. 242. Indeed, Putnam went so far as to assert that "most terms are *rigid*" (ibid., p. 265). Cf. Carney, "A Kripkean Approach," p. 150 ("I also believe that it can be plausibly argued that 'art' is a rigid designator and that even aesthetic terms such as 'unified,' 'graceful,' and 'balanced' are also rigid designators").

71. Putnam, *Mind, Language and Reality*, p. 232. Cf. ibid., p. 241.

72. Ibid., pp. 235, 239, 240–41.

73. "What the essential nature is is not a matter of language analysis but of scientific theory construction; today we would say it was chromosome structure, in the case of lemons, and being a proton-donor, in the case of acids" (Putnam, "Is Semantics Possible?", p. 104).

74. Putnam, "Meaning and Reference," p. 121; idem, *Mind, Language and Reality*, pp. 223–24.

75. Idem, *Mind, Language and Reality,* p. 224, and "Meaning and Reference," p. 121.

76. Putnam, "Meaning and Reference," p. 130 ("At this point I will be able to say that the stuff on Twin-Earth that I earlier *mistook* for water isn't really water"); idem, *Mind, Language and Reality,* pp. 232–33.

77. Cf. Kripke, "Naming and Necessity," pp. 319–20, 323.

78. Putnam sometimes gives the impression of wishing to *demonstrate* the alleged essentialism of our concepts, rather than account for it, by means of an origin which appears quite mythical in its uniformity and simplicity: "To use a term suggested by Alan Berger, when we teach the meaning of the word 'water,' we *focus* on certain samples. A substance which doesn't behave as *these* examples do will be counted as not the same substance (barring a special explanation)" (*Representation and Reality,* p. 33).

79. Putnam, *Realism and Reason,* pp. 73, 74.

80. Cf. Dupré, "Natural Kinds and Biological Taxa," p. 72 ("After all, it is surely just the absence of experiences like the one Putnam describes that makes it reasonable to attach to molecular structure at least most of the importance that Putnam ascribes to it").

81. Hallett, *Language and Truth,* p. 91. I shall cite this principle half a dozen times hereafter, but shall not rely heavily on its acceptance. A full explanation and defense, duplicating that in *Language and Truth,* is not possible here; and a mere summary would occasion as many doubts as it resolved.

82. Ibid., pp. 91–92, 96–102, 170–75.

83. Note the nature of the "we" implicit in Putnam's remark: "The reason we *don't* use 'cat' as synonymous with a description is surely that we know enough about cats to know that they do have a hidden structure, and it is good scientific methodology to use the name to refer rigidly to the things that possess that hidden structure, and not to whatever happens to satisfy some description" (*Mind, Language and Reality,* p. 244).

84. Carnap, *Logical Foundations of Probability,* p. 6.

85. Achinstein, "Rudolf Carnap," pp. 527 ("the fact that for other purposes and in other areas it may be advisable to use the term in a different way is not a sufficient reason for changing its use in the first areas"), 531 ("the fact that *scientists* (as well as oth-

ers) may stretch or otherwise modify the use of an ordinary term (e.g., 'force,' 'mass,' 'work') for their special purposes does not require adopting this use in ordinary contexts or even in all scientific ones").

86. Dupré, "Natural Kinds and Biological Taxa," pp. 83–84.

87. Ibid., p. 82. See Quine, "Natural Kinds," p. 173.

88. Achinstein, "On the Meaning of Scientific Terms," pp. 500–01; Quine, "Natural Kinds," p. 174; Goosens, "Underlying Trait Terms," p. 135; Gemes, "The World in Itself," pp. 314–17.

89. Achinstein, "On the Meaning of Scientific Terms," p. 501.

90. Compare Cajetan in chapter 2.

91. To some extent, the theory is self-verifying: the more people state its restrictions with assurance, the more rigid usage is likely to become. Thus Robert Martin, for example, accepts unquestioningly that H_2O is the essence of water, as "nondescriptivists" claim (*The Meaning of Language,* pp. 199–200).

92. See, e.g., Ackerman, "Natural Kinds"; Averill, "Essence and Scientific Discovery"; Campbell, "Extension and Psychic State"; Canfield, "Discovering Essence"; Cassam, "Science and Essence"; Chandler, "Sources of Essentialism," pp. 379–82; Churchland, *Scientific Realism,* pp. 70–74; Donnellan, "Kripke and Putnam," pp. 98–104; Double, "Twin Earths," pp. 302–4; Dupré, "Natural Kinds and Biological Taxa"; Ebersole, "Stalking the Rigid Designator," pp. 255–65; Farrell, "Metaphysical Necessity"; Fodor, "Cognitive Science"; Forbes, "An Anti-Essentialist Note"; Goosens, "Underlying Trait Terms"; Grayling, "Internal Structure and Essence"; Katz, "Logic and Language," pp. 87–101; Leplin, "Is Essentialism Unscientific?", pp. 506–7; Mellor, "Natural Kinds"; Moravcsik, "How Do Words"; Platts, "Natural Kind Words"; Rosen, *The Limits of Analysis,* pp. 87–89; Shapere, "Reason"; Zemach, "Putnam's Theory."

93. See, e.g., Schwartz, "Putnam on Artifacts," pp. 573–74; idem, *Naming, Necessity, and Natural Kinds,* pp. 34–41; idem, "Natural Kinds and Nominal Kinds."

94. Hollinger, "Natural Kinds," p. 333. Cf. Copi, "Essence and Accident," pp. 187–90; Wiggins, *Sameness and Substance,* pp. 80–83.

95. Hollinger, "Natural Kinds," p. 333. Cf. Copi, "Essence and

Accident," p. 190: "To derive conclusions about *all* accidental properties of a substance, we should need to know both its real essence and all relevant causal laws. That is an ideal towards which science strives, rather than its present achievement, of course. To the extent to which one small group of properties of a substance can serve as a basis from which its other properties can be causally derived, to that extent we can be justified in identifying that group of properties as its real essence."

96. Hollinger, "Natural Kinds," p. 328.

97. Ibid., p. 326.

98. Ibid., p. 330.

99. Idem, "A Defense of Essentialism," p. 336. Elsewhere, Hollinger is more tentative and guarded in his claims. See ibid., pp. 327, 334.

100. Idem, "Aspects," pp. 321–22. See ibid., pp. 330, 337–38.

101. Idem, ibid., p. 338. See idem, "A Defense of Essentialism," p. 333. Cf. Copi, "Essence and Accident," p. 187 ("Modern science seeks to know the *real* essences of things, and its increasing successes seem to be bringing it progressively nearer to that goal"). Peirce envisaged convergence toward the truth, but the same truth can be differently expressed, in very different categories.

102. Hollinger, "A Defense of Essentialism," p. 337.

103. Ibid., pp. 337–38.

104. Wilkerson, "Natural Kinds."

105. Copi, "Essence and Accident," p. 190.

106. Weckert, "Putnam, Reference and Essentialism," p. 516.

107. Ibid., p. 520.

108. Ibid., p. 518.

Chapter 2: The Persistence of Essentialistic Theorizing

1. Hallett, *Logic for the Labyrinth*, p. 19. (The aptness of both its focus and its progression accounts for this self-quotation.)

2. Foreword to de Vio (Cajetan), *The Analogy of Names*, p. ix.

3. de Vio, *The Analogy of Names*, pp. 10–11; *Scripta philosophica*, pp. 4–6; McInerny, *The Logic of Analogy*, p. 3.

4. de Vio, *The Analogy of Names,* e.g., pp. 11, 13, 23–24. McInerny comments indignantly: "When St Thomas says something about analogous names, Cajetan tells us the saint is abusing terms. Surely what a commentator should do is determine how an author uses his terms. There is no justification whatsoever in the texts of St Thomas for saying that 'healthy' and 'true' (said of intellect and things) are only abusively called analogous names. What must be found is an interpretation of St Thomas's doctrine on the analogy of names which does not entail the dismissal of most of what he has to say on the subject" (*The Logic of Analogy,* p. 22).

5. "How often," writes McInerny (ibid., p. 35), "in commenting on the *Metaphysics* does St Thomas speak of analogy where Aristotle has not used the Greek term, but rather the phrase 'things said in many ways.' Are we to discount St Thomas' remarks because κατ'άναλογιαν or άναλογια does not occur in Aristotle? How absurd, and yet we have seen that this is precisely the tendency of Cajetan and, less clearly, Sylvester. To strive for a one-to-one correspondence between the use of άναλογια and *analogia* is wrongheaded at best, since the correspondence is obviously lacking."

6. "Aside from holding Latin authors to Greek usage, Cajetan's procedure is curious on the level of Greek alone. In the latter language, it is only by an extension of its meaning that άναλογ ια can be used in other than mathematical discussions. Why is not such usage abusive? Doubtless because it became a matter of usage. Apart then from other considerations, it seems odd to berate Latin authors for abuse of terminology while at the same time admitting that the Greek term had been extended to include non-mathematical relations" (McInerny, *The Logic of Analogy,* pp. 10–11).

7. Lash, "Ideology, Metaphor and Analogy," p. 82. Aquinas often gives a contrary impression. See Klubertanz, *St. Thomas Aquinas on Analogy,* pp. 37–38 ("The 'general' descriptions are not general").

8. Russell, *Logic and Knowledge,* pp. 201, 243.

9. Wittgenstein, *Notebooks 1914–1916,* p. 39.

10. Idem, *Philosophical Investigations,* §96. See, e.g., idem, *Notebooks 1914–1916,* pp. 6–7; idem, *Tractatus Logico-Philosophicus,* 4–4.001 ("A thought is a proposition with a sense. The totality of propositions is language").

11. Idem, *Notebooks 1914–1916,* p. 7.

12. Idem, *Philosophical Investigations,* §23.

13. Ibid., §65.

14. Ibid., §66.

15. For similar critiques of other illustrations, see Hallett, *Darkness and Light,* pp. 97–101, and idem, *Language and Truth,* p. 62.

16. In keeping with his prescriptions in 3.325, the author of the *Tractatus* avoided the use of *Satz* for both propositions and sentences and spoke instead of *Sätze* and *Satzzeichen.*

17. Wittgenstein, *Philosophical Investigations,* §§114–15.

18. Williams, "Knowledge and Reasons," p. 1.

19. Ibid., p. 5.

20. Ibid., p. 7.

21. Ibid.

22. Ayer, "Comments," pp. 15–16.

23. In concrete confirmation, consider, for example, Wittgenstein's misgivings, in *On Certainty,* concerning Moore's applications of *know,* and note the implications for the general populace.

24. See chapter 5 and Hallett, *Wittgenstein's Definition,* pp. 151–56.

25. For similar pragmatic queries, complementing mine, see Schlesinger, *Metaphysics,* p. 141.

26. Kenny, *Faith and Reason,* p. 43.

27. In chapter 2 of *Logic for the Labyrinth* I have argued that the discovery of an accurate all-and-only definition, in which the defined and defining expressions perfectly match, far from demonstrating the existence of some single essence common to all the things thus defined, would actually lessen the probability of there being any such essence—any such single *reality.*

28. Hallett, *Companion,* p. 56.

29. Dretske, "Conclusive Reasons," pp. 3–4.

30. Ibid., pp. 12–13.

31. Ibid., p. 22.

32. See, e.g., Harman, "Knowledge, Inference, and Explanation," p. 173.

33. Boardman, "Conclusive Reasons and Scepticism," pp. 33–34, 36. A case in Harman, "Knowledge, Inference, and Explanation," p. 172, might be exploited in the same sense.

34. Pappas and Swain, "Some Conclusive Reasons," pp. 73–76. Pappas and Swain conclude: "We suspect . . . that *any* interpretation of the conclusive reasons requirement will yield a conception of knowledge that is too strong" (ibid., p. 76).

35. See, e.g., Sorell, "The Analysis of Knowledge," pp. 130–33, for a survey of post-Gettier proposals and critiques of the proposals.

36. See, e.g., Boyd, "Metaphor and Theory Change," pp. 374–75 (on reference); Parkinson, "Different Types of Causation," pp. 292–95 (on goal-directed behavior); Feinberg, "Analytic Jurisprudence," p. 110 (on legal concepts); Geisler and Feinberg, *Introduction to Philosophy*, pp. 13–14 (on philosophy); Uyl and Machan, "The Concept of Happiness"; Parent, "The Concept of Privacy"; Martin and Nickel, "The Concept of Rights," pp. 165–72.

37. Dretske, "Conclusive Reasons," p. 12.

38. Wittgenstein, Manuscript 219, p. 10.

39. Harman, "Knowledge, Inference, and Explanation," p. 164.

40. Cf. Schlesinger, "The Method of Counterexample," pp. 163–64; idem, *Metaphysics*, pp. 143–44.

41. Wittgenstein, *Philosophical Investigations*, p. 216.

42. Fuller backing for negative answers to these queries can be found in chapter 5, second section ("Real Concepts, Unreal Worlds").

Chapter 3: Calculus and Mosaic

1. Mill, *System of Logic*, p. 19.

2. Hazo, *The Idea of Love*, p. 6.

3. Pitcher, *The Philosophy of Wittgenstein*, pp. 251–52.

4. Hallett, *Wittgenstein's Definition*, pp. 140–41.

5. Gustafson, "On Pitcher's Account," p. 253.

6. Ibid., p. 255.

7. Ibid., pp. 255–56 (paragraph break omitted).

8. For criticism of such reasoning, see Black, *The Labyrinth of Language,* pp. 161–62; Wheatley, "How to Give a Word a Meaning," p. 123.

9. Gustafson, "On Pitcher's Account," pp. 257–58. In *The Philosophy of Wittgenstein,* p. 253, Pitcher adduces similar data, similarly, to suggest that "Wittgenstein himself occasionally divorces, at least by implication, the notions of meaning and use."

10. See, e.g., Wittgenstein, *Philosophical Investigations,* §§1–2, 116–17, and Hallett, *Companion,* p. 75.

11. Cf. ibid., pp. 122–23.

12. Wavell, "Wittgenstein's Doctrine of Use," p. 253.

13. Ibid., p. 254.

14. Black, *The Labyrinth of Language,* p. 163.

15. On this particular instance, see Champlin, "The Elusiveness of Meaning," p. 294. And compare: "A reliable definition of religion must capture the sense in which a person can *be* 'religious'" (Kapitan, "Devine on Defining Religion," p. 208).

16. Montagu, Introduction, p. v.

17. Aristotle, *De interpretatione* 16a.

18. Wavell, "Wittgenstein's Doctrine of Use," p. 255.

19. Ibid., p. 258. For further instances of calculus-reasoning in Wavell, see, e.g., ibid., pp. 262–63.

20. In confirmation of his objection, Wavell adduces a comparison with the uses of chess pieces before and after the names of the pieces are learned by an observer, not noticing that only if the children acquired their "concepts" by observing adult linguistic behavior, rather than merely "interacting with their nonhuman environments," would the comparison become relevant—but also useless for his purposes (since the concepts learned would then be the words' uses in the language).

21. Brown, "Meaning and Rules of Use," p. 494.

22. Röper, Review, p. 427.

23. Abelson, "Meaning," p. 51.

24. Ibid.

25. Ibid., p. 52.

26. Ibid., p. 53.

27. Ibid.

28. Hill, *The Concept of Meaning,* p. 251.

29. Ibid., p. 274.

30. Ibid., p. 252.

31. Ibid., pp. 316–17.

32. Ibid., p. 316.

33. In addition to Abelson, above, and Wheatley, below, see Gustafson, "Pitcher's Account," p. 253, and Pitcher, *The Philosophy of Wittgenstein,* p. 252.

34. Wheatley, "Some Aspects," pp. 643–44.

35. Hallett, *Wittgenstein's Definition,* p. 161. See idem, *Logic for the Labyrinth,* pp. xvi–xvii.

36. Paul Ziff, for instance, argues: "It is wrong to say, 'the meaning of a word is its use in the language' for the use of a word depends on many factors many of which have nothing to do with questions of meaning" (*Semantic Analysis,* p. 158). Wittgenstein's saying is, indeed, a rough indication; and what works as a description or identification may not as a strict definition, enunciating sufficient and necessary conditions. However, the use of the word *definition* in the translation of *Investigations* §43, though justifiable, does not indicate that Wittgenstein was attempting an all-and-only characterization. All and only members of *what* class would the definition describe? Wittgenstein's allusion to "a *large* class of cases," without further identification, sounds one clear signal, among others, that he had no intention of continuing the essentialistic enterprise of real definition. For a critique similar to Ziff's, but fuller, see Cooper, *Philosophy,* pp. 37–39.

37. Waismann, "Analytic-Synthetic," p. 29.

38. See also Brown, "Meaning and Rules of Use," p. 510; Charlesworth, "Meaning and Use," p. 302.

39. Putnam, "Psychological Concepts," p. 96.

40. Ibid.

41. Pitcher, *The Philosophy of Wittgenstein*, p. 252.

42. See Hallett, *Wittgenstein's Definition*, pp. 139–40.

43. Hallett, *Companion*, p. 122. See Wittgenstein, *The Blue and Brown Books*, p. 1, and *Philosophical Grammar*, pp. 59–60, 68.

44. In Bouwsma, *Wittgenstein: Conversations 1949–1951*, p. 25, Wittgenstein himself appears dissatisfied with such reasoning. In its defense it might be suggested that the Tractarian, Russellian view that was his chief concern did in fact require the continuing existence of a name's bearer if the name was to have meaning. So perhaps he was careless in his wording? Perhaps the argument of §40 would work better if directed more specifically at that intended target? On the contrary, it would lose all semblance of validity. Tractarian object-meanings do not die or go out of existence. Their "dying" would be an absurdity; their ceasing to exist was precluded by their absolute logical simplicity. Hence the situation envisaged in §40 does not occur. Even if it did, the fact that *Mary* or *Spartansburg* does not cease to have meaning when Mary or Spartansburg ceases to exist, or that their meanings do not then go out of existence, would warrant no automatic inference with regard to Tractarian meanings. For the *Tractatus* denied any parallel between the meaning of genuine names and the meanings of everyday names. The latter were veiled propositions.

45. Alston, "Meaning," p. 234.

46. Wittgenstein, *Tractatus Logico-Philosophicus*, 4.002.

47. Frege, *The Foundations of Arithmetic*, p. 71. See ibid., pp. x, 116; cf. Hallett, *Wittgenstein's Definition*, pp. 9–14.

48. Hallett, *Wittgenstein's Definition*, pp. 96–98.

Chapter 4: Network-Reasoning

1. Wittgenstein, *Philosophical Investigations*, §97. Compare idem, *Tractatus Logico-Philosophicus*, 5.4541. After noting Wittgensteinian objections to Kant's eternal, universal system of categories, Stuart Hampshire writes: "It still seems to me that Kant was right in looking for some few categories, or elements of grammar, which are the most fundamental of all, and in trying to show some systematic connection between them" ("Metaphysical Systems," p. 35).

2. Descartes, *The Philosophical Works*, p. 155 (Meditation II).

3. Waismann, "How I See Philosophy," p. 365.

4. Baker and Hacker, *Wittgenstein: Understanding and Meaning,* p. 664.

5. Ibid.

6. Ibid.

7. Ibid., p. 665.

8. Ibid., p. 667.

9. Wittgenstein, *Philosophical Investigations,* §81.

10. Moore, *Commonplace Book 1919–1953,* p. 330.

11. Hallett, *Language and Truth,* p. 151.

12. Graham, *J. L. Austin,* pp. 67–72.

13. Ibid., pp. 76–79; Hallett, *Language and Truth,* pp. 138–40.

14. Hallett, *Language and Truth,* pp. 144–45.

15. Malcolm, *Thought and Knowledge,* p. 127.

16. Chapman and Henle, *The Fundamentals of Logic,* p. 11.

17. Pollock, *Language and Thought,* p. 4.

18. Ibid.

19. Ibid., p. 5.

20. Hallett, *Companion,* p. 237.

21. Hill, *The Concept of Meaning,* p. 242.

22. Spang-Hanssen, *Recent Theories,* p. 75, and Lyons, *Structural Semantics,* p. 54.

23. Lehrer, "Meaning in Linguistics," p. 14. See Parent, "The Concept of Privacy," p. 347.

24. Lyons, *Introduction to Theoretical Linguistics,* pp. 429–30.

25. Ibid., pp. 429–30. Compare Lyons, *Structural Semantics,* p. 39 (less freighted with assertions of necessity).

26. Cf. Hallett, *Language and Truth,* p. 207: "Such operational dependence should also be distinguished from definitional dependence of the kind Gilbert Ryle asserts, rightly or wrongly, when he writes: 'Knowing is not one definable species of "consciousness

of…" among others, it is something anyhow partly in terms of which believing, fancying, guessing, wanting and the rest have to be defined. Belief, *e.g.*, is a state of mind involving *ignorance* of such and such a *knowledge* of so and so; it involves more than that, but at least it involves this double reference to knowledge' ('Phenomenology,' in *Analytic Philosophy and Phenomenology*, ed. H. Durfee [The Hague: Nijhoff, 1976], p. 26). From the fact that I cannot define X without using the word Y, it does not follow that I cannot use X without applying the criteria for Y."

27. Strawson, Review, p. 32.

28. Wilson, "Problem," p. 17.

29. Ramsey, *The Foundations of Mathematics*, p. 264.

30. Ryle, "Proofs in Philosophy," pp. 156–57.

31. Strawson, "Construction and Analysis," pp. 101–2.

32. Wuellner, *A Dictionary of Scholastic Philosophy*, p. 248.

33. Ewing, *Ethics*, p. 19.

34. Moore, *Principia Ethica*, p. 5.

35. Ibid., pp. 9–10.

36. Moore, *Philosophical Papers*, p. 89. For a fuller explanation of *good*'s indefinability, see Hallett, *Christian Moral Reasoning*, pp. 31–35.

37. Schlick, "Meaning and Verification," p. 148.

38. Wittgenstein, *The Blue and Brown Books*, p. 2.

39. Feinberg, "Analytic Jurisprudence," p. 110.

40. Compare Frege, *Philosophical Writings*, pp. 42–43: "One cannot require that everything shall be defined, any more than one can require that a chemist shall decompose every substance. What is simple cannot be decomposed, and what is logically simple cannot have a proper definition."

41. Aune, *Knowledge, Mind and Nature*, p. 228.

42. Findlay, "Use, Usage, and Meaning," p. 233.

43. Ibid., p. 233.

44. Wittgenstein, *Philosophical Investigations*, §87.

45. Baker and Hacker, *Wittgenstein: Understanding and Meaning*, p. 7.

46. Ibid., pp. 77, 82. Compare Dummett, *Frege: Philosophy of Language*, p. 92; idem, *The Interpretation of Frege's Philosophy*, pp. 74, 77.

47. Dummett speaks of "the intuitive equivalence between 'to understand *A*' and 'to know what *A* means'" (*The Interpretation of Frege's Philosophy*, p. 77).

48. Idem, *Frege: Philosophy of Language*, p. 84.

49. Wittgenstein, *Philosophical Investigations*, p. ix.

50. Ibid.

Chapter 5: Other Worlds

1. Kitcher, "On Appealing to the Extraordinary," p. 99.

2. Waismann, "How I See Philosophy," p. 368.

3. Ibid.

4. Wittgenstein, *Philosophical Investigations*, §117.

5. E.g., Wittgenstein, *Philosophical Investigations*, pp. 193 ("But we can also *see* the illustration now as one thing now as another.—So we interpret it, and *see* it as we *interpret* it"), 197 ("if you are having the visual experience expressed by the exclamation, you are also *thinking* of what you see"), 200, 212. Pp. 194–213 of the *Investigations*, appropriately translated, are sprinkled with iterative forms of *see*.

6. Graham, *J. L. Austin*, p. 50.

7. Hallett, *Language and Truth*, p. 134 (paragraph break omitted).

8. Teichman, "The Definition of Person," p. 177.

9. Wheeler, "Attributives and Their Modifiers," p. 319. See also Wallace, "Positive, Comparative, Superlative," p. 777.

10. Hallett, *Language and Truth*, p. 210. See Wittgenstein, *Philosophical Investigations*, p. 230; Hallett, *Companion*, p. 747.

11. Putnam, *Mind, Language and Reality*, pp. 314–15.

12. Ibid.

13. Wittgenstein, *Philosophical Investigations*, §282.

14. Hill, *The Concept of Meaning*, p. 239.

15. Ibid., pp. 238–39.

16. Ibid., p. 239.

17. Fodor, "On Knowing What We Would Say," p. 303.

18. Ibid., p. 305.

19. Hill, *The Concept of Meaning*, p. 242.

20. Wittgenstein, *Philosophical Investigations*, p. 216.

21. Ibid.; Hallett, *Companion*, p. 707.

22. Borowski, Synopsis, p. 297. See idem, "Puzzle Cases," p. 252. Compare Weitz, "The Role of Theory in Aesthetics," pp. 31–32, and Margolis, "Mr. Weitz," pp. 88–89.

23. Gettier, "Is Justified True Belief Knowledge?", pp. 36–37.

24. Kitcher, "On Appealing to the Extraordinary," p. 100.

25. Ibid., p. 101.

26. Ibid.

27. Cf. Hallett, *Companion*, pp. 51–52.

28. Pollock writes: "Gettier's paper was followed by a spate of articles attempting to meet his counterexamples by adding a fourth condition to the analysis of knowing" (*Contemporary Theories of Knowledge*, p. 180). "I think that such a fourth condition will ultimately provide the solution to the Gettier problem, but no proposal of this sort has been worked out in the literature" (ibid., p. 182). Compare Williams in chapter 2.

29. Schwartz, *Naming, Necessity, and Natural Kinds*, p. 27.

30. Putnam, "It Ain't Necessarily So," p. 660.

31. Ibid.

32. Seddon, "Logical Possibility," pp. 491–92.

33. Wittgenstein, *Philosophical Investigations*, p. 230.

34. Ibid., §200.

35. Putnam, "It Ain't Necessarily So," pp. 660–61.

36. Goosens, "Underlying Trait Terms," pp. 146–47.

37. Ibid., p. 147.

38. Ibid., p. 148.

39. Putnam, "It Ain't Necessarily So," p. 661.

40. Descartes, *The Philosophical Works,* p. 150 (Meditation II).

41. Wittgenstein, *On Certainty,* §114.

42. This surmise is strengthened by the fact that contemporary analytic thinkers like Schlick and Waismann, who entertained similar hypotheses, proceeded with similar unconcern about the methodological implications of language. See Hallett, *Companion,* p. 312. There would be no incoherence, notice, if Descartes merely questioned whether we *know* that persons and bodies exist, while continuing to believe that they do, or merely abstracted from their existence, as in Husserl's epoché.

43. Descartes, *The Philosophical Works,* p. 149 (Meditation II).

44. Ibid., p. 151 (Meditation II).

45. Ibid., p. 152.

46. Ibid., p. 153.

47. Compare Husserl, *Cartesian Meditations,* p. 25: "If I keep purely what comes into view—for me, the one who is meditating—by virtue of my free epoché with respect to the being of the experienced world, the momentous fact is that I, with my life, remain untouched in my existential status, regardless of whether or not the world exists and regardless of what my eventual decision concerning its being or non-being might be. This Ego, with his Ego-life, who necessarily remains for me, by virtue of such epoché, is not a piece of the world; and if he says, 'I exist, *ego cogito,*' that no longer signifies, 'I, this man, exist.'"

48. Cf. Wittgenstein, *Philosophical Investigations,* §§281, 360.

49. Ibid., §580.

50. See, e.g., Geach, *God and the Soul,* chapter 2.

51. Hallett, *Language and Truth,* pp. 177–80.

52. Descartes, *The Philosophical Works,* p. 152 (Meditation II).

53. Ibid., p. 190 (Meditation VI).

54. Kenny, *Descartes,* p. 89.

55. Descartes, *The Philosophical Works,* p. 240.

56. Ibid.

57. Williams, *Descartes,* pp. 116–17. Williams prefers his reconstruction to Malcolm's:

> *x* is my essence if it is the case that (a) if I am aware of *x* then (necessarily) I am aware of myself, and (b) if I am aware of myself then (necessarily) I am aware of *x*. Thinking satisfies these conditions.
> *Ergo,* thinking is my essence ("Descartes's Proof," p. 331).

58. Williams, *Descartes,* p. 117.

59. Ibid., p. 118. Williams adds: "I have argued elsewhere ('Are Persons Bodies?', in *Problems of the Self* (Cambridge, 1973): see pp. 70–73), without using the notion of an essential property, that the possibility of *becoming* disembodied, at any rate, would imply a Cartesian account of persons." His reasoning there looks as essentialistic, in its way, as the reasoning he opposes.

60. Swinburne, *The Evolution of the Soul,* p. 146.

61. Ibid., p. 151.

62. Ibid., p. 152.

63. Ibid., p. 153.

64. Plantinga, *The Nature of Necessity,* pp. 67–68. Compare idem, "Replies," p. 369, especially: "perhaps, if I am a material object, I am my *brain,* or some part of my brain, or perhaps some other part of my body (but of course I should argue in the same way that I could exist when no *part* of my body existed)."

65. That is, the principle that for any object *x* and any object *y*, if *x* is identical with *y*, then every property of *x* is a property of *y*, and vice versa.

66. Vendler, "Possibility," p. 65; Chisholm, "Identity through Possible Worlds," pp. 81–82. Chisholm reveals his own essentialism when, after imagining a gradual, total exchange of properties between Adam and Noah in this world and another, he writes: "Is there a way, then, in which we might reasonably countenance identity through possible worlds and yet avoid such extreme conclusions? The only way, so far as I can see, is to appeal to some version of the doctrine that individual things have essential properties" (ibid., p. 84). PRS would serve equally well to preclude such a

total exchange. Anyone that similar to Adam would be Adam; anyone that similar to Noah would be Noah.

67. Kripke, "Naming and Necessity," p. 277. "My view is that proper names (except perhaps, for some quirky and derivative uses, that are not uses as *names*) *are* always rigid" (idem, "Speaker's Reference and Semantic Reference," p. 272).

68. Idem, "Identity and Necessity," p. 83. See idem, "Naming and Necessity," p. 270.

69. The present discussion does not require closer consideration of weaker and stronger senses of this claim. See, e.g., Cook, "Names and Possible Objects," pp. 304–5.

70. Quine, "Introduction: Problèmes de la Reference," p. 226.

71. Kripke, "Naming and Necessity," pp. 351–52.

72. Ibid., p. 279.

73. Kripke, "Identity and Necessity," p. 81.

74. Idem, "Naming and Necessity," p. 268.

75. Ibid., p. 270. See ibid., p. 273.

76. Compare Russell, *Logic and Knowledge*, p. 168 ("'This' is the point from which the whole process starts, and 'this' itself is not defined, but simply given").

77. Kripke, "Naming and Necessity," p. 268.

78. Ibid., pp. 268–69.

79. For clear contrast, compare Kripke's essentialism with Zeno Vendler's. "Following some of Saul Kripke's suggestions," Vendler writes, "we can make a creditable attempt at establishing [Napoleon's] individual essence: pare away the accidental features by the scalpel of the counterfactual, i.e., remove all those facts of his life-history that could have been otherwise. What is left, his essence, seems to be the following: he is the person born to his biological parents as a result of the fusion of two individual gametes" ("The Possibility of Possible Worlds," p. 68). It is difficult to conceive how, without explicit definition of the kind Kripke rightly considers atypical, such an essence might be fixed, for instance at the moment of naming, and difficult to conceive what evidence might establish its existence.

80. Compare Russell, *Logic and Knowledge*, p. 202: "In order

to understand a name for a particular, the only thing necessary is to be acquainted with that particular. When you are acquainted with that particular, you have a full, adequate, and complete understanding of the name, and no further information is required."

81. Kripke, "Identity and Necessity," p. 77, and "A Puzzle about Belief," p. 243.

82. Idem, *Naming and Necessity,* pp. 3–4.

83. Kripke's reasoning might have taken a different tack than that he reports. Let origin be a necessary but not a sufficient condition of identity. It will then be necessary that Butch derive from Steve, his earlier self, and Steve from Martha and Thomas, his parents, and Martha and Thomas from their progenitors, and so on, back to the beginning of the species and beyond. From such linkage it would appear that the Big Bang may be included among Butch's necessary antecedents. Kripke traces no such implications, but he does mention origin as a necessary property. And this stipulation, by itself, precludes the nonidentity of Steve and Butch. Butch would not be Butch if, in some world, he did not derive from Steve. Hence Steve and Butch, if identical, cannot be contingently identical.

84. Kripke, "Naming and Necessity," p. 334. See idem, "Identity and Necessity," p. 101.

Chapter 6: Sources of Essentialism

1. Moody, "Progress in Philosophy," p. 39.

2. Drury, "A Symposium," p. 69.

3. For fuller discussion of these and other causes of slight linguistic awareness, see Hallett, *Logic for the Labyrinth,* pp. 9–14.

4. See Hallett, *Companion,* pp. 26–34.

5. Wittgenstein, *The Blue and Brown Books,* p. 26.

6. Hallett, *Logic for the Labyrinth,* pp. 25–27. (In the case of a perfect match, in order for the defined term to designate an essence, each of the defining terms—more numerous than the term defined and more general—must also designate an essence.)

7. Wittgenstein, *Philosophical Investigations,* §72.

8. Russell, *The Problems of Philosophy,* p. 91.

9. Hallett, *Companion*, pp. 28–34.

10. Wittgenstein, *The Blue and Brown Books*, p. 18. Cf. idem, *Philosophical Investigations*, §§1, 10, 120; Stroll, "Meaning," p. 110; Pears, "Universals," p. 44, and those he cites: J. S. Mill, *Examination*, p. 381, and Berkeley, *Principles of Human Knowledge*, Introduction §18.

11. Russell, *The Problems of Philosophy*, p. 93.

12. Aristotle, *Sophistical Refutations* 178b38 (quoted in Kretzmann, "Semantics," p. 362).

13. "Our use of expressions like 'names of numbers,' 'names of colours,' 'names of materials,' 'names of nations' may spring from two different sources. One is that we might imagine the functions of proper names, numerals, words for colours, etc., to be much more alike than they actually are" (Wittgenstein, *The Blue and Brown Books*, p. 82).

14. This is not to deny, nor is it contradicted by the fact, that the inference often goes the other way, proper names being said to have "meanings," as general terms do. Both types of meanings may still be conceived as unitary, essentialistic.

15. Plato, *Theaetetus* 146e (F. M. Cornford translation).

16. Hallett, *Logic for the Labyrinth*, pp. 9–14.

17. Moore, *Principia Ethica*, p. 6.

18. Samples from Moore are cited and critiqued in Hallett, *Language and Truth*, pp. 18–19, 150–52.

19. Moore, *Principia Ethica*, p. 147.

20. Donagan, *Choice*, p. 24.

21. Ibid.

22. Ibid., p. 107.

23. Ibid., p. 108.

24. Hallett, *Language and Truth*, pp. 117–18.

25. Ibid., pp. 110–13.

26. Ibid., p. 117.

27. Wittgenstein, Manuscript 112, p. 221.

28. de Vio, *The Analogy of Names,* p. 27.

29. McInerny, *The Logic of Analogy,* p. 3.

30. Russell, "On Scientific Method in Philosophy."

31. Idem, *Logic and Knowledge,* p. 193.

32. "I have not found in Wittgenstein's *Philosophical Investigations* anything that seemed to me interesting . . . I realize, however, that I have an overpoweringly strong bias against it, for, if it is true, philosophy is, at best, a slight help to lexicographers, and at worst, an idle tea-table amusement" (Russell, *My Philosophical Development,* pp. 216–17).

33. James, *Pragmatism,* p. 18. Compare the text Max Black aptly chose as the motto for his commentary on the *Tractatus:* "At this period an insatiate appetite is accompanied by a fastidious palate. Nothing but the quintessences of existence, and those in exhaustless supplies, will satisfy this craving, which is not to be satisfied! Hence this bitterness. Life can furnish no food fitting for him . . ." (*Companion,* p. v; from *The Ordeal of Richard Feverel*).

34. "Often it is only after immense intellectual effort, which may have continued over centuries, that humanity at last succeeds in achieving knowledge of a concept in its pure form, in stripping off the irrelevant accretions which veil it from the eyes of the mind" (Frege, *The Foundations of Arithmetic,* p. vii).

35. James, *Pragmatism,* pp. 38–39. Compare Russell, *The Problems of Philosophy,* p. 100: "The world of universals, therefore, may also be described as the world of being. The world of being is unchangeable, rigid, exact, delightful to the mathematician, the logician, the builder of metaphysical systems, and all who love perfection more than life. The world of existence is fleeting, vague, without sharp boundaries, without any clear plan or arrangement, but it contains all thoughts and feelings, all the data of sense, and all physical objects, everything that can do either good or harm, everything that makes any difference to the value of life and the world. According to our temperaments, we shall prefer the contemplation of the one or of the other." If inclined at all toward the former, we shall at least be inclined to suppose that it exists.

36. Wittgenstein, *Philosophical Investigations,* §107.

37. James, *Pragmatism,* pp. 96–97.

38. Ibid., p. 102.

39. Ibid., p. 65.

40. Frege, *Philosophical Writings,* p. 159.

41. See, e.g., Russell, *Logic and Knowledge,* p. 179. Cf. Wittgenstein, *Philosophical Investigations,* §70; Levi, *Philosophy and the Modern World,* p. 449.

42. See, e.g., Russell's introduction to Wittgenstein's *Tractatus,* p. x.

43. Russell, *Introduction to Mathematical Philosophy,* p. 172.

44. As a typical illustration of such aspirations, recall Baker and Hacker's words: "The aim of a philosophical investigation of meaning is to reveal, or perhaps to introduce some order into this apparent chaos, i.e. to survey and organize the multiple applications of the concept of meaning and the welter of conceptual connections between meaning and other notions."

45. Wittgenstein, *Zettel,* §173.

46. For fuller development of points in this paragraph, see Hallett, *Logic for the Labyrinth,* pp. 40–41, 46–49.

47. Pears, "Universals," p. 45.

48. A sociological explanation—vague, general, and unconvincing—of realism versus nominalism can be found in Stark, *The Sociology of Knowledge,* pp. 37–43 (recounting a fuller treatment by Paul Landsberg).

49. Compare, for example, the essentialistic reading of "same" implicit in Frege's remark: "Common usage inaccurately calls signs of similar shape one and the same sign, although every time I write an equality sign I produce a different object. These structures differ in their positions, times of origin, and probably in shape" (*Philosophical Writings,* p. 194).

50. Russell, *The Problems of Philosophy,* pp. 96–97.

51. Frege, *Philosophical Writings,* p. 194.

52. Cf. Frege, *Funktion, Begriff, Bedeutung,* p. 90.

53. On this line of reasoning, see Berkeley, *The Principles of Human Knowledge,* Introduction §§19–20.

54. James, *Pragmatism,* p. 96.

55. Hallett, *Language and Truth,* pp. 19–24.

56. Locke, *An Essay concerning Human Understanding*, pp. 14–15 (book 3, chapter 3, nn. 1–2).

57. Ibid., pp. 16–17 (book 3, chapter 3, n. 6).

58. Ibid., p. 247 (book 4, chapter 5, n. 6).

59. Wittgenstein, *The Blue and Brown Books*, p. 35.

60. Pears, "Universals," pp. 45–48.

61. It was not always so. For a summary of arguments for Platonic forms ("the most important arguments that seem to have been used in the Academy"), see Grube, *Plato's Thought*, pp. 5–6. Here, as previously, I pass over arguments that do not clearly relate to "essences" as understood in this study. For example, Stanley Rosen's brief *plaidoyer* for essences, to the effect that "objects are unthinkable except as having properties" (*The Limits of Analysis*, p. 67), is compatible with the most varied understanding of these "properties" (family resemblance, rope structure, qualitative continuum, or whatever).

Chapter 7: Diagnoses and Prognosis

1. Wittgenstein, *Zettel*, §273.

2. Maslow, *A Study in Wittgenstein's* Tractatus, p. x.

3. Scheler, *Formalism in Ethics*, pp. 108–9. See idem, *On the Eternal in Man*, pp. 163, 169.

4. Scheler, *Selected Philosophical Essays*, p. 153: "To be sure, the special cognitive goal of a phenomenological investigation is the source of a special problem of the possibility and method of *communicating* what is known in this way. This problem should not be concealed. It does not exist for any philosophy which openly or—as is mostly the case—covertly starts by assuming that the only fit subject of knowledge is that about which one can *talk* in unambiguous symbols, that which can be socially communicated to anyone one pleases, that which can be the subject of debate, etc."

5. Scheler, *On the Eternal in Man*, p. 170.

6. Ibid. See idem, *Späte Schriften*, p. 246.

7. Scheler, *Selected Philosophical Essays*, pp. 152–53.

8. Ibid., p. 145.

9. Ibid., p. 178.

10. Ibid. Cf. ibid., p. 143 ("In this sense *phenomenological* philosophy is a continual *desymbolization of the world*"); Spiegelberg, *The Phenomenological Movement,* p. 279 ("A particularly important aspect of Scheler's phenomenological experience is its de-symbolizing quality, i.e., its role as a guide from symbolizing thought to the symbolized self-given phenomenon").

11. Scheler, *Selected Philosophical Essays,* p. 138.

12. Spiegelberg, *The Phenomenological Movement,* p. 279.

13. Scheler, *Selected Philosophical Essays,* p. 220.

14. Ibid., p. 218.

15. Pöll, *Wesen und Wesenserkenntnis,* pp. 70–71.

16. Scheler, *Vom Umsturz der Werte,* p. 180.

17. Ibid., p. 178.

18. Dupuy, *La philosophie de Max Scheler,* vol. 1, p. 10.

19. Ferretti, *Max Scheler,* p. 10. See Spiegelberg, *Doing Phenomenology,* p. 6.

20. On the advantages essences assured in relation to empirical science, see Pöll, *Wesen und Wesenserkenntnis,* pp. 1–2.

21. "Max Scheler hat mit besonderem Nachdruck die Wesenserkenntnis als diejenige Leistung der Philosophie bezeichnet, wodurch sie sich gegenüber der Wissenschaft abhebt" (ibid., p. 1). "Die Philosophie," wrote Scheler, "ist aber nicht ancilla, sondern regina scientiarum—oder sie est überhaupt nicht" (*Erkenntnislehre und Metaphysik,* p. 52).

22. "Contro l'empirismo in genere, [Scheler] afferma che le essenze non possono venire ricavate da una induzione astrattiva, che procede per generalizzazioni da molteplici osservazioni empiriche, poiché in tal modo non si potrebbe mai giungere ad avere delle autentiche essenze, di cui si sappia con certezza che sono applicabili apriori non solo a tutti i casi singoli osservati, ma anche ad ogni altro caso osservabile in futuro o al di là di ogni possibile osservazione" (Ferretti, *Max Scheler,* p. 53).

23. Lauer, "Phenomenological Ethics," pp. 274–75. Cf. Kersten, "Husserl's Phenomenology of Essence," pp. 63–65; Scheler, *On the Eternal in Man,* pp. 202–3 ("a *realm of essences* which offers a constitutional model for all possible worlds and realities

made from matters of fact"), 211 ("in this way the originally objective a-priori *becomes* the subjective a-priori; the thing thought becomes a 'form' or pattern of thinking").

24. Dupuy, *La philosophie de Max Scheler*, vol. 2, p. 739.

25. Scheler, *Philosophical Perspectives*, p. 47.

26. Ibid., p. 37. Cf. idem, *On the Eternal in Man*, pp. 89 ("Philosophy is *one*, in contrast with the sciences, which—essentially—are many"), 90–91.

27. Copleston, *A History of Philosophy*, p. 164.

28. Gould, *The Development of Plato's Ethics*, p. 67.

29. Lauer, "Phenomenological Ethics," p. 281.

30. Chisholm, "Comments," pp. 304–5.

31. See Hallett, *Christian Moral Reasoning*, pp. 31–35.

32. Wittgenstein, *Notebooks 1914–1916*, p. 89.

33. Idem, *Tractatus Logico-Philosophicus*, 4.027.

34. Ibid., 4.03.

35. Ibid., 4.5.

36. Wittgenstein, *The Blue and Brown Books*, p. 17.

37. Idem, *Philosophical Investigations*, §§1–8.

38. Ibid., §23.

39. Ibid.

40. Wittgenstein, *Notebooks 1914–1916*, p. 96.

41. Hallett, *Companion*, pp. 37–41. Cf. Moore, *Philosophical Papers*, p. 264.

42. Wittgenstein, *Remarks on the Philosophy of Psychology*, §498.

43. Idem, *Philosophical Investigations*, §102.

44. Hallett, *Companion*, p. 40. Cf. Moore, *Philosophical Papers*, p. 264.

45. Wittgenstein, *Lectures and Conversations*, p. 2.

46. Idem, *The Blue and Brown Books*, p. 17.

47. Hallett, *Companion,* pp. 142–43.

48. Manuscript 108, p. 203; Malcolm, *Ludwig Wittgenstein: A Memoir,* pp. 7, 68–69.

49. Wittgenstein, *Notebooks 1914–1916,* p. 7.

50. Ibid. Note the resemblance to Husserl and Scheler.

51. Idem, *Zettel,* §444 (the word *clear* is omitted in the translation). See Hallett, *Companion,* p. 95.

52. Cf. Wittgenstein, *Philosophical Grammar,* p. 75.

53. Idem, *The Blue and Brown Books,* p. 18.

54. Ibid., pp. 19–20.

55. Warnock, *English Philosophy since 1900,* p. 57; Wittgenstein, *Philosophical Grammar,* p. 75.

56. Wittgenstein, *Notebooks 1914–1916,* p. 112.

57. Idem, *The Blue and Brown Books,* p. 18.

58. Russell, "On Scientific Method in Philosophy"; Hallett, *Companion,* p. 193.

59. Wittgenstein, *Tractatus Logico-Philosophicus,* 5.472 ("The description of the most general propositional form is the description of the one and only general primitive sign in logic").

60. Idem, *Philosophical Investigations,* §97.

61. Ibid., §96.

62. Idem, *Tractatus Logico-Philosophicus,* 5.511.

63. Ibid., 6.13.

64. Ibid., 5.511, 6.13.

65. Idem, *Philosophical Investigations,* §203.

66. Ibid., §18.

67. Idem, *Notebooks 1914–1916,* p. 53.

68. Ibid., p. 39. See Hallett, *Companion,* pp. 36–37.

69. Wittgenstein, *Tractatus Logico-Philosophicus,* 5.4541.

70. Idem, *Notebooks 1914–1916,* p. 7. Cf. idem, *Philosophical Investigations,* §97 ("this order, it seems, must be *utterly simple*").

71. Paragraph break omitted. See Wittgenstein, *Tractatus Logico-Philosophicus,* 4.114–4.115.

72. Wittgenstein, *Philosophical Investigations,* §69.

73. Ibid.

74. Engelmann, *Letters,* p. 143.

75. Ibid., p. 97.

76. Quoted by Levi, *Philosophy and the Modern World,* p. 449. Cf. Frege, *Philosophical Writings,* p. 159; Wittgenstein, *Philosophical Investigations,* §§70, 99; idem, *Notebooks 1914–1916,* p. 64 ("We might demand definiteness in this way too: if a proposition is to make sense then the syntactical employment of each of its parts must be settled in advance").

77. Russell, *Logic and Knowledge,* p. 179.

78. Wittgenstein, *Philosophical Investigations,* §105.

79. Hallett, "Picture Theory," p. 315.

80. Wittgenstein, *Philosophical Investigations,* §116.

81. Four steps can be noted: 1) "Notice that Wittgenstein is careful to qualify his claim" (p. 249); 2) "it is clear that he regards the exceptions as trivial and unimportant" (ibid.); 3) "We may safely ignore the exceptions in the discussion that follows, then" (pp. 249–50); 4) Pitcher's refutation adduces such relatively trivial and unimportant (alleged) exceptions as *amen* and *Q.E.D.* (p. 252). The will to refute looks strong.

82. Pitcher, *The Philosophy of Wittgenstein,* p. 218.

83. See note 81, above.

84. Graham, *J. L. Austin,* p. 68.

85. Ibid., p. 76.

86. For a longer, complementary account, and critique, see Hallett, *Language and Truth,* pp. 135–42.

87. Austin, *Philosophical Papers,* p. 182.

88. Graham, *J. L. Austin,* pp. 36–37.

89. Ibid., pp. 37–38.

90. Ibid., p. 149.

91. Ibid., p. 39.

92. Cf. Hallett, *Language and Truth*, pp. 135–40. In his review (p. 465), Mats Furberg makes a similar criticism. The same conflation appears in Michael Seidler's admiring review, p. 382 ("We would be entitled to hold this only if our present language presented a complete and adequate account of the world—which we have no reason to assume") and in Graham's article, "A Note on Reading Austin," pp. 145–46.

93. Graham, *J. L. Austin*, p. 46.

94. Ibid., p. 68.

95. E.g., ibid., p. 228. One advantage of revision that attracts Graham is the solution it provides to the problem of analysis. An analysis of a concept that merely spelled out the meaning of the word would, he thinks, be an uninteresting tautology. To be interesting, an analysis must present a concept in novel terms. Revision permits this. It allows him to satisfy "the apparently contradictory demand that the terms of the analysis both be and not be closely connected with the concept being analysed. They must stand in the properly intimate relation to the concept if I am to reproduce its meaning, but it must not be too *obvious* that they stand in such a relation" (ibid., p. 25).

96. Ibid., p. 98. See ibid., pp. 83, 120, 122 ("On the general grounds outlined in Chapter IV, section 3, if we can give an explanatory account of some concept which is also unitary and simple, then so much the better").

97. Ibid., pp. 98–99. Graham (ibid., p. 268) expresses his gratification at discovering "not only advocacy of a narrow theory but also some of the same arguments in support of it" in Wertheimer, *The Significance of Sense*, chapter 2.

98. Graham, *J. L. Austin*, pp. 149–50.

99. Ibid., p. 149.

100. Ibid., pp. 31–32.

101. Hallett, *Logic for the Labyrinth*, pp. xxii–xxiii.

102. Graham, *J. L. Austin*, p. 83.

103. Ibid., pp. 84–85.

104. Hallett, *Language and Truth*, pp. 140–42.

105. Idem, *Logic for the Labyrinth*, pp. xx–xxi, xxiii.

106. Graham, *J. L. Austin*, p. 178.

107. Ibid., pp. 79–81.

108. Ibid., p. 83. See Hallett, *Language and Truth*, p. 139.

109. Graham, *J. L. Austin*, p. 76.

110. Hallett, *Language and Truth*, pp. 138–39.

111. Ibid., p. 145.

112. Ibid., p. 140.

113. On the etiology of this conflation, see chapter 6 and Hallett, *Language and Truth*, pp. 117–18.

114. Kripke, "Naming and Necessity," p. 273.

115. Ibid., p. 335.

116. Chandler, "Rigid Designation," p. 366.

117. Kripke, "Naming and Necessity," p. 268.

118. Idem, "Identity and Necessity," p. 81.

119. Wittgenstein, *Remarks on the Philosophy of Psychology*, §38.

120. Hacker, "Wittgenstein on Ostensive Definition," p. 271.

121. Ibid.

122. Kripke, "A Puzzle about Belief," p. 243.

123. Cf. Føllesdal, "Reference and Sense," pp. 230–31: "In order to make sense of quantified modal logic there has to be one kind of singular terms that stay with their objects regardless of all the changes they undergo . . . All genuinely referring expressions that refer to the same objects, must be freely substitutable for one another in these positions . . . If it were impossible to get around Quine's arguments, not only would modal logic have to go, but so would also our talk about causality, probability, counterfactuals, belief, knowledge, obligation etc. in short almost all the key notions in science, epistemology and ethics."

124. Kripke, "Naming and Necessity," pp. 327–42, e.g., p. 341: "In sum, the correspondence between a brain state and a physical state seems to have a certain obvious element of contingency. We have seen that identity is not a relation that can hold contingently."

125. Wittgenstein, Manuscript 108, p. 160.

126. Kripke, "Naming and Necessity," p. 280.

127. Ibid., p. 300.

128. Ibid., p. 301.

129. Blackburn, "The Elusiveness of Reference," pp. 192–93 ("*Our* use of 'refers' may be justified and debated through appeal to a variety of considerations, but it is not governed by any general rules that the theorist can hope to reveal").

130. Kripke, "Naming and Necessity," p. 313.

131. Disagreeing, Don Locke can only cite his "conflicting intuitions" ("Who I Am," p. 312). This typical impasse (see Hallett, *Language and Truth,* pp. 142–43, 157–58, and *Logic for the Labyrinth,* pp. 163–78) tips off neither author to the worthlessness of such intuitions nor to their origin (semantic backing for one or the other of two conflicting claims in most instances; the lack of such backing in this instance; the disputants' inattention to this fact and its relevance; the presence of both similarities and dissimilarities, beckoning in both directions, in the semantic in-between zone where they debate).

132. Kant, *Critique of Pure Reason,* p. 300.

133. Ibid., p. 299.

WORKS CITED

Abelson, Raziel. "Meaning, Use and Rules of Use." *Philosophy and Phenomenological Research* 18 (1957–58): 48–58.

Achinstein, Peter. "On the Meaning of Scientific Terms." *Journal of Philosophy* 61 (1964): 497–509.

———. "Rudolf Carnap." *Review of Metaphysics* 19 (1965–66): 517–49, 758–79.

Ackerman, Diana. "Natural Kinds, Concepts, and Propositional Attitudes." *Studies in Epistemology.* Ed. Peter A. French, Theodore E. Uehling, Jr., and Howard K. Wettstein. Midwest Studies in Philosophy 5. Minneapolis: University of Minnesota Press, 1980. 469–85.

Agassi, Joseph and Paul T. Sagal. "The Problem of Universals." *Philosophical Studies* 28 (1975): 289–94.

Alston, William P. "Meaning." *The Encyclopedia of Philosophy.* 1967.

Aune, Bruce. *Knowledge, Mind, and Nature: An Introduction to Theory of Knowledge and the Philosophy of Mind.* New York: Random House, 1967.

Austin, J. L. *Philosophical Papers.* Ed. J. O. Urmson and G. J. Warnock. London: Oxford University Press, 1970.

Averill, Edward. "Essence and Scientific Discovery in Kripke and Putnam." *Philosophy and Phenomenological Research* 43 (1982–83): 253–57.

Ayer, A. J. "Comments on Professor Williams' 'Knowledge and Reasons.'" *Problems in the Theory of Knowledge.* Ed. G. H. von Wright. The Hague: Nijhoff, 1972. 12–16.

Baker, G. P. and P. M. S. Hacker. *Wittgenstein: Understanding and Meaning.* Volume 1 of *An Analytical Commentary on the* Philosophical Investigations. Chicago: University of Chicago Press; Oxford: Blackwell, 1980.

Bennett, Jonathan. "Analytic-Synthetic." *Proceedings of the Aristotelian Society* 59 (1958–59): 163–88.

Black, Max. *A Companion to Wittgenstein's 'Tractatus.'* Ithaca: Cornell University Press, 1964.

———. *The Labyrinth of Language.* New York: Praeger, 1968.

Blackburn, Thomas. "The Elusiveness of Reference." *Realism and Antirealism.* Ed. Peter A. French, Theodore E. Uehling, Jr., and Howard K. Wettstein. Midwest Studies in Philosophy 12. Minneapolis: University of Minnesota Press, 1988. 179–94.

Boardman, William S. "Conclusive Reasons and Scepticism." *Australasian Journal of Philosophy* 56 (1978): 32–40.

Borowski, E. J. "Puzzle Cases: The Wrong Approach to Personal Identity." *Metaphilosophy* 9 (1978): 252–58.

———. Synopsis of idem, "Puzzle Cases: The Wrong Approach to Personal Identity." *Philosopher's Index* 13 (1979): 297.

Bouwsma, O. K. *Wittgenstein: Conversations 1949–1951.* Ed. J. L. Craft and Ronald E. Hustwit. Indianapolis: Hackett, 1986.

Boyd, Richard N. "Metaphor and Theory Change: What is 'Metaphor' a Metaphor for?" *Metaphor and Thought.* Ed. Andrew Ortony. Cambridge, England: Cambridge University Press, 1979. 356–408.

Brown, Robert. "Meaning and Rules of Use." *Mind* 71 (1962): 494–511.

Bunge, Mario. "The Complexity of Simplicity." *Journal of Philosophy* 59 (1962): 113–35.

Cairns, Dorion. "An Approach to Husserlian Phenomenology." *Phenomenology and Existentialism.* Ed. Richard M. Zaner and Don Ihde. New York: Putnam's, 1973. 31–46.

Campbell, John. "Extension and Psychic State: Twin Earth Revisited." *Philosophical Studies* 42 (1982): 67–89.

Canfield, John V. "Discovering Essence." *Knowledge and Mind: Philosophical Essays.* Ed. Carl Ginet and Sydney Shoemaker. New York: Oxford University Press, 1983. 105–129.

Carnap, Rudolf. *Logical Foundations of Probability.* 2nd ed. Chicago: University of Chicago Press, 1962.

———. *Meaning and Necessity: A Study in Semantics and Modal Logic.* 2nd ed. Chicago: University of Chicago Press, 1956.

————. "Replies and Systematic Expositions." *The Philosophy of Rudolf Carnap*. Ed. Paul Arthur Schilpp. La Salle: Open Court, 1963. 859–1013.

Carney, James D. "A Kripkean Approach to Aesthetic Theories." *British Journal of Aesthetics* 22 (1982): 150–57.

Cassam, Quassim. "Science and Essence." *Philosophy* 61 (1986): 95–107.

Champlin, T. S. "The Elusiveness of Meaning." *Philosophical Investigations* 6 (1983): 276–300.

Chandler, Hugh S. "Rigid Designation." *Journal of Philosophy* 72 (1975): 363–69.

————. "Sources of Essence." *Studies in Essentialism*. Ed. Peter A. French, Theodore E. Uehling, Jr., and Howard K. Wettstein. Midwest Studies in Philosophy 11. Minneapolis: University of Minnesota Press, 1986. 379–89.

Chapman, Frank M. and Paul Henle. *The Fundamentals of Logic*. New York: Scribner, 1933.

Charlesworth, Maurice. "Meaning and Use." *Australasian Journal of Philosophy* 44 (1966): 301–15.

Chisholm, Roderick M. "Comments on the 'Proposal Theory' of Philosophy." *Journal of Philosophy* 49 (1952): 301–6.

————. "Identity through Possible Worlds: Some Questions." *Nous* 1 (1967): 1–8. Rpt. in *The Possible and the Actual: Readings in the Metaphysics of Modality*. Ed. Michael J. Loux. Ithaca: Cornell University Press, 1979. 80–87.

Churchland, Paul M. *Scientific Realism and the Plasticity of Mind*. Cambridge, England: Cambridge University Press, 1979.

Clarke, Bowman L. *Language and Natural Theology*. The Hague: Mouton, 1966.

Cook, Monte. "Names and Possible Objects." *Philosophical Quarterly* 35 (1985): 303–9.

Cooper, David E. *Philosophy and the Nature of Language*. London: Longman, 1973.

Copi, Irving M. "Essence and Accident." Schwartz, *Naming*, 176–91.

Copleston, Frederick. *A History of Philosophy*. Vol. 1, 2nd ed. London: Burns and Oates, 1966. 9 vols. 1946–75.

Descartes, René. *The Philosophical Works of Descartes*. Trans. Elizabeth S. Haldane and G. R. T. Ross. Vol. 1. Cambridge, England: Cambridge University Press, 1931. 2 vols. 1931.

deVio, Thomas (Cardinal Cajetan). *The Analogy of Names* and *The Concept of Being*. Trans. and ed. Edward A. Bushinski and Henry J. Koren. Duquesne Studies: Philosophical Series 4. Pittsburgh: Duquesne University Press, 1953.

———. *Scripta philosophica: De nominum analogia. De conceptu entis*. Ed. N. Zammit. Rome: Angelicum, 1934.

Donagan, Alan. *Choice: The Essential Element in Human Action* London: Routledge, 1987.

———. "Universals and Metaphysical Realism." *The Monist* 47 (1963): 211–46.

Donnellan, Keith S. "Kripke and Putnam on Natural Kind Terms." *Knowledge and Mind: Philosophical Essays*. Ed. Carl Ginet and Sydney Shoemaker. New York: Oxford University Press, 1983. 84–104.

Dorrough, Douglas Charles. *A Prolegomenon to Some Future Considerations of the Notion of Analogy*. Diss. University of North Carolina, 1964. Ann Arbor: University Microfilms, 1965.

Double, Richard. "Twin Earths, Ersatz Pains, and Fool's Minds." *Metaphilosophy* 17 (1986): 300–10.

Dretske, Fred. "Conclusive Reasons." *Australasian Journal of Philosophy* 49 (1971): 1–22.

Drury, M. O'C. "A Symposium: Assessments of the Man and the Philosopher, II." *Ludwig Wittgenstein: The Man and His Philosophy*. Ed. K. T. Fann. New York: Delta-Dell, 1967. 67–71.

Dummett, Michael. *Frege: Philosophy of Language*. 2nd ed. Cambridge: Harvard University Press, 1981.

———. *The Interpretation of Frege's Philosophy*. Cambridge: Harvard University Press, 1981.

Dupré, John. "Natural Kinds and Biological Taxa." *Philosophical Review* 90 (1981): 66–90.

Dupuy, Maurice. *La philosophie de Max Scheler: Son évolution et son unité.* 2 vols. Paris: Presses Universitaires de France, 1959.

Ebersole, Frank B. "Stalking the Rigid Designator." *Philosophical Investigations* 5 (1982): 247–66.

Engelmann, Paul. *Letters from Ludwig Wittgenstein, with a Memoir.* Trans. L. Furtmüller. Ed. B. F. McGuinness. Oxford: Blackwell, 1967.

Ewing, A. C. *Ethics.* New York: Free, 1953.

Farrell, Robert. "Metaphysical Necessity Is Not Logical Necessity." *Philosophical Studies* 39 (1981): 141–53.

Feinberg, Joel. "Analytic Jurisprudence." *The Encyclopedia of Philosophy.* 1967.

Ferretti, Giovanni. *Max Scheler.* Vol. 1: *Fenomenologia et antropologia personalistica.* Milan: Università Cattolica del Sacro Cuore, 1972. 2 vols. 1972.

Findlay, J. N. "Use, Usage, and Meaning." *Proceedings of the Aristotelian Society,* supp. vol. 35 (1961): 231–42.

Fodor, J. A. "Cognitive Science and the Twin-Earth Problem." *Notre Dame Journal of Formal Logic* 23 (1982): 98–118.

———. "On Knowing What We Would Say." *Philosophical Review* 73 (1964): 198–212. Rpt. in *Philosophy and Linguistics.* Ed. Colin Lyas. New York: Macmillan, 1971. 297–308.

Føllesdal, Dagfinn. "Reference and Sense." *Philosophy and Culture.* Ed. Venant Cauchy. Vol. 1. Montreal: Montmorency, 1988. 229–39. 5 vols. 1988.

Forbes, Graeme. "An Anti-Essentialist Note on Substances." *Analysis* 41 (1981): 32–37.

Frege, Gottlob. *The Foundations of Arithmetic: A Logico-Mathematical Enquiry into the Concept of Number.* Trans. J. L. Austin. 2nd ed. Evanston: Northwestern University Press, 1953.

———. *Funktion, Begriff, Bedeutung: Fünf logische Studien.* Ed. Günther Patzig. Göttingen: Vandenhoeck and Ruprecht, 1962.

———. *Translations from the Philosophical Writings of Gottlob Frege.* Ed. Peter Geach and Max Black. 2nd ed. Oxford: Blackwell, 1960.

Furberg, Mats. Review of *J. L. Austin: A Critique of Ordinary Language Philosophy,* by Keith Graham. *Synthese* 42 (1979): 465–73.

Geach, Peter. *God and the Soul.* New York: Schocken, 1969.

Geisler, Norman L. and Paul D. Feinberg. *Introduction to Philosophy: A Christian Perspective.* Grand Rapids: Baker, 1980.

Gemes, Ken. "The World in Itself: Neither Uniform nor Physical." *Synthese* 73 (1987): 301–18.

Gettier, Edmund L. "Is Justified True Belief Knowledge?" *Analysis* 23 (1962–63): 121–23. Rpt. in *Knowing: Essays in the Analysis of Knowledge,* ed. Michael D. Roth and Leon Galis. New York: Random House, 1970. 35–38.

Goosens, William K. "Underlying Trait Terms." Schwartz, *Naming,* 133–54.

Gorovitz, Samuel and Merrill Hintikka, Donald Provence, and Ron G. Williams. *Philosophical Analysis: An Introduction to Its Language and Techniques.* 3rd ed. New York: Random House, 1979.

Gould, John. *The Development of Plato's Ethics.* Cambridge, England: Cambridge University Press, 1955.

Graham, Keith. *J. L. Austin: A Critique of Ordinary Language Philosophy.* Atlantic Highlands: Humanities, 1977.

―――. "A Note on Reading Austin." *Synthese* 46 (1981): 143–47.

Grayling, A. C. "Internal Structure and Essence." *Analysis* 42 (1982): 139–40.

Griffin, N. "Einstein's Simplicism." *Scientia* 106 (1971): 1029–54.

Grube, G. M. A. *Plato's Thought.* Indianapolis: Hackett, 1980.

Gustafson, Donald. "On Pitcher's Account of *Investigations* §43." *Philosophy and Phenomenological Research* 28 (1967–68): 252–58.

Hacker, P. M. S. "Wittgenstein on Ostensive Definition." *Inquiry* 18 (1975): 267–87.

Hallett, Garth L. *Christian Moral Reasoning: An Analytic Guide.* Notre Dame: University of Notre Dame Press, 1983.

―――. *A Companion to Wittgenstein's "Philosophical Investigations."* Ithaca: Cornell University Press, 1977.

———. *Darkness and Light: The Analysis of Doctrinal Statements.* New York: Paulist, 1975.

———. "Is There a Picture Theory of *Language* in the *Tractatus*?" *Heythrop Journal* 14 (1973): 314–21.

———. *Language and Truth.* New Haven: Yale University Press, 1988.

———. *Logic for the Labyrinth: A Guide to Critical Thinking.* Lanham: University Press of America, 1984.

———. *Wittgenstein's Definition of Meaning as Use.* Orestes Brownson Series on Contemporary Thought and Affairs 6. New York: Fordham University Press, 1967.

Hampshire, S. N. "Metaphysical Systems." *The Nature of Metaphysics.* Ed. D. F. Pears. London: Macmillan, 1957. 23–38.

Hanna, Joseph F. "An Explication of 'Explication.'" *Philosophy of Science* 35 (1968): 28–44.

Harman, Gilbert. "Knowledge, Inference, and Explanation." *American Philosophical Quarterly* 5 (1968): 164–73.

Hazo, Robert G. *The Idea of Love.* New York: Praeger, 1967.

Hill, Thomas E. *The Concept of Meaning.* New York: Humanities, 1971.

Hollinger, Robert. "Aspects of the Theory of Classification." *Philosophy and Phenomenological Research* 36 (1975–76): 319–38.

———. "A Defense of Essentialism." *Personalist* 57 (1976): 327–44.

———. "Natural Kinds, Family Resemblances, and Conceptual Change." *Personalist* 55 (1974): 323–33.

Husserl, Edmund. *Cartesian Meditations: An Introduction to Phenomenology.* Trans. Dorion Cairns. The Hague: Nijhoff, 1960.

———. *Experience and Judgment: Investigations in a Genealogy of Logic.* Trans. James S. Churchill and Karl Ameriks. Ed. Ludwig Landgrebe. Evanston: Northwestern University Press, 1973.

———. *Ideas: General Introduction to Pure Phenomenology.* Trans. W. R. Boyce Gibson. London: Allen and Unwin; New York: Humanities, 1931.

James, William. *Pragmatism.* The Works of William James 1. Cambridge: Harvard University Press, 1975.

224 *Works Cited*

———. *The Principles of Psychology.* 2 vols. London: Macmillan, 1901.

Kant, Immanuel. *Critique of Pure Reason.* Trans. Norman Kemp Smith. 1929. New York: St. Martin's, 1965.

Kapitan, Tomis. "Devine on Defining Religion." *Faith and Philosophy* 6 (1989): 207–14.

Katz, Jerrold J. "Logic and Language: An Examination of Recent Criticisms of Intensionalism." *Language, Mind, and Knowledge.* Ed. Keith Gunderson. Minnesota Studies in the Philosophy of Science 7. Minneapolis: University of Minnesota Press, 1975. 36–130.

Kennick, W. E. "Philosophy as Grammar and the Reality of Universals." *Ludwig Wittgenstein: Philosophy and Language.* Ed. Alice Ambrose and Morris Lazerowitz. London: Allen and Unwin; New York: Humanities, 1972. 140–85.

Kenny, Anthony. *Descartes: A Study of His Philosophy.* New York: Random House, 1968.

———. *Faith and Reason.* New York: Columbia University Press, 1983.

Kersten, Fred. "The Occasion and Novelty of Husserl's Phenomenology of Essence." *Phenomenological Perspectives: Historical and Systematic Essays in Honor of Herbert Spiegelberg.* The Hague: Nijhoff, 1975. 61–92.

Kitcher, Patricia. "On Appealing to the Extraordinary." *Metaphilosophy* 9 (1978): 99–107.

Klubertanz, George P. *St. Thomas Aquinas on Analogy: A Textual Analysis and Systematic Synthesis.* Chicago: Loyola University Press, 1960.

Kretzmann, Norman. "Semantics, History of." *The Encyclopedia of Philosophy.* 1967.

Kripke, Saul. "Identity and Necessity." Schwartz, *Naming,* 66–101.

———. "Naming and Necessity." *Semantics of Natural Language.* Ed. Donald Davidson and Gilbert Harman. 2nd ed. Dordrecht, Netherlands: Reidel, 1972. 253–355, 763–69.

———. *Naming and Necessity.* Cambridge: Harvard University Press, 1980.

————. "A Puzzle about Belief." *Meaning and Use: Papers Presented at the Second Jerusalem Philosophical Encounter April 1976.* Ed. Avishai Margalit. Dordrecht, Netherlands: Reidel; Jerusalem: Magnes, 1976. 239–83.

————. "Speaker's Reference and Semantic Reference." *Studies in the Philosophy of Language.* Ed. Peter A. French, Theodore E. Uehling, Jr., and Howard K, Wettstein. Midwest Studies in Philosophy 2. Morris: University of Minnesota, Morris, 1977. 255–76.

Lash, Nicholas. "Ideology, Metaphor and Analogy." *The Philosophical Frontiers of Christian Theology: Essays Presented to D. M. MacKinnon.* Ed. Brian Hebblethwaite and Stewart Sutherland. Cambridge, England: Cambridge University Press, 1982. 68–94.

Lauer, Quentin. "The Phenomenological Ethics of Max Scheler." *International Philosophical Quarterly* 1 (1961): 273–300.

Lehrer, Adrienne. "Meaning in Linguistics." *Theory of Meaning.* Ed. Adrienne Lehrer and Keith Lehrer. Englewood Cliffs: Prentice–Hall, 1970. 9–16.

Leplin, Jarrett. "Is Essentialism Unscientific?" *Philosophy of Science* 55 (1988): 493–510.

Levi, Albert William. *Philosophy and the Modern World.* Bloomington: Indiana University Press, 1959.

Locke, Don. "Who I Am." *Philosophical Quarterly* 29 (1979): 301–18.

Locke, John. *An Essay concerning Human Understanding.* Ed. Alexander Campbell Fraser. Vol. 2. Oxford: Clarendon, 1894. 2 vols. 1894.

Lyons, John. *Introduction to Theoretical Linguistics.* Cambridge, England: Cambridge University Press, 1968.

————. *Structural Semantics: An Analysis of Part of the Vocabulary of Plato.* Publications of the Philological Society 20. Oxford: Blackwell, 1963.

Malcolm, Norman. "Descartes's Proof That His Essence Is Thinking." *Philosophical Review* 74 (1965): 315–38.

————. *Ludwig Wittgenstein: A Memoir.* London: Oxford University Press, 1958.

————. *Thought and Knowledge.* Ithaca: Cornell University Press, 1977.

Margolis, Joseph. "Mr. Weitz and the Definition of Art." *Philosophical Studies* 9 (1958): 88–95.

Martin, Rex and James W. Nickel. "Recent Work on the Concept of Rights." *American Philosophical Quarterly* 17 (1980): 165–80.

Martin, Robert M. *The Meaning of Language*. Cambridge: MIT Press, 1987.

Maslow, Alexander. *A Study in Wittgenstein's* Tractatus. Berkeley: University of California Press, 1961.

McGreal, Ian Philip. "An Analysis of Philosophical Method." *The Monist* 48 (1964): 513–32.

McInerny, Ralph M. *The Logic of Analogy: An Interpretation of St Thomas*. The Hague: Nijhoff, 1961.

Mellor, D. H. "Natural Kinds." *British Journal for the Philosophy of Science* 28 (1977): 299–312.

Mill, John Stuart. *Examination of Sir William Hamilton's Philosophy*. 5th ed. London: Longmans, Green, 1878.

———. *A System of Logic Ratiocinative and Inductive*. Ed. J. M. Robson. Collected Works of John Stuart Mill 7–8. Vol. 2. Toronto: University of Toronto Press; London: Routledge, 1974. 2 vols. 1973–74.

Montagu, Ashley. Introduction. *The Meaning of Love*. Ed. Montagu. New York: Julian, 1953. v–viii.

Moody, Todd C. "Progress in Philosophy." *American Philosophical Quarterly* 23 (1986): 35–46.

Moore, George Edward. *Commonplace Book 1919–1953*. Ed. C. Lewy. London: Allen and Unwin; New York: Macmillan, 1962.

———. *Philosophical Papers*. London: Allen and Unwin, 1959.

———. *Principia Ethica*. Cambridge, England: Cambridge University Press, 1903.

———. *Some Main Problems of Philosophy*. London: Allen and Unwin; New York: Humanities, 1953.

Moravcsik, J. M. E. "How Do Words Get Their Meanings?" *Journal of Philosophy* 78 (1981): 5–24.

Pappas, George S. and Marshall Swain. "Some Conclusive Reasons against 'Conclusive Reasons.'" *Australasian Journal of Philosophy* 51 (1973): 72–76.

Parent, W. A. "Recent Work on the Concept of Privacy." *American Philosophical Quarterly* 20 (1983): 341–55.

Parkinson, G. H. R. "Different Types of Causation." *The Handbook of Western Philosophy*. Ed. by Parkinson. New York: Macmillan, 1988. 279–300.

Pears, David. "Universals." *Philosophical Quarterly* 1 (1951): 218–27. Rpt. in *Universals and Particulars: Readings in Ontology*. Ed. Michael J. Loux. 2nd ed. Notre Dame: University of Notre Dame Press, 1976. 44–58.

Pitcher, George. *The Philosophy of Wittgenstein*. Englewood Cliffs: Prentice-Hall, 1964.

Plantinga, Alvin. *The Nature of Necessity*. Oxford: Clarendon, 1974.

———. "Replies." *Alvin Plantinga*. Ed. James E. Tomberlin and Peter van Inwagen. Dordrecht, Netherlands: Reidel, 1985. 313–96.

Platts, Mark. "Natural Kind Words and 'Rigid Designators.'" *Proceedings of the Aristotelian Society* 82 (1981–82): 103–14.

Pöll, Wilhelm. *Wesen und Wesenserkenntnis: Untersuchungen mit besonderer Berücksichtigung der Phänomenologie Husserls und Schelers*. Munich: Reinhardt, 1936.

Pollock, John L. *Contemporary Theories of Knowledge*. Totowa: Rowman, 1986.

———. *Language and Thought*. Princeton: Princeton University Press, 1982.

Putnam, Hilary. "Is Semantics Possible?" Schwartz, *Naming*, 102–18.

———. "It Ain't Necessarily So." *Journal of Philosophy* 59 (1962): 658–71.

———. "Meaning and Reference." Schwartz, *Naming*, 119–32.

———. *Mind, Language and Reality*. Vol. 2 of *Philosophical Papers*. Cambridge, England: Cambridge University Press, 1975.

———. "Psychological Concepts, Explication, and Ordinary Language." *Journal of Philosophy* 54 (1957): 94–100.

———. *Realism and Reason*. Vol. 3 of *Philosophical Papers*. Cambridge, England: Cambridge University Press, 1983.

———. *Representation and Reality*. Cambridge: Bradford-MIT Press, 1988.

Quine, Willard V. O. "Introduction: Problèmes de la Reference" [in English]. *Philosophy and Culture.* Ed. Vincent Cauchy. Vol. 1. Montreal: Montmorency, 1988. 225–27. 5 vols. 1988.

———. "Natural Kinds." Schwartz, *Naming,* 155–75.

Ramsey, Frank Plumpton. *The Foundations of Mathematics and Other Logical Essays.* Ed. R. B. Braithwaite. London: Routledge, 1931.

Röper, Peter. Review of *Wittgenstein's Definition of Meaning as Use,* by Garth Hallett. *Heythrop Journal* 9 (1968): 427–28.

Rosen, Stanley. *The Limits of Analysis.* 1980. New Haven: Yale University Press, 1985.

Ross, William David. *Plato's Theory of Ideas.* Oxford: Clarendon, 1951.

Russell, Bertrand. *An Introduction to Mathematical Philosophy.* 2nd ed. London: Allen and Unwin, 1920.

———. *Logic and Knowledge: Essays 1901–1950.* Ed. Robert Charles Marsh. London: Allen and Unwin, 1956.

———. *My Philosophical Development.* London: Allen and Unwin, 1959.

———. "On Scientific Method in Philosophy." Oxford: Clarendon, 1914. Rpt. in *Mysticism and Logic.* By Russell. 1917. London: Allen and Unwin, 1963. 75–93.

———. *The Problems of Philosophy.* 1912. New York: Galaxy-Oxford University Press, 1959.

Ryle, Gilbert. "Proofs in Philosophy." *Revue Internationale de Philosophie* 8 (1954): 150–57.

Scheler, Max. *Erkenntnislehre und Metaphysik.* Ed. Manfred S. Frings. Schriften aus dem Nachlass 2. Bern: Francke, 1979.

———. *Formalism in Ethics and Non-Formal Ethics of Values: A New Attempt toward the Foundation of an Ethical Personalism.* Trans. Manfred S. Frings and Roger L. Funk. Evanston: Northwestern University Press, 1973.

———. *Man's Place in Nature.* Trans. Hans Meyerhoff. New York: Noonday-Farrar, 1962.

———. *On the Eternal in Man.* Trans. Bernard Noble. London: SCM Press, 1960.

———. *Philosophical Perspectives.* Trans. Oscar A. Haac. Boston: Beacon, 1958.

———. *Selected Philosophical Essays.* Trans. David R. Lachterman. Evanston: Northwestern University Press, 1973.

———. *Späte Schriften.* Ed. Manfred S. Frings. Bern: Francke, 1976.

———. *Vom Umsturz der Werte: Abhandlungen und Aufsätze.* Bern: Francke, 1955.

Schlesinger, George N. *Metaphysics: Methods and Problems.* Totowa: Barnes and Noble, 1983.

———. "The Method of Counterexample." *Principles of Philosophical Reasoning.* Ed. James H. Fetzer. Totowa: Rowman, 1984. 151–71.

Schlick, Moritz. "Meaning and Verification." *Philosophical Review* 45 (1936): 339–69. Rpt. in *Readings in Philosophical Analysis,* ed. Herbert Feigl and Wilfrid Sellars. New York: Appleton-Century-Crofts, 1949. 146–70.

Schwartz, Stephen P., ed. *Naming, Necessity, and Natural Kinds.* Ithaca: Cornell University Press, 1977.

———. "Natural Kinds and Nominal Kinds." *Mind* 89 (1980): 182–95.

———. "Putnam on Artifacts." *Philosophical Review* 87 (1978): 566–74.

Seddon, George. "Logical Possibility." *Mind* 81 (1972): 481–94.

Seidler, Michael J. Review of *J. L. Austin,* by Keith Graham. *Modern Schoolman* 56 (1979): 380–82.

Shapere, Dudley. "Reason, Reference, and the Quest for Knowledge." *Philosophy of Science* 49 (1982): 1–23.

Shimony, Abner. "The Status and Nature of Essences." *Review of Metaphysics* 1.3 (1948): 38–79.

Sokolowski, Robert. "What is Moral Action?" *New Scholasticism* 63 (1989): 18–37.

Solomon, Robert C. "Sense and Essence: Frege and Husserl." *International Philosophical Quarterly* 10 (1970): 378–401.

Sorell, T. "The Analysis of Knowledge." *The Handbook of Western*

Philosophy. Ed. G. H. R. Parkinson. New York: Macmillan, 1988. 127–36.

Spang-Hanssen, Henning. *Recent Theories on the Nature of the Language Sign*. Travaux du Cercle Linguistique de Copenhague 9. Copenhagen: Nordisk sprog-og Kulturforlag, 1954.

Spiegelberg, Herbert. *Doing Phenomenology: Essays on and in Phenomenology*. The Hague: Nijhoff, 1975.

———. *The Phenomenological Movement: A Historical Introduction*. 3rd ed. The Hague: Nijhoff, 1982.

Stark, W. *The Sociology of Knowledge: An Essay in Aid of a Deeper Understanding of the History of Ideas*. London: Routledge, 1958.

Strawson, P. F. "Construction and Analysis." *The Revolution in Philosophy*. By Strawson and others. London: Macmillan, 1956.

———. Review of *Philosophical Investigations*, by Ludwig Wittgenstein. *Mind* 63 (1954): 70–99. Rpt. in *Wittgenstein: The Philosophical Investigations*. Ed. George Pitcher. 1966. Notre Dame: University of Notre Dame Press, 1968. 22–64.

Stroll, Avrum. "Meaning, Referring, and the Problem of Universals." *Inquiry* 4 (1961): 107–22.

Swinburne, Richard. *The Evolution of the Soul*. Oxford: Clarendon, 1986.

Teichman, Jenny. "The Definition of Person." *Philosophy* 60 (1985): 175–85.

Uyl, Douglas Den and Tibor R. Machan. "Recent Work on the Concept of Happiness." *American Philosophical Quarterly* 20 (1983): 115–34.

Vendler, Zeno. "On the Possibility of Possible Worlds." *Canadian Journal of Philosophy* 5 (1975): 57–72.

von Hildebrand, Dietrich. *What Is Philosophy?* Chicago: Franciscan Herald, 1973.

Waismann, Friedrich. "Analytic-Synthetic, II." *Analysis* 11 (1950–51): 25–38.

———. "How I See Philosophy." *Contemporary British Philosophy*. Third Series. Ed. H. D. Lewis. London: Allen and Unwin, 1956.

447–90. Rpt. in *Logical Positivism*. Ed. A. J. Ayer. New York: Free Press, 1959. 345–80.

Wallace, John. "Positive, Comparative, Superlative." *Journal of Philosophy* 69 (1972): 773–82.

Walton, Douglas N. *On Defining Death: An Analytic Study of the Concept of Death in Philosophy and Medical Ethics*. Montreal: McGill-Queen's University Press, 1979.

Warnock, G. J. *English Philosophy since 1900*. 2nd ed. London: Oxford University Press, 1969.

Wavell, Bruce B. "Wittgenstein's Doctrine of Use." *Synthese* 56 (1983): 253–64.

Weckert, John. "Putnam, Reference and Essentialism." *Dialogue* 25 (1986): 509–21.

Weitz, Morris. "The Role of Theory in Aesthetics." *Journal of Aesthetics and Art Criticism* 15 (1956–57): 27–35.

Wertheimer, Roger. *The Significance of Sense: Meaning, Modality, and Morality*. Ithaca: Cornell University Press, 1972.

Wheatley, Jon. "How to Give a Word a Meaning." *Theoria* 30 (1964): 119–36.

———. "Some Aspects of Meaning and Use" [abstract]. *Journal of Philosophy* 60 (1963): 643–44.

Wheeler, Samuel C., III. "Attributives and Their Modifiers." *Nous* 6 (1972): 310–34.

Wiggins, David. *Sameness and Substance*. Cambridge: Harvard University Press, 1980.

Wilkerson, T. E. "Natural Kinds." *Philosophy* 63 (1988): 29–42.

Williams, Bernard. *Descartes: The Project of Pure Enquiry*. Atlantic Highlands: Humanities, 1978.

———. "Knowledge and Reasons." *Problems in the Theory of Knowledge*. Ed. G. H. von Wright. The Hague: Nijhoff, 1972. 1–11.

Wilson, Mary. "A Problem in the Relation between Use and Meaning." *Analysis* 10 (1949–50): 16–21.

Wittgenstein, Ludwig. *The Blue and Brown Books*. 2nd ed. Oxford: Blackwell, 1960.

———. *Lectures and Conversations on Aesthetics, Psychology and Religious Belief.* Ed. Cyril Barrett. Oxford: Blackwell, 1966.

———. *Notebooks 1914–1916.* Trans. G. E. M. Anscombe. Ed. G. H. von Wright and G. E. M. Anscombe. Oxford: Blackwell, 1961.

———. *On Certainty.* Trans. Denis Paul and G. E. M. Anscombe. Ed. G. E. M. Anscombe and G. H. von Wright. Oxford: Blackwell, 1969.

———. *Philosophical Grammar.* Trans. Anthony Kenny. Ed. Rush Rhees. Oxford: Blackwell, 1974.

———. *Philosophical Investigations.* Trans. G. E. M. Anscombe. 2nd ed. Oxford: Blackwell, 1967.

———. *Remarks on the Philosophy of Psychology.* Vol. 1. Trans. G. E. M. Anscombe. Ed. G. E. M. Anscombe and G. H. von Wright. Chicago: University of Chicago Press, 1980. 2 vols. 1980.

———. *Tractatus Logico-Philosophicus.* Trans. D. F. Pears and B. F. McGuinness. London: Routledge, 1961.

———. *Zettel.* Trans. G. E. M. Anscombe. Ed. G. E. M. Anscombe and G. H. von Wright. Oxford: Blackwell, 1967.

Wuellner, Bernard. *A Dictionary of Scholastic Philosophy.* 2nd ed. Milwaukee: Bruce, 1966.

Zemach, Eddy M. "Putnam's Theory on the Reference of Substance Terms." *Journal of Philosophy* 73 (1976): 116–27.

Ziff, Paul. *Semantic Analysis.* Ithaca: Cornell University Press, 1960.

INDEX